English Grammar Pedagogy

Designed for ESL and ELT pedagogy courses around the world, this text describes English grammar from a World Englishes perspective. It is distinguished by its focus on the social setting for English as a global language, the latest thinking about grammatical theory, and new theories of how first and second languages are learned and taught. The fundamental premise is that teaching and learning grammar cannot be isolated from the local, regional, and global sociocultural contexts in which the teaching and learning take place.

Part I presents different attitudes toward English as a global language and some challenges that learners of English share, no matter where they are in the world. Attention is given to how language learning affects cognition and identity, and to how language is learned both implicitly through interaction and explicitly through direct instruction, and that both can result in accuracy and fluency. Part II is about the features of English that educated speakers consider the most likely and probable in Academic English. Part III describes the flexible and fluid features of English that might be susceptible to change or modification over time. Each chapter includes engaging Study, Discussion, and Essay Questions and Activities.

Barbara M. Birch is Professor in the Department of Linguistics at California State University, Fresno.

ESL & Applied Linguistics Professional Series
Eli Hinkel, Series Editor

English Grammar Pedagogy

Pedagogy

A Global Perspective

BARBARA M. BIRCH

Routledge
Taylor & Francis Group

NEW YORK AND LONDON

First published 2014
by Routledge
711 Third Avenue, New York, NY 10017

Simultaneously published in the UK
by Routledge
2 Park Square, Milton Park, Abingdon, Oxon OX14 4RN

Routledge is an imprint of the Taylor & Francis Group, an informa business

Library of Congress Cataloging-in-Publication Data
Birch, Barbara M.
English grammar pedagogy : a global perspective / By Barbara M. Birch.
pages cm. —(ESL & Applied Linguistics Professional series)
Includes bibliographical references and index.
1. English language–Grammar–Study and teaching. 2. English
language–Study and teaching–Foreign speakers. 3. Second language
acquisition. I. Title.
PE1065.B43 2013
428.0071–dc23
2013006245

ISBN: 978–0–415–88584–3 (hbk)
ISBN: 978–0–415–88585–0 (pbk)
ISBN: 978–0–203–83874–7 (ebk)

Typeset in Dante and Avenir
by Keystroke, Station Road, Codsall, Wolverhampton

Printed and bound in the United States of America by Publishers Graphics, LLC on sustainably sourced paper.

Dedication

For my family

Contents

Preface

This book is intended for pre-service teachers, instructors, or students of grammar who want to understand the social setting for English as a global language, the latest thinking about grammatical theory, and new theories of how first and second languages are learned and taught. In particular, this book is aimed at those who intend to learn to speak and write a more formal form of English called Academic English (AE). This book is different from other grammar books because it takes as a fundamental premise that teaching and learning grammar cannot be isolated from the local, regional, and global sociocultural contexts in which the teaching and learning take place.

For instance, in this book the concept of World Englishes (WE) is the foundation for learning and teaching. World Englishes is an umbrella term for the wonderful diversity of spoken and written varieties of English. Within this diversity, more formal written Englishes share areas of agreement about forms and usages. Formal written Englishes are both internal and external to local or regional varieties. They are internal because when people speak of Jamaican English, they are referring to a continuum of varieties from informal speech with local vocabulary and structures to formal Jamaican writing which is probably indistinguishable from British English writing. When people speak of Filipino English, Ugandan English, or English as a lingua franca (ELF), similar continua exist. Everywhere, the local varieties of English are each a microcosm of a global situation with diverse spoken usages on one end of a spectrum and similar written usages on the other. Because of the consensus on the features of formal written usage at one end of the World Englishes spectrum, there appears to be a common external variety of Academic English.

Part I of this book begins by presenting different attitudes toward English as a global language and some challenges that learners of English share, no matter where they are in the world. This book adopts a theory of grammar that explains how the learning of one, two, or multiple languages occurs within sociocultural contexts, and how language learning affects cognition and identity. It takes as primary the idea that language is learned implicitly through interaction, but also explicitly through direct instruction, and that both of these routes can result in accuracy and fluency. The book also addresses pedagogy, with innovative as well as traditional suggestions that can be implemented in the classroom without embracing any particular methodology.

Part II is about the features of English that educated speakers consider the most likely and probable in Academic English. These features are called **consensus features**, not because everyone agrees with them but because their high likelihood and probability are shown by statistical studies. In any consensus there may be disagreements and lack of harmony among individual opinions and judgments, but overall there is some agreement and solidarity behind these norms of usage. Consensus is not unanimity. Part II is about the morphology, word formation, phrases, sentences, and discourse of Academic English.

Part III describes the flexible and fluid features of English that might be susceptible to change or modification over time. These features have been considered fragile, vulnerable, or breakable, but in this book the term **instability** is adopted as a cover term that includes both diverse forms and unstable forms. **Diverse forms** are the stable features that differ in the varieties of English, such as the presence or absence of forms of the verb *be* (*he is coming, he be coming, he coming*). **Unstable forms** are less firmly fixed; they are features that are used unpredictably or undependably in people's speech or writing, especially in the English as a lingua franca (ELF) setting, such as the presence or absence of verbal inflections. As it turns out, there is overlap between diverse forms and unstable forms. It goes without saying that the discussion in this book will just scratch the surface of this important issue, but there is an invitation for readers to consider their own diverse or unstable forms.

This book adopts both a meaning-oriented perspective and a message-oriented perspective; that is, quotes (with citations) are used for their meaning and relevance to a chapter topic as well as for a source of realistic examples of Academic English. All of the excerpts in the book were placed into a simple database or mini-corpus (without citations). The corpus for this book is a representative sample of Academic English, but not restricted to any subset of the population of writers that use AE. The writers of the excerpts represent many different points of view and backgrounds, but they are all successful AE writers, although their work may have been subject to editing by someone else, just as my own writing is. At least one of the excerpts in the corpus is a translation, and a few reflect older written AE norms. Many of the examples in the book are drawn from the corpus.

Each chapter is followed by **Study, Discussion, and Essay Questions** and **Activities**, such as these examples:

Study, Discussion, and Essay Questions

Create a Language Notebook as a file or folder on a computer or a hard copy notebook. The Language Notebook will hold your answers to these questions, as assigned, as well as a glossary of new words in each chapter.

1. Start a glossary as part of your Language Notebook. Begin by adding these terms: consensus features, instability, diverse forms, unstable forms.
2. Based on the information in this preface, write a paragraph about how these concepts differ and how are they the same. The concepts are World Englishes (WE), Academic English (AE), and English as a lingua franca (ELF).

Activity

Study this short quote (Hockett, 1968, p. 95) using both a meaning-based and a message-based approach. What does it mean? What kind of English is it? Where might you find it? What linguistic features do you notice about the words, punctuation, and sentence structure? Put your understanding of the quote in your own words in your Language Notebook. Compare your answers with those of your classmates.

> Is it possible that the brains of speakers and hearers coin [invent] and understand utterances on the basis of "abstract patterns" of some sort, extracted over the months and years of language-learning and language-use from actual utterances of similar shapes?

You will learn the answer to Hockett's question by reading this book.

Acknowledgments

I am very grateful to Naomi Silverman and Eli Hinkel for their patience, support, and understanding throughout the process of writing this book.

Part I

Global Trends in English Grammar Pedagogy

Overall, Part I is meant to make a strong case for teachers' own preparation for teaching language, especially in the area of formal grammar. Chapter 1 begins with a look at the global context of English language instruction and a discussion of what issues in the global spread of English influence English language teachers and learners in their local settings. Academic English (AE) is not the native language of anyone; its features are so specialized and conventionalized that it is a different variety of English. Although some English speakers are privileged because their "native" language is similar to it, in fact everyone faces linguistic obstacles when it comes to learning to write and speak AE, in contrast to his or her colloquial varieties. Grammatical obstacles like proper word choice, accurate grammatical forms, and complex sentence patterns form a barrier between AE and colloquial varieties of English. Grammar teachers across the globe have the job of helping learners who want to overcome the linguistic barrier.

Chapter 2 presents a new theory of grammar, Construction Grammar, that has been emerging in recent years. Construction Grammar offers a way of reconciling first language acquisition and second or later language learning as similar cognitive and linguistic processes. In Chapter 3, some factors in second language acquisition theory are explored for their influence on identity, language awareness, interaction, feedback, with special attention to the psychological processes involved in language learning. Finally, Chapter 4 is about the best practices in grammar instruction, in light of new ideas of language learning and acquisition. Some of the recommendations are innovative and some are traditional practices that are taken off the storeroom shelf, dusted off, and brought back into the classroom.

Global Perspectives on English

1

It goes without saying that, in the real world, all users of English are equal partners in ELF (English as a Lingua Franca); in the classroom, we will expose learners to those forms and varieties of English which will empower them to meet the challenges of globalism and to resist the hegemony of one culture over another.

(Prodomou, 2008, p. xiii)

Prodomou's quote is a good introduction to a global perspective on English because it encapsulates three common ideas about what English is in the world today. First, there is the broad-based English that refers to a language used by many people the world over. This English has varieties that range from local to global, standard to non-standard, or halting to fluent. It has different users, mother-tongue monolinguals, second language learners, and bilingual and multilingual users. People use English for many purposes, from the integrative purposes of immigrants, refugees, and people who wish to participate actively in a globalized culture, to the instrumental purposes of entrepreneurs, students, and politicians who want to increase their social and economic capital through language learning. This broad concept of the English language is often called World Englishes (WE).

English as a Global Language

1. World Englishes (WE)
2. English as a lingua franca (ELF)
3. Academic English (AE)

The second idea about English has to do with English used as a lingua franca (ELF), which refers to a spoken variety of English used as a medium of communication among speakers of various levels of proficiency. For Prodomou (2008), any user of World Englishes can speak it as a lingua franca with others; for others, ELF is a more specialized concept. However, there is also a third concept of English in the quote: the forms and varieties within World Englishes that will empower learners to accomplish the professional or educational purposes they have set for themselves. This is the English of the classroom, Academic English (AE). This chapter is about these three concepts of English as a global language and some specific characteristics and challenges of Academic English.

English as a Global Language

English as a global phenomenon is described metaphorically in a number of different ways. It is part of a global system of language **constellations**. It is the result of processes of intentional **diffusion** as a form of imperialism and colonialism. It is a **place of resistance** to imperialism and colonialism. It is a set of concentric **circles** of multicultural speakers, and finally it is a language spoken at the **intersection** of different populations and purposes.

Constellations

English is a language of wider communication (LWC). Languages of wider communication are resources that allow speakers to communicate with people beyond their local context and setting. They are official languages like Mandarin in China, international languages like French or Arabic, or trade languages like Hiri Motu in Papua New Guinea. LWCs are at the center of linguistic constellations and galaxies with local languages clustered around them, and with regional dialects clustered around national languages.

> The languages of the world together constitute a global system held together by multilingual people who can communicate with several language groups. The position of each language in this system may be characterized by its "communication value" (Q), the product of its prevalence and its centrality. Languages represent a very special class of economic goods: they are not only collective goods but also display network effects ... The special characteristics of language, language

groups and their accumulated textual capital help to explain the dynamics of language acquisition, conservation, and abandonment.

(de Swaan, 1998, p. 63)

This dynamic system of languages was not intentionally created but is the result of many individual actions. People learn second and third languages (or not), speak and write languages, stop using languages, and neglect to teach their languages to their children. Their actions create a global system of languages held together by people who are positioned by their languages to interact with people in other positions. The way that people position themselves reveals the prevalence and centrality of a language in the constellation of languages.

An example that de Swaan gives is the position of Russian among former Soviet Union countries and satellites. Among the people of those regions, Russian was at the center as a LWC because, among multilingual people, Russian was the most frequently known. By de Swaan's reckoning, English is now the most central LWC, with the highest communication value and strategic importance because of its number of speakers and sociopolitical and economic importance. English also has a very high textual capital, which is a term for written or memorized texts that are part of the cultural capital or heritage produced by the users of that language in media, art, music, scholarship, and so on. More and more, the texts created by people across the globe are in English.

The constellation metaphor that applies to languages of the world can also describe World Englishes. It is a constellation of different spoken and written varieties with different communicative values, network effects, and textual capital that affect acquisition, conservation, and abandonment. In each English-speaking country there are national standard varieties as well as regional standards that differ in pronunciation and some grammatical patterns. There are a lot of differences between spoken English and formal written English, so many differences that a language barrier called *diglossia* has arisen. Diglossia is a social and cultural situation in which there are dual linguistic systems, one of which is learned at home and one of which is learned in school. AE is the learned variety with spelling rules, subject–verb agreement, and complete sentences; it is not the native language of anyone.

Diffusion and Resistance

Some people celebrate the spread of English into international contexts. The quote below from noted Italian-born American linguist Mario Pei shows that the diffusion of English was already uppermost in his mind in the 1960s. Explicit in the mid-century attitudes expressed by Pei are the assumptions that the English language belongs to a certain territory and that it is associated with specific cultural values. It would be a mistake to assume that these ideas have gone out of fashion, although nowadays proponents of this position are often more circumspect.

Global Metaphors

Constellations
Diffusion and Resistance
Concentric Circles
Intersection of Circles

> To begin with, there is little question that English is . . . the carrier of Anglo-American cultural imperialism, neo-colonialism, commercialism. There is little point in English speakers, American or British, apologizing for these three things. Shorn of the semantic changes that have been attached to these words, they represent progress—the type of progress every nation, including the communist ones, is trying to achieve. We, the speakers of English, should proudly flaunt the banners of cultural imperialism, neo-colonialism, and commercialism. The first places us in the forefront of intellectual and educational progress; the second proves that we are scientifically and technologically in the lead; the third points the way to a better material life for everyone concerned.
>
> (Pei, 1967, p. 174)

For some people, English is still a language that is associated with Anglo-American culture and the good that the association entails. For some, English means access to and progress in intellectual pursuits, education, science, technology, and material well-being.

For others, the diffusion of English is to be resisted. This resistance is often expressed as a dichotomy between two ideologies. One, Global English, represents the point of view that English as a language of wider communication cannot be separated from its imperialist past. Global English refers to one standard language that is used internationally. The other, World Englishes, represents the point of view that there is no standard global English variety, but there are rather multiple varieties. English has a place in the world's constellation of languages, but only if it re-creates itself with standards and norms that do not depend on English as it is spoken in its home countries and does not threaten other languages or multilingualism. The main distinctions between the two ideologies of language are spelled out in Phillipson (2007, p. 128, citing Tsuda, 1994 and Skutnabb-Kangas, 2000) and adapted here in Figure 1.1.

Global English Paradigm	World Englishes Paradigm
assimilationist	celebration of diversity
monolingual orientation	multilingual orientation
US/UK norms	cross-national linguistic common core
English monopolizes prestige domains	local languages have high prestige
no concern for other languages	linguistic rights
target norm: the "native speaker"	target norm: the good ESL user

Figure 1.1 Diffusion and Resistance: Two World Views

Global English and World Englishes are two opposing paradigms or world views. One world view is that English is threatening to local identities and languages, learning English means belonging to an imperialist speech community, and speaking English implies acceptance of the cultural baggage that comes along with English. In the other world view, English spins away from native speaker control, loses its cultural baggage, and becomes a cross-national linguistic common core, or a consensus, among numerous local norms. The question of what the consensus features are is the topic of Part II of this book, while Part III discusses some of the diverse features.

Not everyone is satisfied with a strict dichotomy model between diffusion and resistance, between Global English and World Englishes. House (2003) argues that:

> In conceptualizing and researching ELF, we need "a third way", which steers clear of the extremes of fighting the spread of English for its linguistic imperialism, and accepting it *in toto* for its benefits. Accepting hybridity and using English creatively for one's own communicative purposes seems to be one such "third way" . . . I find it better to try to do more (and more varied) empirical research on how ELF is actually used and what it does to local languages.
>
> (House, 2003, p. 574)

House (2003) questions the idea that English is a threat to other languages because many people who use it do not identify with it and continue using their local languages. English users have different proficiency levels and mix their languages, making their lingua franca usage highly variable and fluid "hybrids." ELF is a resource for communication, not a source of identity.

Concentric Circles

Kachru (1985) offers another metaphor to understand the relationship between English, local linguistic situations, and speakers (see Figure 1.2). He sees the relationship in terms of three concentric circles. The *inner circle* refers to the countries where English is spoken natively by populations historically tied to England by colonialism and immigration (including, along with England itself, Australia, Canada, Ireland, New Zealand, Scotland, South Africa, and the USA).

Surrounding the inner circle is the *outer (or extended) circle*, where people of other ethnicities speak varieties of English along with other local languages in multilingual societies, as in Bangladesh, Hong Kong, India, Kenya, Nigeria, Pakistan, or the Philippines. In the outer circle, people use English in many domains with varying degrees of fluency and proficiency.

The *expanding circle* refers to the speakers who learn English in classrooms. Their countries do not have a history of colonialism by English-speaking countries. In the extended and the expanding circles, Kachru notes that the diffusion of English is initiated and controlled by non-native users. Kachru also believes that there is a process of de-Englishization taking place. Kachru writes:

> English ceases to be an exponent of only one culture—the Western Judaeo-Christian culture; it is now perhaps the world's most multicultural language, a fact which is, unfortunately, not well recognized. The present multicultural character of English is clearly revealed in its uses around the globe, especially in creative writing. In other words, English is now the language of those who use it; the users give it a distinct identity of their own in each region. As this transmuting alchemy of English takes effect, the language becomes less and less culture-specific.
>
> (Kachru, 1985, pp. 19–20)

For Kachru and many others, World Englishes is already detached from its identity with the inner circle speakers, regions, and cultures.

Intersection of Circles

Prodomou (2008, p. xiv) redraws Kachru's concentric circles model. He over-laps circles of English speakers, with ELF as a linguistic commodity shared among them. In his view, English is used as a lingua franca by anyone who knows it or knows part of it. In this area of common ground among all English users, there is room for hybrid cultures that are culturally de-Englishized or de-Americanized, re-Islamized, re-Europeanized, re-Africanized, and so on, depending on the identities and affiliations of the speakers in any given con-versation. Prodomou's model is adapted here in Figure 1.2.

This discussion offers some take-away points. There is a dynamic system of languages in the world, in which languages "gain" or "lose" based on the individual choices of people to use or not to use a language. It is important for people to maintain the use of their local language(s) and when they decide to learn English, they may choose from a variety of perspectives. They may participate in diffusion or resist it, they may reinvent English as part of their own identity, or they may use it simply for communication. They may define English as someone's culture-bound native language, as a lingua franca that offers a path to greater opportunity, or as a loose collection of diverse varieties spoken across the globe that have some consensus features that permit communication. World Englishes offers all of these choices, and more.

**World Englishes:
Common Ground**

English as a lingua franca
Diglossia
Academic English

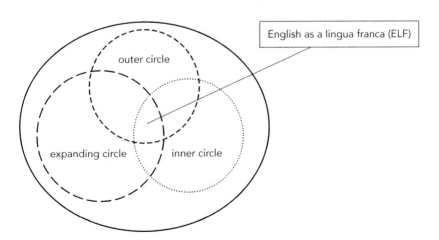

English as a lingua franca (ELF)

outer circle

expanding circle   inner circle

Figure 1.2 ELF at the Intersection of All English Users

World Englishes

World Englishes (WE) includes varieties of English spoken in Europe, Asia, Africa, some of which are known as Singlish, Chinglish, Spanglish, Euro-English, and so on. Within this diversity, there are three areas of common ground. One area is English as a lingua franca as the intersection of speakers who use English. Second, there is the shared problem of diglossia, that spoken and written versions of English are inevitably distant from each other, creating learning difficulties. Third, there are consensus features of language for those who wish to speak and write fluently and accurately in a professional or academic setting. These features set the goals for Academic English in the classroom.

English as a Lingua Franca

English as a lingua franca is at the intersection of the various populations of English users. Some researchers argue that the characteristics of ELF simply emerge from a combination of the speakers and their first languages, their proficiency in English, and situational factors. Firth (1996), after analyzing ELF conversations on the telephone, described ELF talk as "fleeting," with fluid norms because the participants are often insecure about what the norms were. Participants use a strategy ("'let it pass") of ignoring problems as long as comprehension was successful. ELF speakers use shorter turns and more non-verbal communication (Meierkord, 1996), and numerous repetitions (Lichtkoppler, 2007).

In this example of an ELF conversation between a German speaker and a Japanese speaker recorded at a housing office in a German-speaking university (Lichtkoppler, 2007, pp. 55–58, adapted

ELF Conversation 1

S1: *Can you print er the new address for me? PRINT.*

S2: *Sorry. hh You need a confirmation or . . . just a second. I just think.*

. . .

S2: *Thank you s- so: . . . You're now living in [place 1]*

S1: *Yeah yeah yeah.*

S2: *and then move in [place 2]*

S1: *Yeah yeah yeah yeah.*

S2: *and you need?*

S1: *Can you print*

S2: *ah*

S1: PRINT {drawing a paper in the air}

S2: *mhm*

S1: *The address for me.*

S2: *The confirmation for your visa?*

S1: *Yeah yeah yeah yeah.*

for readability), it is possible to see how overall efficient and understandable the conversations are. It appears that at times where native speakers might choose to use yes/no questions, Subject 2 uses only the intonation to mark the question, which is a simpler option.

Some researchers believe that ELF is becoming a unique variety of English with its own phonological and syntactic features, and not a mistake-ridden form of Standard English. For instance, Seidlhofer (2007, p. 145) sees an ELF as an entity whose features of usage transcend first language influence and levels of proficiency. The features are those that attract a lot of attention from English teachers and yet don't interfere with successful communication, like omitting the third person singular present tense on verbs, interchanging the relative pronouns *who* and *which*, using definite and indefinite articles in unconventional ways, overuse of generic verbs like *do, have, make, put, take*. She also notes redundant expressions like *discussed about* and *black color*. Mauranen and Ranta (2010) distinguish the English spoken as a lingua franca in academic settings from ELF with the acronym ELFA (Mauranen and Ranta, 2010). (There is an example of spoken ELFA in the Activities section of the chapter.)

Diglossia in World Englishes

Seidlhofer (2007) makes the case that a standard exists for certain kinds of writing in World Englishes, in academic, professional, or diplomatic settings, although spoken English has a less rigid standard. An international discourse community adheres to these established norms in order to maintain intelligibility among writers of different linguistic and cultural backgrounds. These standards are also maintained by editors and publishers of internationally distributed books and articles because they seek to be non-controversial.

> It stands to reason that in written language use, where there is no possibility of the overt reciprocal negotiation of meaning typical of spoken interaction, there is more reliance on established norms, and these are naturally maintained by a process of self-regulation whereby these norms are adhered to in the interest of maintaining global mutual intelligibility . . . However, as these written modes become increasingly used and appropriated by non-native users, one might speculate that, in time, self-regulation might move towards less dependence on native norms so that these written modes also take on the kind of distinctive features that are evident in spoken ELF.
>
> (Seidlhofer, 2007, p. 146)

Seidlhofer leaves the door open to change if writers, editors, and publishers cease to rely exclusively on the linguistic and textual features of formal prose. However, that is not likely to happen in the near future, and the question remains: just how different is formal language from informal speech?

Biber (1988) used a large database of spoken and written English as a native langue (ENL) texts to pinpoint how they vary in formal and informal **registers**. Registers are the different words and grammar used in different types of situations, for example in telephone conversations, spontaneous speeches, personal letters, fiction, official documents, and academic prose. He found that speech and writing showed variety along a number of dimensions: informational versus emotionally involved communication, explicit versus implied reference to things and people in the situation, and abstract versus concrete information. Each dimension correlates with different vocabulary and syntactic choices that the speakers/writers make. There is a continuum formed by these three dimensions, with informational, explicit, and abstract characteristics like official documents on one end and emotionally involved, implied, and concrete characteristics like phone conversations on the other.

For example, phone conversations have contractions, pronouns like *you* and *it*, questions, and few nouns. They have words like *today, tomorrow, now, here, there*, and few multi-syllabic nouns. Phone conversations have active sentences (*He goes . . . She walks . . .*). In contrast, official documents have many nouns and few questions. They have many complex multi-syllabic nouns (*development* or *construction*) and few adverbs like *tomorrow, here, now*. Official documents have passive sentences like *It was observed that . . .* or *The findings were shown to . . .* because passive sentences show detachment. People choose the linguistic features that are appropriate for the type of communication they are trying to achieve, but successful mastery of the more formal registers happens only after many years of schooling.

ENL Conversation

A: *Where do you go for that, Bath Travel for that then Neil?*

B: *Where?*

A: *For that brochure.*

B: *Bath Travel, where's that?*

A: *No, where do you get the—thing from then?*

B: *What?*

A: *Butlins?*

B: *Well—I got it from that travel agent's.*

A: *Oh.*

B: *er the one*

A: *In the precinct?*

B: *by, yeah, by Boots.*

A: *Oh yeah.*

(Biber et al., 1999, p. 225)

Academic English

Writers of English in business, legal, political, and academic registers follow the AE norms. Seidlhofer (2007, p. 146) thinks that, in written language, native speaker norms are more stable because writers must make their message comprehensible to readers without the benefit of context. ELF writers will adhere to these stricter standards "in the interest of maintaining global mutual intelligibility." Formal registers of English are not anyone's native language because of their differences from normal speech. Although some inner and outer circle English users may find it easier to learn Academic English, not all native speakers learn to use it effectively.

Academic English

Language is a dynamic system. It comprises the ecological interactions of many players: people who want to communicate and a world to be talked about. It operates across many different agents (neurons, brains, and bodies; phonemes, morphemes, lexemes, constructions, interactions, and discourses), different human conglomerations (individuals, social groups, networks, and cultures), and different timescales (evolutionary, diachronic, epigenetic, ontogenetic, interactional, neurosynchronic). Cognition, consciousness, experience, embodiment, brain, self, communication and human interaction, society, culture, and history are all inextricably intertwined in rich, complex, and dynamic ways in language. Yet despite this complexity, despite its lack of overt government, instead of anarchy and chaos, there are patterns everywhere, patterns not preordained by God, by genes, by school curriculum, or by other human policy, but patterns that emerge—synchronic patterns of linguistic organization at numerous levels (phonology, lexis, syntax, semantics, pragmatics, discourse, genre, etc.), dynamic patterns of usage, diachronic patterns of language change (linguistic cycles of grammaticization, pidginization, creolization, etc.), ontogenetic developmental patterns in child language acquisition, global geopolitical patterns of language growth and decline, dominance and loss, and so forth. As a complex system, the systematicities of language are emergent and adaptive. Only by adopting an integrative, dynamic framework will we understand how they come about.

(Ellis, 2008, p. 232)

In a recent article, Biber and Gray (2010) shed more light on the differences between informal and academic registers. Spoken English is more "verbal," while Academic English is more "nominal" because it has complex noun phrases with descriptions and modifiers. Formal Academic English is compressed, with a lot of information packed into each noun phrase. It is not always easy to interpret complex noun phrases with many layers of description. They argue that less compressed expressions like "the theory that explains relativity" are clearer and more specific than more compressed expressions like "relativity theory." In the shorter and compressed noun phrases, the relationship between the two words is left to the reader to figure out.

In the Ellis quote in the box above, many of the characteristics that Biber and Gray identified in Academic English are apparent: the use of many modifiers and prepositional phrases, increased use of lists of examples, words in parentheses, and the use of the colon. While not everyone wants to write or read such compressed texts, it is clear that English users who intend to read and write Academic English must be prepared for linguistic challenges that go beyond what they would need to be successful ELF speakers.

Figure 1.3 shows the types of writing that English users need along the two dimensions of proficiency and carefulness. Bisecting this figure is a line that demarcates two registers of English with different norms and characteristics.

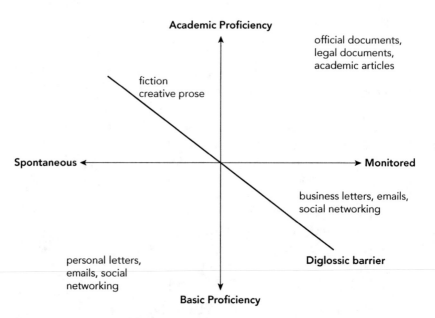

Figure 1.3 Diglossia in World Englishes

On one side of the diglossic barrier, formal writing is carefully written, closely monitored, accurate, complex, and compressed. On the other side, informal writing is spontaneous, lightly monitored, and simple.

English users the world over find themselves immersed in a diglossic situation in which the standards for speech and writing and the different registers complicate learning. What kind of English should be the goal of learning? What about tests and testing?

Standards and Tests

Timmis (2002) discusses a dilemma for teachers: should they offer some kind of informal variety such as ELF as a target for learning, which may not meet student aspirations, or should they teach a variety that meets international standards? ELF emerges naturally as interlocutors interact in speech and writing in the intersection of English usage in conversations and email. As a variety with "fleeting" and context dependent features, ELF may not offer a teachable goal at present. Academic English, with its stricter and more rigid norms, can be taught in the classroom when both fluency and accuracy are important.

Standards

Academic English has common core standards for international English in terms of pronunciation and grammar. Donesch-Jezo (2011) argues that mastery of these common standards is still crucial because professionals and students need to function at an advanced level to perform appropriately on high-stakes standardized tests, to fulfill professional obligations, and to succeed in advanced studies.

> The need to achieve an adequate proficiency in English language use has never been greater. Its position as the primary language of international communication in almost every field of professional activity means that its acquisition at a sufficiently advanced level is expected from graduates of secondary and tertiary education. Correct English language use in speech and in writing requires the possession of a competence which includes the knowledge of grammar rules and vocabulary items, as well as the ability to use them in real-life contexts.
>
> (Donesch-Jezo, 2011, p. 754)

The standards for Academic English across the globe are close to those of formal English in the inner circle countries. However, many students do not achieve these standards. For instance, after studying a large number of university student essays written by both English natives and L2 writers from various backgrounds, Hinkel (2002, p. 258) concludes that, despite many years of learning English and reading English texts, the English L2 writers were not entirely successful. Using the abbreviation NNS for non-native speaker, she says:

> Overall, in their writing, NNSs employ a great number of lexical and syntactic features of text that may not be particularly appropriate in constructing academic texts. On the other hand, various advanced syntactic constructions that are commonly associated with academic texts seem to be largely missing from NNS essays.

Despite the reality of ELF as a legitimate variety of English, the need for grammar instruction in core standards has never been more important. For one thing, Academic English is what prepares English learners to pass the gatekeeping tests that they may need to take.

Tests

Gatekeeping tests are proficiency tests that serve to distinguish two groups of people: those who are included in employment and higher education because of their "superior" English knowledge, and those who are excluded from opportunities because of their "inferior" fluency and accuracy. The costs for these tests average from $100 to $200 depending on the location and medium (paper or web-based) of the test, so taking these tests is expensive to start with, and multiple failures are even more expensive.

More than 27 million people have taken the TOEFL (Test of English as a Foreign Language) test, according to its website (http://www.ets.org/toefl, retrieved 4/3/2012). Over one million people a year take the IELTS test, from the International English Language Testing System (http://www.british council.org/learning-ielts-what-is-it.htm). The TOEIC (Test of English for International Communication) administers four million tests per year for people who want to demonstrate their English proficiency for potential employers.

These tests include items on listening, speaking, reading, and writing, and their focus is accuracy and fluency in standard varieties of formal English. These

The TOEIC promises to "help people achieve career success through three steps:

1) Take the TOEIC to demonstrate your English ability and include your score on your resume.
2) Apply for your dream job.
3) Accept job offer!"

(http://www.etscanada.ca/students/, retrieved 4/3/2012)

tests are controversial because they have become multinational money-makers beyond the tests themselves (e.g. overseas testing sites, preparation, English teaching programs). These tests are also controversial because they do not take into account diverse usages from outer circle or expanding circle English varieties; for the present, these tests reflect inner circle norms.

Despite their own preferences, teachers may find themselves teaching to the test; that is, they may be required by the school administration or pressured by students or parents to adjust their teaching toward the standard usages found on international tests. Teachers, be they native-speaking or expert non-native-speaking, may feel unprepared to teach the sometimes subtle and advanced grammar points or discourse organization required for written Academic English. However, Derewianka has a larger perspective on the goals of English grammar instruction:

> In summary, contemporary approaches to English language teaching and learning emphasize the need for learners to engage in purposeful inter-action using spoken, written, and visual modes. Learners are expected to be critically literate and able to create accurate, contextually appro-priate texts. A grammar that is responsive to such challenges needs to go beyond simply describing the "parts of speech" and their combination. It would require reconceptualizing grammar as a dynamic system of text-forming choices relevant to the students' communicative needs.
>
> (Derewianka, 2007, p. 855)

If grammar is a system of text-forming choices, then grammatical choices take place within the creation of spoken and written texts: conversations, emails, social networking, business correspondence, academic lectures, standardized tests and essays, and the like. Such discourses serve different functions, meet different needs, and require different linguistic abilities, all of which must be taken into account in our study of grammar, grammar teaching, and grammar learning.

At the turn of the century, Conrad (2000) made three predictions about the future of grammar instruction in the twenty-first century. As will be seen in later chapters, these predictions are already coming true. Grammarians now have access to descriptions of English that are specific to different registers and varieties such as conversational ELF, fiction, and academic texts. Concurrently, the importance of structural accuracy is balanced with the students' understanding of and ability to use spoken or written alternatives that are appropriate within a register and variety. Finally, in recent grammatical theories, grammar and lexicon have become two sides of the same coin. What Conrad did not predict was that a new theory of grammar would emerge that would make these predictions more likely; that is the topic of the next chapter.

> **Conrad's Predictions about the Future of Grammar Instruction**
>
> 1. Monolithic descriptions of English grammar will be replaced by register-specific descriptions.
> 2. The teaching of grammar will become more integrated with the teaching of vocabulary.
> 3. Emphasis will shift from structural accuracy to the appropriate conditions of use for alternative grammatical constructions.
>
> (Conrad, 2000, p. 549)

Study, Discussion, and Essay Questions

Create a Language Notebook as a file or folder on a computer or a hard copy notebook . The Language Notebook will hold your answers to these questions as well as a glossary of new words in the chapter.

1. Add these words to your glossary in your Language Notebook: World Englishes (WE), English as a lingua franca (ELF), Academic English (AE), languages of wider communication (LWC), diglossia, register. 12
2. Discuss the idea of a global system of language constellations with reference to the languages in your region. Key ideas are local languages, national languages, international languages or LWCs.

3. Contrast the metaphors of the diffusion of English (Global English) and the resistance to English (World Englishes) by going over the points in Phillipson's 2007 dichotomy. How do you see these attitudes operating in your setting?

4. What is the inner circle? The outer (or extended) circle? The expanding circle? How are Kachru's and Prodomou's ideas similar? How do they differ? What is your assessment of them?

5. Can a language be purged of its cultural heritage and traditional associations? What are the potential consequences? Do you think English can be a neutral language?

6. What examples of diglossia in English can you find? Use Figure 1.3 to help you find examples of differences. How can diglossia create special problems for teachers?

7. Look up five words you don't know from the Ellis (2008, p. 232) quote and add them to your glossary. Try to put the definitions into your own words.

8. Go over the characteristics of academic texts found by Biber and his colleagues to see what examples you can find in the Ellis quote.

9. Timmis raises the issue of standards in English as a target for learning. From your experience, what relevance do you see for proficiency testing? What kind of English do you want to know? If you are or are going to be a teacher, what kind of English do you want to teach?

Activities

1. Sinclair and Mauranen (2006, pp. 111–113) reproduce this ELFA conversation among Dutch, Lithuanian, and Finnish speakers in a university seminar session. How is this example like and unlike the ELF and ENL conversations cited in this chapter? What factors might account for the similarities and differences? Write your answer as a 100 word paragraph and be prepared to discuss.

    A: *Yeah but ca- can I legally if I'm a Russian living in Estonia like (if) I don't speak Estonian, can I legally open a shop or er work at this shop?*

    B: *You have to use their you have to use their language even in in business. It's its law now.*

    C: *Yeah.*

    B: *You have to use it if you can't if you can't prove that you have the sufficient well that's what I believe if you don't have that you have a sufficient er knowledge*

A: *Yeah*

B: *of Estonian then you can't do.*

A: *Then you can't even get a job officially.*

B: *Well I think in certain areas you can but for example in service you can't if you have to*

A: *mhm*

B: *erm If you have a direct contact with the people and you don't have s- efficient Estonian then you can't get it.*

A: *Yeah yeah okay.*

B: *And I mean it's funny thing because the Estonian it was an article I read. It was a famous Estonian tele- television I don't know reporter or something he went on strike on the hunger strike because er the Estonian government they made some kind of simplifying towards the citizenship law for the Russians so he went to the hunger strike because of the(ir) thinking that it's unfair.*

2. Using your answer to Activity 1 (or another paragraph you have written), find five examples of nouns. Copy your nouns, with the words before them and the words after them, in a list in your Language Notebook. Then answer this question about your experience: what strategies did you come up with for finding the nouns in the document? How did you find the nouns? (If you have a word-processed document, you may be able to use the FIND feature.)

3. How does the paragraph you wrote in Activity 1 fit on a scale of informal vs formal writing? Go over these terms to make sure you understand what they mean.

Informal	**Formal**
Emotion	Information
Implied reference	Explicit reference
Concreteness	Abstractness

4. Rewrite your paragraph twice, once to make it more informal and once to make it more formal. Which style seems more appropriate for the topic?

New Trends in Grammatical Theory

2

A powerful solution to the acquisition problem is the assumption that innate linguistic structure helps the child overcome the (possible) under-specification of language structure in the input. In this view, the input has to be mapped onto innate linguistic categories, but the categories or principles of core syntax do not have to be learned because they are there right from the beginning. But innate structure, as rich as it may be, cannot account for the acquisition of language-specific properties, such as the lexicon of a language or the inflectional properties of German or Dutch. These language-specific properties must be derived from the input over a number of years. In contrast, the so-called emergentist and usage-based approaches to language acquisition, that have become prominent in the past decade, are based on the assumption that language structure can be learned from language use by means of powerful generalization abilities ... The rationale of acquisition theory has changed accordingly, if the child has to learn the irregular and peculiar aspects of language by general learning mechanisms, these mechanisms should suffice to learn the more general and predictable patterns of that language as well.

(Behrens, 2009, p. 384)

This long and complex quote requires a message-oriented approach but it is worth the trouble because it outlines some fundamental issues in the connection between grammatical theory and language acquisition. The "acquisition problem" is the difficulty that researchers have explaining how infants go from babbling at one year of age to speaking like adults at age six. How do children accomplish such a complex task in such a short time despite the wide variety of cultural norms around the world? Generally, children hear incomplete and underspecified fragments of language, with little obvious grammatical structure and unclear meanings. There must be an explanation for how they acquire an adult grammar that has both common abstract patterns like subject–verb, as well as those features idiosyncratic to individual languages like words (lexical items) or verb endings (inflections).

Do they have innate knowledge in the form of categories or principles of grammar to help them, or can they learn both abstract common patterns and language-specific features from usage and exposure to normal language during infancy and childhood? Are general cognitive abilities powerful enough to work with incomplete and insufficient linguistic data and explain how a fully formed adult grammar emerges over time? Furthermore, although the acquisition problem and its solutions have been posed in terms of first language acquisition, as Behrens does in the quote above, they are also relevant to second language acquisition because theories from first language are applied to second, and are often the basis for second language pedagogy. This chapter will further explain these ideas.

Language Acquisition Hypotheses

Behrens alludes to two possible solutions to the acquisition problem (see Figure 2.1). The first explanation, the **Innatist Hypothesis**, emerged in the 1960s. The hypothesis is that babies are born with a mental capacity that allows them to map the words they hear and learn onto predetermined universal grammatical structures. As long as children are exposed to normal language, the innate capacity for language will cause them to form abstract adult grammars identical to the grammars of other people. The acquisition problem is reduced to mastery of any idiosyncratic properties of languages which must be acquired from social interaction. From the people around them, children learn that the past tense of *go* is *went*, not **goed*, or that the suffix *-ing* marks the progressive in English. Thus, the Innatist Hypothesis needs two separate systems to explain language acquisition: an innate capacity for universal syntactic structures, and general learning capacities for language-specific features. This hypothesis also rests on a critical period of childhood during which language acquisition must take place.

More recently, researchers have proposed another solution, the **Usage/ Exposure Hypothesis**. These researchers argue that since children succeed in

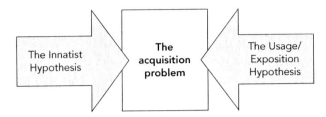

Figure 2.1 Two Explanations for the "Problem" of First Language Acquisition

learning language-specific features from the surrounding usage and exposure, they can also learn syntactic structures as well. Babies may come equipped with powerful but normal mental capacities (e.g. the ability to generalize from specific experiences or the ability to derive analogies) so that they can acquire language from the interaction around them. The Usage/Exposure Hypothesis is simpler because it requires only one mechanism to explain language acquisition, and its explanation is in terms of mental capacities that people need for other tasks besides language.

The Innatist Hypothesis

Linguistic theory is concerned primarily with an ideal speaker-listener, in a completely homogeneous speech-community, who knows its language perfectly and is unaffected by such grammatically irrelevant conditions as memory limitations, distractions, shifts of attention and interest, and errors (random or characteristic) in applying his knowledge of the language in actual performance . . . We thus make a fundamental distinction between *competence* (the speaker-hearer's knowledge of his language) and *performance* (the actual use of language in concrete situations) . . . A grammar of a language purports to be a description of the ideal speaker-hearer's intrinsic competence.
                                     (Chomsky, 1965, pp. 3–4)

Chomsky thinks that linguistic theory can advance only if certain assumptions limit the research questions. One assumption is that there is an ideal native

Grammaticality

An utterance or sentence is grammatical if it conforms to a set of rules that describes or generates a language, or part of the native speaker's competence.

speaker of a language who lives in a monolingual speech community. The linguistic knowledge of this ideal speaker-hearer is called **competence**, and it has none of the sloppiness of actual use of language in specific settings, or **performance**. Another assumption is that performance (e.g. slips of the tongue, mispronunciations, or speech errors) is too messy to deal with. It is the job of the linguist to describe a set of rules that determines the grammaticality of utterances or sentences, to discover the innate categories and principles in the linguistic system.

This research agenda presents some serious dilemmas for those interested in second language acquisition. For instance, if syntactic theories are based on an ideal speaker-hearer in a homogeneous speech community with linguistic competence, what about second language learners who live in heterogeneous speech communities, and whose language has speech errors? If there is a critical period for successful first language acquisition, is successful language learning outside of the critical period possible?

The Usage/Exposure Hypothesis

Meanwhile, some of Chomsky's assumptions have been questioned. Firth and Wagner (1997) argue that the identities of the native speaker and non-native speaker are not homogeneous but rather multi-faceted. They suggest that language users are largely successful at communicating using a variety of resources and strategies, as, for example, the ELF speakers described in Chapter 1. Language users may not want to become native-like speakers; instead, they may want to acquire just the amount of the language to suit their needs and no more.

More questions about the Innatist Hypothesis arise from the use of technology. Since the 1980s computers have been used to analyze speech and written texts so that linguistic performance has become more accessible to analysis. Linguists can now examine huge amounts of data from real language usage and from real language users. From these studies, the concept of **naturalness** has taken the place of competence.

> **Naturalness**
>
> An utterance or sentence is natural if it conforms to people's knowledge of their normal usage and exposure or if the words occur together with a certain frequency or probability.

First and foremost, the ability to examine large text corpora in a systematic manner allows access to a quality of evidence that has not been available before. The regularities of pattern are sometimes spectacular and, to balance the variation seems endless. The raw frequency of differing language events has a powerful influence on evaluation . . . What is more, the growing respect for real examples led in the mid-1980s to a notion of textual well-formedness, which was dubbed *naturalness*.

(Sinclair, 1991, pp. 4–5)

The goal of a linguistic theory is not to describe what sentences are possible or grammatical in an ideal speaker-hearer's linguistic system, but what sentences are natural in a corpus of real spoken utterances and written sentences. These sentences from Ellis (2008, p. 232) are naturally occurring sentences in Academic English.

Language is a dynamic system. It comprises the ecological interactions of many players: people who want to communicate and a world to be talked about.

The sentences are natural because there are syntactic, semantic, pragmatic, and textual associations between words, phrases, and grammatical structures. The words occur with their expected grammatical roles, like subject of the sentence or object of a preposition, and their normal categories, like noun or verb. In contrast, the following hypothetical sentences are unnatural, even though they are grammatical and possible:

A dynamic system is language. Many communicating people's interactions are ecological because they discuss the world.

The Usage/Exposure Hypothesis, with its dependence on multi-faceted multilingual learners, actual performance data from corpora, and naturalness rather than grammaticality, seems to be a fruitful direction for second language grammatical theory and pedagogy, so it is adopted for this book.

Models of Construction

Databases of conversations, letters, fiction, and academic prose reveal the most likely and frequent usages and, based on those, language users form expectations of what is natural. These expectations form the basis for a grammatical system that is used to construct utterances and sentences as well as comprehend them. Sinclair's examination of natural linguistic data led him to propose two different models of how language users construct utterances using their linguistic system.

The Open Choice Principle

The first model of construction follows the **open choice principle**, that "[a]t each point where a unit is completed (a word or phrase or a clause), a large range of choice opens up and the only restraint is grammaticalness" (Sinclair, 1991, p. 109). This is the way that people often think of grammar, that people construct sentences creatively starting from words and building larger structures more or less freely by following grammatical patterns. However, in reality, there are strong grammatical preferences that constrain the choice of words in typical phrases and sentences, so the choice is not really open. These grammatical preferences are called colligational constraints or **colligations**. Hoey (2005, p. 43) defines colligation as "the grammatical company a word or word sequence keeps or avoids keeping, the grammatical functions preferred or avoided by a group in which the word participates, the place in a sequence that a word or word sequence prefers or avoids."

Colligation

$[[put]_V [NP] [Place]]_{VP}$

For instance, the verb *put* requires both an object and a location: *put the shoes in the closet*. The colligation is written $[[put]_V [NP] [Place]]_{VP}$ to represent the idea that the verb *put* requires a noun phrase (NP) and something that refers to a place in order to be a complete verb phrase (VP). Bracketed representations illustrate the frequently occurring abstract patterns that language users acquire. The knowledge of abstract grammar patterns in a linguistic system allows language users to construct innovative but natural phrases and sentences by making lexical choices at crucial moments.

The Idiom Principle

Nevertheless, Sinclair (1991, p. 110) notes: "It is clear that words do not occur at random in a text, and that the open-choice principle does not provide for substantial enough restraints on consecutive choices. We would not produce normal text simply by operating the open-choice principle." He proposes another model of utterance construction called the **idiom principle**, whereby "a language user has available a large number of semi-preconstructed phrases

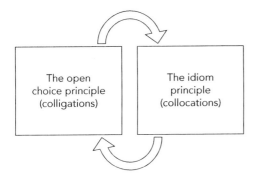

Figure 2.2   Two Models of How Spoken Utterances or Written Sentences Are Constructed or Understood during Language Processing

that constitute segments" (1991, p. 110) These prefabricated phrases called **collocations** allow speakers to construct and comprehend utterances more easily in real-time communication. As people construct sentences, they may choose to access a prefabricated phrase as a whole unit from memory instead of constructing a phrase word by word using the open choice principle.

Computer analysis of large corpora reveals the immensity of prefabrication and collocation in language. In constructing an utterance, speakers often choose more than one word at a time. Instead of choosing individual words and inserting them into phrases, collocations like *set eyes on* or *learn your way around* are available as whole units that fit within utterances and sentences. A lot of the normal usage found in corpus data consists of such prefabricated segments and they contribute to the fluency and accuracy found in natural language.

Collocation

put the kettle on

Wray's Idiomatic Paradox

The dual nature of the language system (colligation and collocation) presents a paradox in second language acquisition: what makes language natural, fluent, and accurate for native speakers is exactly what is most difficult for learners of a language. Native speakers acquire knowledge of numerous prefabricated expressions and collocations that facilitate language production and comprehension. Language learners, on the other hand, make good use of such memorized prefabrications early on, but as they advance, there isn't enough usage and exposure for them to learn enough collocations. Instead, they must rely on the open choice principle to create new utterances and sentences to communicate. That is why, even though their utterances and sentences are grammatically correct, their speech or writing may sound less natural. Native speakers may say *Put the kettle on* when they want tea, but an English learner may say *Start the water to boil*. The latter is not incorrect, but it is less natural than the former. For many learners, living, working, and studying in the country where the second language is spoken, or some other kind of total immersion, is what ultimately makes learners expert.

Wray's Idiomatic Paradox

I had been reading about formulaic language in the context of language proficiency, and had been struck by three observations made in the literature. The first was that native speakers seem to find formulaic (that is, prefabricated) language an easy option in their processing and/or communication. The second was that in the early stages of first and second language acquisition, learners rely heavily on formulaic language to get themselves started. The third observation, however, seemed to fly in the face of the first two. For L2 learners of intermediate and advanced proficiency, the formulaic language was the biggest stumbling block to sounding nativelike. How could something that was so easy when you began with a language, and so easy when you were fully proficient in it, be so difficult in between?

(Wray, 2002, p. ix)

Construction Grammar

In the quote at the beginning of the chapter, Behrens alludes to the idea that grammatical theory must place both productive experiences (usage and exposure) with language and general cognitive abilities as the primary raw materials for language acquisition, as shown in Figure 2.3. Insights like Behrens' are part of a new theory of grammar called **Construction Grammar**.

People's participation in a society and a culture, along with general cognitive abilities, are the only raw materials necessary for language acquisition. Humans control and monitor their experiences with the world and store them as traces in memory. The memory traces accumulate over time and what is created is a linguistic system (or "architecture") that allows for rapid and accurate decision-

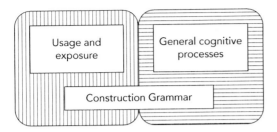

Figure 2.3 The Raw Materials for Learning Language in Construction Grammar

making during language use. The linguistic architecture is never complete or perfect because learning spans the life-time of the individual, so there is no disconnect between the child's language and the adult's language. There is no inherent difference between first language learners and second language learners.

Constructions

Psychologists and other brain scientists now understand more about memory and learning. Using general cognitive processes, people notice, represent, and store memory traces that keep track of language forms and their communicative functions. Over time, with sufficient usage and exposure, memory traces accumulate, acquire stability, and turn into linguistic symbols that are the building blocks called **constructions**. Croft (2001, pp. 17–18) suggests that constructions model a speaker's grammatical knowledge in form and meaning pairs, as shown in Figure 2.4.

Constructions

Cognitive symbols that encode the connections between language forms (e.g. words, phrases, colligations, collocations) and communicative functions or meanings relevant to something in the world.

A construction can be any unit of language: a sound, a prefix or a suffix, a word, a colligation, a collocation, a sentence, and even a text. A single word construction contains information about its sounds, structure, spelling, category information like noun or verb, animacy (living, dead, or inanimate) and other meaning-related information, and its pragmatic and discourse uses. Figure 2.5 is a representation of a form-meaning pairing for the prefabricated greeting *How do you do?*

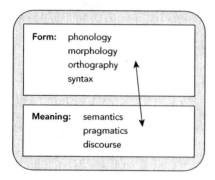

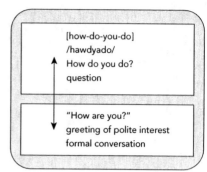

Figure 2.4 Constructions Are Symbols That Pair Forms with Their Meanings and Functions

Figure 2.5 A Construction for the Collocation *How Do You Do?*

The construction *how do you do* contains a form (a set of sounds pronounced a certain way, a set of morphemes or words) as well as a meaning (*how are you*), a pragmatic use (polite interest in a greeting), and a discourse context (formal conversation). Like Croft, Tomasello (2003) suggests that constructions encode regularities and general patterns like the plural construction [Noun + s], as well as irregularities and unusual patterns like [child + ren]. Tomasello (2003, p. 100) defines the construction as "a unit of language that comprises multiple linguistic elements used together for a relatively coherent communicative function."

Acquisition and Attunement

Babies learn simple form/function constructions and gradually fill in more information inside each construction and acquire more constructions. By the age of five, children are rapid and accurate language users, able to make the right decisions as they speak fluently and listen with good comprehension. They become attuned to the language in their environment because their memories keep track of the probabilities and frequencies with which constructions occur in certain

Development of Constructions from Concrete to Abstract

Item-based constructions:
Single word: *cookie*
Two words: *eat cookie*
Three words: *daddy eats cookie*

Mixed construction:
[[X] eats [Z]]

Pattern-based construction:
[[NP] [[V] [NP]]$_{VP}$]$_{SENTENCE}$

contexts. In this process, an architecture of small and large, concrete and abstract constructions is used for rapid decision-making while processing and producing utterances and sentences.

Tomasello (2003, p. 139) proposes several stages of development in children's acquisition of grammar. Children first acquire single words and then simple two-word constructions like *daddy bye-bye* or *gimme juice*. The third stage consists of concrete **item-based constructions** with ordered words and grammatical suffixes like *daddy eats cookie*. Next, children begin to generalize and analogize from numerous item-based constructions to form **mixed item-based and pattern-based constructions**, like [[X] *eats* [Z]], where X stands for something or someone that can eat (animate) and Z stands for something that can be eaten (food). These abstract symbols (or variables) are associated with the word *eats* in a construction. Around the same time, children begin to acquire a concept of what can be the subject of a sentence (a NP, usually animate) and what can be a direct object (a NP, usually inanimate). Finally, Tomasello (2003, p. 145) argues that "the learner groups together into categories those linguistic items that function similarly—that is, consistently play similar communicative roles—in different utterances and constructions." In other words, children acquire unconscious knowledge of lexical categories like noun and verb, syntactic categories like NP and VP, and common sentence structures as part of a linguistic architectural system.

The system includes fully abstract **pattern-based constructions** which stand for common sentence patterns with variables for the noun phrase subject (NP) and the verb phrase predicate (VP). The verb phrase is composed of any verb (V) (not just *eats*) with any direct object noun phrase (NP). There are no actual words associated with a pattern-based construction like [[NP] [V NP]$_{VP}$]$_{SENTENCE}$, so it has no pronounceable form. The pattern has only a grammatical meaning or function: to express the idea "someone/something does something to someone."

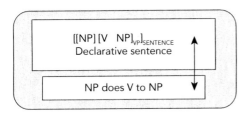

Figure 2.6 An Abstract Construction for a Pattern-Based Construction

Priming

The "glue" that holds constructions together in the linguistic architecture is a psychological process called priming. Priming is pervasive in the processing and comprehension of language. In priming, the use of one construction, the "prime" (a word or phrase), results in the same construction or a similar or related construction (the "target" or "response") being used subsequently by the speaker or the listener. Priming is strong when the prime and the target have a high probability of co-occurring in normal (as shown by statistical studies) language usage. Thus, what speakers and listeners have been exposed to influences the production or recognition of subsequent language. McDonough and Trofimovich (2009, p. 2) remark that:

> Priming is "the phenomenon in which prior exposure to specific language forms or meanings either facilitates or interferes with a speaker's subsequent language processing."
>
> (McDonough and Trofimovich, 2009, p. xvi)

> A speaker's sensitivity to previous encounters with language forms and meanings suggests that language use is sensitive to the occurrence of language forms and meanings in the environment. In other words, the exact forms and meanings that speakers use can be affected by the language that occurred in discourse they recently engaged in.

Priming actually refers to a variety of phenomena. **Semantic priming** refers to facilitation in the processing of a response word because of similar or related meanings. For instance, it is easier to read the target word *hospital* after exposure to the word *doctor* because their meaning connection facilitates recognition of the word. The more closely related the prime and the target, the better the priming will be.

Repetition priming is facilitation in processing words because of prior exposure to those words. Repetition priming operates at the level of prefixes and suffixes, individual words, collocations, colligations, or sentences. For example, Grainger and Carreiras (2009, p. 935) report that there is evidence for priming across forms that share the same prefix (*REmake* primes *REthink*) and suffix (*farmER* primes *walkER*). **Lexical priming** is the tendency for people to process a word, phrase, or collocation more quickly and more accurately because they have had previous exposure to that construction.

Syntactic priming affects the likelihood that a speaker will produce a construction when compared with an equally acceptable alternative. If a speaker uses a sentence with a prepositional dative like *My daughter sold the car to her friend*, the listener is more likely to later use another prepositional dative sentence instead of a double object dative like *My daughter sold her friend the car*. Syntactic priming operates at the level of abstract pattern-based constructions with variables like NP and VP.

Because of these different levels of priming, the effects can be **nested** within each other; the word *set* primes the colligation [*set* NP], and [*set* NP] weakly primes the phrase *set a fire* or *set a standard*, depending on the context of the interaction. However, the word *set* strongly primes the collocation *set the table*, and the collocation *set the table* might prime its occurrence in a common imperative construction like *Please set the table before dinner.*

Types of Priming

Semantic priming from the meaning associations a construction evokes.

Repetition priming from having experienced a construction before, and lexical priming from prior exposure to a word.

Syntactic priming among abstract grammatical constructions.

Hoey (2005) specifically applies the idea of priming to collocations. Priming and nesting create a "thicket" of mental traces, memories, and associations that activate constructions to facilitate rapid decision-making, fluency, and accuracy in language use.

> We can only account for collocation if we assume that every word is mentally primed for collocational use. As a word is acquired through encounters with it in speech and writing, it becomes cumulatively loaded with contexts and co-texts in which it is encountered, and our knowledge of it includes the fact that it co-occurs with certain other words in certain kinds of context. The same applies to word sequences built out of these words; these too become loaded with the contexts and co-texts in which they occur. I refer to this property as nesting, where the product of a priming becomes itself primed in ways that do not apply to the individual words making up the combination.
>
> (Hoey, 2005, p. 8)

In short, different kinds of priming occur among constructions of different types (item-based, mixed, or pattern-based) and at different levels (morphemes, words, phrases, sentences). Priming occurs from the top-down and from the bottom-up. That is, it operates from abstract pattern-based constructions "down" to specific lexical items, and from lexical items "up" to abstract constructions. Priming associations also operate both internally and externally. Internal priming means that constructions of various types are associated with each other inside the mind of the speaker. Priming is external because it spreads to the listener. Use of a construction by a speaker causes activation of that construction and associated constructions in the listener's mind. Priming reduces memory load, helps resolve ambiguities, and aids in understanding intended messages. It also must be involved in language learning.

Processing

Sinclair (1991) proposed two principles to explain why language had a natural quality (the idiom principle) as well as a creative quality (the open choice principle). Wray (2002, p. 14) also proposed a dual systems approach to language processing. The **holistic system** is idiomatic; it depends on formulaic language and prefabricated chunks to express ideas fluently and reduce cognitive load in both comprehension and production of language. The **analytical system** is open choice; it is the use of pattern-based constructions to process novel utterances and sentences. However, the notion of priming allows these two systems to be unified. The differences between holistic and analytic processing are due to the amount of priming among the constructions selected during the processing of utterances and sentences.

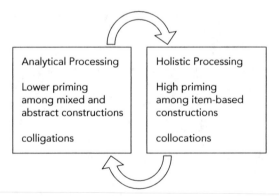

Figure 2.7 One Neural Architecture with Different Amounts of Priming and Different Types of Constructions Derived from Usage and Exposure and General Cognitive Abilities

Analytic processing involves greater use of mixed and pattern-based constructions with variables, like $[put \ [NP] \ [PLACE]]_{VP}$, $[be \ [V]_{PAST}$ $_{PARTICIPLE}]_{PASSIVE}$ or $[set \ [NP]]$, to produce utterances and sentences. The priming associations among abstract constructions are fewer and weaker due to the presence of the "open choice" variables. Language users must work hard to match and merge word-level constructions with pattern-based constructions, so producing or comprehending involves more cognitive work and results, perhaps, in less fluent or less natural but more creative language use.

In contrast, **holistic processing** makes use of item-based constructions closely related to each other through nested priming associations with high probabilities of appearing together. In holistic processing, language production and comprehension operate closer to the "bottom" of the grammatical architecture, where priming is strong among words and formulaic expressions, such as *set the table, please set the table before dinner,* or *how-do-you-do.* Once a word is selected, collocational primings almost force a language user to access a related prefabricated structure, so processing is easier, faster, and leads to more fluent and natural language.

To summarize, the linguistic architecture is a system of item-based, mixed, and pattern-based constructions primed to occur and co-occur in a "thicket" of associations. The same architecture produces and comprehends language analytically or holistically. Analytical processing relies on abstract constructions with less or weaker priming, while holistic processing relies on item-based constructions with more or stronger priming associations. Although it is convenient to refer to dual systems in language production and comprehension, in fact there is one linguistic system involved in the processing of utterances and sentences. For the purposes of exposition in this book, the linguistic system is modeled as an architecture of construction types in Figure 2.8. Priming

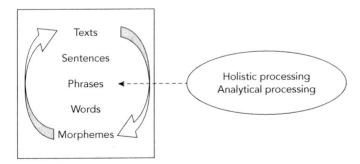

Figure 2.8   A Schema of the Linguistic Architecture with Its Main Construction Types

trickles down from texts to sentences to phrases to words and to morphemes to influence rapid decision-making at each decision-point in language processing and use.

Bottom-up priming also influences choices during language use. The lowest part of the language system is the level of morphemes and word formation. Word-level constructions participate in collocational or colligational choices to access larger phrasal constructions (e.g. collocations and colligations), which in turn take part in accessing sentence-level constructions. Utterances and sentences participate in discourse creation to produce texts like conversations, emails, paragraphs, letters, and research articles. The chapters in Part II of this book take up each of these levels in turn.

Construction Grammar and Language Learning

In Construction Grammar, language learning is a process of attunement in which people use general cognitive abilities to process large amounts of language data in usage and exposure. As such, in any one individual, the linguistic system is always being modified by experience. Grammar is not mastered once and for all; instead, it must be used, replenished, and maintained through new contexts and negotiations of meaning. The learning curve is steeper for children than it is for adults, who reach a point where their learning is only in very small increments. Hopper (1998, p. 170) put it like this:

> This means that the task of "learning a language" must be reconceived. Learning a language is not a question of acquiring grammatical structure but of expanding a repertoire of communicative contexts. Consequently, there is no date or age at which the learning of a language can be said to be complete. New contexts, and new occasions of negotiation of meaning, occur constantly. A language is not a circumscribed object but a loose confederation of available and overlapping social experiences.

L1/L2 Similarities

Learning a second language is similar to learning a first language because it involves exposure and usage to acquire constructions. If learning is dependent on general cognitive capacities, then first language learners and learners of second languages face a similar task: to continuously update and maintain item-based, mixed, and pattern-based constructions throughout the life-span. Since learning abilities develop and continue throughout the life-span, successful second language learning can take place after childhood. Language acquisition begins through exposure to words and collocations that are learned slowly. Over time, more abstract pattern-based constructions emerge; a "top," an abstract system of grammar, is created. Once the grammatical system exists, top-down influences on learning, comprehension, and production occur. Priming is implicated in this process in both first and second language acquisition, and so are holistic and analytical processing abilities.

L1/L2 Differences

There are obvious and important differences between first and later language learners. First language learners have unpressured time and high motivation to acquire their language, but the amount of exposure and repetition that first language learners enjoy contrasts with the "poverty" of the language-learning environments of most second language learners. Normal first language learning takes place with massive amounts of interaction, input, and natural feedback, offering the learner multiple exposures as fodder for generalization, analogy, and internalization. Most second language learning takes place in classrooms for a few hours a week and offers reduced exposure and few repetitions of experiences. This may not be enough exposure for people to become attuned to priming associations to allow for quick and easy decision-making holistically or analytically.

In first language acquisition, ample usage and exposure result in differing amounts of priming among constructions, and hence holistic and analytical processing abilities naturally emerge. Holistic processing is associated with increased fluency because prefabricated expressions simply need to be retrieved. For the listener, dealing with collocations that have high frequencies of occurring together assists in comprehension and makes it faster. Nevertheless, although beginning second language learners rely on prefabricated units, their lack of exposure and usage in the classroom leads ultimately to a greater reliance on analytic processing which, because of the lack of priming associations, can result in unnatural sounding language. (Wray's paradox will be discussed further in Chapter 15.)

Second language users are usually older so they have more cognitive capacities (e.g. greater memory, well-developed cognition, better abilities to analyze, more world and culture knowledge); these facilitate language learning so that it can be less dependent on simple usage and exposure. They have a pre-existing linguistic system that facilitates or interferes with the acquisition of later languages. They have highly evolved knowledge of colligations and collocations with priming associations in their first language. Attunements are habits, and acquiring fluency and accuracy in another language means breaking those habits and forming new ones.

Instruction and Purpose

There are limitations on what can be done in all but the most privileged of educational settings. Grammar teachers, in their pedagogical planning and implementation, have at least these purposes:

- to find shortcuts to acquisition that can make up for the inevitable lack of usage and exposure, such as direct instruction and explicit feedback;
- to take advantage of all cognitive capacities for learning, including memorization, rote practice, inductive or data-based learning;
- to balance vocabulary and grammar through holistic methods with collocations and analytical methods with colligations;
- to provide opportunities for individualized practice designed to substitute L2 habits for L1 habits for both fluency and accuracy;
- to make grammar instruction register-specific by embedding grammar instruction in highly interactive communicative contexts about diverse genres and texts.

In an ideal world, everyone wishing to perfect a second or third language or maintain language skills would be able to travel or do a home-stay in the country whose language they are interested in. Short of that, it may be necessary to reinvent the grammar classroom or, perhaps, repurpose successful methods from the past. Learners need to use active strategies for acquisition inside and outside the classroom. At the very least, it is abundantly clear that the amount of classroom time for exposure and usage needs to be increased. As Butzkamm and Caldwell (2009, p. 29) suggest, "[o]nly sufficient time in language bath contexts can furnish the multitudinous examples of language expressions for the discernment of recurring grammatical structure and lexical meanings and choices."

Study, Discussion, and Essay Questions

Write the answers to these questions in your Language Notebook.

1. Add these terms to your glossary and define them according to their usage in this chapter: competence, performance, grammaticality, naturalness, colligation, and collocation.
2. How do judgments of naturalness differ from grammaticality judgments?
3. Describe Sinclair's two models of how language users create sentences.
4. What is Wray's idiomatic paradox?
5. What are the two "raw materials" for Construction Grammar? Does Construction Grammar conform to the Innatist Hypothesis or the Usage / Exposure Hypothesis? What potential benefits does Construction Grammar offer in thinking about second language acquisition?
6. What are constructions? How do they differ from grammar rules?
7. Put the quote from Tomasello (2003, p. 145) into your own words. What does it have to say about how learners learn the grammar of their first language? Do you think second language acquisition could be the same?
8. What are item-based, mixed, and pattern-based constructions?
9. What is priming? How does the idea of priming allow the analytical and the holistic models of language processing to be collapsed into one?
10. How is the linguistic system described in this chapter?
11. How is second language learning similar to first language learning? How is it different? Can you think of any ways they are similar / different that are not mentioned in the chapter?

Activities

1. What is the "acquisition problem"? What are the "solutions" to the problem? Describe the differences between the Innatist Hypothesis and the Usage / Exposure Hypothesis and the implications of each for second language instruction. Write your answer as a 100 word paragraph and be prepared to discuss your answer.
2. Following the examples in the text, draw a construction with an example of a common noun, a proper name, or an active verb. Be prepared to share your constructions with the class.
3. Take a "natural" sentence you wrote in your answer to Activity 1 and try to make it "unnatural." How did you do that? What makes the difference

between the natural and the unnatural sentences? Then try to make your sentence ungrammatical. How did you do that?

4. Using your answer to Activity 1 as a text or document, find three examples of noun phrases with the determiner *the* and noun phrases with the determiner *a/an*. List them in your Language Notebook. Can you articulate a difference in meaning between *the* and *a/an* or a syntactic difference between them based on your examples?

New Trends in Second Language Acquisition   **3**

> If we believe that learning an L2 is a process of socialization where we are learning to construct new sociocultural identities and to reshape our subjectivity, then we need a theory of language that enables us to understand how grammar is implicated in such processes.
>
> (Derewianka, 2007, pp. 854–855)

It cannot be disputed that people's first language is acquired as part of general processes of socialization and enculturation that inevitably shape people's identities and subjectivities as individuals and as members of social groups. However, the idea that second language acquisition affects people's identities and subjective experiences, and even their cognitive abilities, is more controversial, as shown by the attitudes toward English discussed in Chapter 1. Construction Grammar, with its strong foundation in cognition and sociocultural usage, seems useful as a "theory of language" that helps teachers understand how grammar learning takes place and can shape people's identity and their subjective experiences.

For one thing, teachers are becoming more sensitive to students' emotional responses to learning English. Referring to the connections among language, tradition, identity, and subjectivity, Kazmi said:

> As more and more attention is given to English, the first language is marginalized. The marginalization of my mother tongue creates a temporal tension in my being-in-the-world—a tension which is the result of the power differential between the two languages . . . It, to put it

simply, breaks the continuity between my past and my present. My past is my tradition and the tradition of my community / society … To withdraw or abandon the language through which tradition speaks is to render tradition mute … As a result of the break, I feel somewhat removed from my tradition and hence less capable of drawing support and getting guidance from it.

(Kazmi, 1997, p. 11)

People who experience a disconcerting loss of identity through learning another language merit understanding and possibly research. More study has been devoted to positive changes in identity, subjectivity, and even cognition when learners acquire language awareness.

Language Awareness

Discussions about the positive effects of language awareness began in the 1970s when researchers studied children's awareness of language, how it related to play, schooling, and literacy, and how it influenced cognitive development in different socioeconomic groups. Researchers distinguished two types of language awareness among children. With the first type, children are able to manipulate and make judgments about language without knowing or being able to articulate what they know in exact terms. This language awareness is based on children's implicit or unconscious learning of language through usage, exposure, and practice. In terms from Construction Grammar, the children know which sentences sound natural or possible based on their attunement to probabilities and frequency information.

Implicit Language Awareness

Adult: How about this one: *I am knowing your sister.*
Child: No, *I know your sister.*
Adult: Why not *I am knowing your sister?* You can say *I am eating your dinner.*
Child: It's different! (shouting) You say different sentences in different ways! Otherwise it wouldn't make sense.

(Cazden, 1974, p. 14)

For instance, Cazden (1974) cites an example of language awareness in response to questions about sentences that sound "funny." Some children know something is funny, but they cannot verbalize problems with abstract grammatical constructions. In this case, there is a mismatch between the verb *know*, which refers to a state of being, and the progressive construction [*be* V + *ing*]$_{VP}$, which implies action in progress. This implicit language awareness remains much the same into adulthood for many people, who know what sounds right but can't explain why.

The second type of language awareness means that children can say what is wrong, as in this example cited in Cazden (1974). In this case, the inanimate expression *the color green* cannot be the direct object of the verb *frighten* because it requires an animate object. It is common for both children and adults to be able to articulate what is "funny" about sentences with semantic or meaning-based anomalies such as this one.

Explicit Language Awareness

Adult: How about *George frightens the color green.*
Child: Sounds okay but it's stupid, it's stupid!
Adult: What's wrong with it?
Child: The color green isn't even alive, so how can it be afraid of George?

(Cazden, 1974, p. 15)

Metalinguistic Awareness

Development in language awareness means that implicit knowledge of language becomes increasingly available as **explicit** knowledge as language users become more mature. Under certain circumstances (e.g. schooling, second language learning, and some forms of bilingualism) language awareness becomes highly sophisticated; it becomes **metalinguistic awareness**. Metalinguistic awareness is the conscious ability to think and speak about language as an object in its own right and to control subtle language functions. Metalinguistic awareness changes people's experience of the world, that is, their subjectivities, their cognitive abilities, and possibly their identities, in positive ways.

Implicit and Explicit Learning

Like those early researchers studying language awareness, Hulstijn (2003, p. 196) also describes a process of language learning with both implicit and explicit components. Implicit learning is natural learning that comes from the accumulated experiences that people normally have as they interact with others. The result of implicit language learning is a diffuse network of memory traces and associations, the linguistic architecture, that gradually builds up strength in the brain through practice. When some of the memory traces and associations build up enough strength, they take on a more symbolic status as independent units (constructions) that are available for conscious cognitive processes like analysis and reasoning. Implicit learning is also called **procedural** because it underlies the ability to "do" language.

> Procedural knowledge comes from implicit learning. It is knowing how to do something that cannot necessarily be explained in words, like cooking, playing a musical instrument, or speaking.
>
> Declarative knowledge comes from explicit learning. It is knowing the "what" of something. It can be articulated like a recipe, musical scores, or, in language, the metalinguistic terminology for syntactic categories and pattern-based constructions.

Implicit knowledge may turn into explicit or declarative knowledge through conscious analysis and reasoning, such as in the examples of language awareness cited above. The lack of explicit grammar terminology impedes the development of language awareness. When people don't have the terms needed for language analysis and reasoning, it is harder for them to accomplish those tasks. Thus, direct instruction in the classroom plays an important part in explicit language awareness.

Indeed, Hulstijn (2003, pp. 206–209) argues that such declarative knowledge (e.g. "concepts" and "rules linking the concepts") may serve as a resource when implicit knowledge is not present.

"Explicit learning" is the construction of explicit, verbalizable, meta-linguistic knowledge in the form of symbols (concepts) and rules, specifying relationships between concepts. Explicit learning is a conscious, deliberative process of concept formation and concept linking. This may either take place when learners are being taught concepts and rules by an instructor or textbook, or when they operate in a self-initiated searching mode, trying to develop concepts and rules themselves . . . I consider explicit knowledge to be a worthwhile, sometimes indeed indispensable, form of knowledge to be used as a resource where and when implicit knowledge is not (yet) available.

The metalinguistic knowledge that children learn in school is the terminology for grammatical concepts (e.g. prefix, suffix, noun, verb, subject, predicate), and rules for pattern-based constructions. For instance, learners acquire explicit knowledge that written sentences need to have subjects and predicates and verbs need to agree with their subjects in singular and plural. The terminology and rules help learners talk about grammar in the same way that knowing cooking terms helps someone learn to cook or knowing how to read music helps someone play a new song. If language users know the metalanguage to describe what they know about language, they have **declarative metalinguistic knowledge**.

Bilingualism

Bilingual people whose natural knowledge of both of their languages is well developed often have high language awareness because they learn multiple words for the same thing, words and word formation processes that can be compared, or collocations and idioms that differ. They acquire multiple different inflections and syntactic forms, so that their usage needs to be monitored and controlled for accuracy. Bialystok (1991) singles out two cognitive abilities linked to language awareness and language proficiency among bilinguals: analysis and control. She hypothesizes that bilinguals have better conscious knowledge of their languages and better control over those languages.

Bromberek-Dyzman and Ewert (2010, p. 318) suggest that the languages of bilinguals are integrated at the lexical, semantic, conceptual, pragmatic, and cultural levels. Metalinguistic awareness of the first language can transfer to the second language through careful use of the first language to scaffold the second. It is possible that more general metalinguistic awareness can develop when languages are compared and contrasted in metalinguistic tasks.

Multicompetence

Cook (1995, p. 94) coined the term **multicompetence** for "an individual's knowledge of a native language and a second language, that is, L1 linguistic competence plus L2 interlanguage." In recent years, others have extended the term to the superior metalinguistic awareness of multilingual people also. Multicompetent people show evidence of increased metalinguistic awareness, creativity, and cognitive flexibility. For example, Jessner (2008, p. 277) says that:

> Metalinguistic awareness developing in individuals living with two or three languages is seen to develop with regard to (a) divergent and creative thinking (e.g. wider variety of associations, original ideas); (b) interactional and/or pragmatic competence (cultural theorems of greeting, thanking); (c) communicative sensitivity and flexibility (language mode); and (d) translation skills that are considered a natural trait in the majority of multilinguals.

Furthermore, with the rise in numbers of people who live with more than two languages, there are identity issues at stake. Jessner (2006) uses the term **multilinguality** for the cognitive style of a multilingual person, different from a monolingual person and perhaps even a bilingual person. This cognitive style includes differences in identity, attitudes, abilities, resources, cognition, and social ties that shape or are shaped by a sociocultural and historical setting. For instance, referring to certain areas of Europe, she says (p. 6):

> As in other countries, increasing integration with the rest of Europe has led to general trends in society like globalization and individualization. A new model of multilingual identity is developing which is oriented towards contemporary transcultural interaction as well as towards regional self-identification.

Thus, a new type of language learner is emerging, one in which transcultural interaction is the norm without jeopardizing a sense of having a homeland. If so, multilingual learners are quite different from those who feel that their identity is threatened by languages of wider communication. This discussion echoes themes from Chapter 1 about ELF speakers, some of whom may be multicompetent individuals with a multilingual identity. Clearly the positive (and the negative) connections between metalinguistic awareness, metacognitive processes, multicompetence, sociocultural identity, and language proficiency must be investigated further.

Factors in Language Learning

People have been learning languages in classrooms for a long time, and one thing seems abundantly clear: few learners acquire language if they sit silently in rows doing worksheets. Learners need active usage and exposure through interaction for implicit learning in the classroom. They need meaningful and motivating activities with a focus on form so that they receive feedback and practice for explicit learning. If learners notice and take up the correct forms, and remember them, they will speak and write more accurately. Accurate forms are practiced for fluency. However, there seems to be a natural order in the developmental stages that learners undergo as they are acquiring advanced grammatical structures like questions and negative sentences, so it is important for teachers to listen to learners to discover what developmental stage they are in, in order to know what stage is next.

Interaction

This example from Kumaravadivelu (2003, p. 116) shows what has been called the I–R–F sequence in which the teacher initiates a topic, the learner responds, and the teacher provides feedback. Construction Grammar is specific about why interaction is necessary but not sufficient for second language learning to be successful. Often there is not enough exposure and usage for holistic processing to develop, and there is simply not enough practice for learners to become adept at creating utterances analytically. Second language learners in classroom settings rarely reach the point of advanced learning where obvious acquisition begins to level off. With limited exposure, usage, and practice, priming associations among constructions remain few and weak. In this view, language learning is slow and error-prone, but there are some possible shortcuts, such as explicit feedback, scaffolding, and practice.

T: How many elephants are there in the picture? . . . How many elephants . . . Keiko?

S: Two.

T: Two . . . good. What are the elephants doing? . . . Carlos, what are the elephants doing?

S: Fight . . . fighting

T: They are fighting. Uh-huh . . . According to the writer, what dies when two elephants fight? What dies . . .? Maria?

S: mm . . . grass.

T: The grass, that's right. When two elephants fight, it's the grass that dies. (Laughs.) OK . . .

Focus on Form

One way for teachers to create a shortcut to learning is by providing a focus on form in the classroom. A focus on form is interaction designed to raise learners' awareness of forms by drawing students' attention to words, collocations, grammatical structures, pragmatic patterns and the like at the time that they come up in lessons whose main focus is on meaning or communication (Long and Robinson, 1998, p. 40). In an interaction, feedback is provided in direct response to a learner's need. Presumably, feedback increases the learner's awareness of and ability to notice linguistic features in the communicative flow of speech. However, it is unclear, despite numerous studies, what type of feedback is the most effective in encouraging learners' language development.

Interaction with a focus on form is sometimes called negotiated interaction. Negotiated interactions are meant to result in modified output on the part of the learner, such as in the example from Mackey and Philp (1998, p. 339). In this example, Speaker 2 requests clarification of what Speaker 1 said; a clarification request is a form of feedback that indicates that the communication failed. S1 is then forced to modify his or her output and produce an utterance that might be better comprehended.

The clarification request directs S1's attention (notice) to a problem with his or her own attempt at communication and encourages an attempt to express the idea in a different way. Finally, S2 provides a recast, a repetition in correct form.

Feedback of this sort within negotiated interaction with a focus on form is thought to lead to language analysis and development. These message-oriented episodes provide valuable negative and positive information for learners. Negative feedback, like the clarification request above, is about the mistake or what people don't say. Positive feedback is acknowledgment of a correct structure, such as when someone comprehends or says "right."

> **Negotiated Interaction with a Focus on Form**
>
> S1: *Here and then the left.*
> S2: *Sorry?* (Clarification request)
> S1: *Ah here and one ah where one ah one of them on the left.* (Modified output)
> S2: *Yeah one's behind the table and then the other's on the left of the table.* (Recast)
>
> (Mackey and Philp, 1998, p. 339)

Uptake

Uptake is the term used to refer to a learner's ability to notice and learn from interactions. Uptake is the first step in learning: noticing a form, representing a form in short-term memory, storing the form in memory so that it can be retrieved later. It takes a number of such episodes of exposure and usage to learn. Uptake may be related to metalinguistic awareness.

In this quote, Zoila, a 25-year-old Spanish speaker, reveals her metalinguistic awareness; she can sort words into two types: "big words" and "small words." She is also clearly aware of an important comprehension strategy that she relies on. She esteems big words over small words for comprehension. Zoila focuses her uptake on words that she thinks she needs to know in the stream of speech and disregards other information.

The efficacy of feedback within a negotiated interaction is dependent on learners' ability or desire to take up the feedback or to learn explicitly while communicating. Learners may be unwilling or unable to notice forms because they are focusing all of their attention on meaning. They may be unable to understand and represent forms in memory because the feedback may be beyond their level of proficiency. If learners, like Zoila, value fluency with "big words"

Zoila: *I never . . . I never listen, you the . . . words little, uh, small words for continue my conversation.*

Rina: *What, like what?*

Zoila: *The /fras/, you know frase?*

Rina: *Sentence.*

Zoila: *The sentence, sentence. In the sentence, I never using this little, little words.*

Rina: *Like what?*

Zoila: *Ah, "and," and "that" mmm /ipidit/ (=examples of "little" words as observed by Zoila). You know? If /bin/ /it/ sometimes (unintelligible) . . . Well, maybe because I no study . . . never, and only hear the people and . . . and talking.*

Rina: *Yeah, but people talk with these words.*

Zoila: *Yeah, pero (ɔs, ɔh), I'm . . . hear and put more attention the big words. You know and . . . something "house." I know "house" is the casa for me. And /ɔsɔs/ and little words is no too important for me.*

(Shapira, 1978, p. 254)

at the expense of accuracy with "little words," then any type of correction will probably have little effect. For students who are interested in accuracy as well as fluency, then correction that encourages productive use of the form in question would better affect notice, representation, storage, and later retrieval.

Scaffolding

In this example, W shows his ability to notice, represent, store, and retrieve words. He initiates a topic (*Kung Fu—fight*), and then takes up the words that T uses and links them with words that he already has stored and can retrieve (*I fight . . . my hand*). He notices a colligation used by the teacher, and either reproduces it or is reminded of it and retrieves it from memory (*I fight with my hand*).

This is an example of scaffolding, in which interlocutors create conversations by helping each other construct utterances from words, collocations, and colligations they only partially know. During the scaffolding, the more knowledgeable interlocutor offers a word, collocation, or colligation for the other to notice, represent, and use (as well as store and retrieve at a future time). Scaffolding is related to the normal priming that goes on during conversations when people interact with each other, but it is also related to the learner's ability to take up constructions. This is why negotiated interaction, scaffolding, and uptake are so important for language acquisition and learning.

> W: *Kung Fu.*
> T: *Kung Fu? You like the movie Kung Fu?*
> W: *Yeah . . . fight.*
> T: *That was about a great fighter? A man who knows how to fight with his hands.*
> W: *I fight . . . my hand.*
> T: *You know how to fight with your hands?*
> W: *I fight with my hand.*
> T: *Watch out guys, Wang knows karate.*
>
> (Ellis, 1999, p. 217)

Natural Order

The natural order hypothesis is based on robust research findings from both first and second language acquisition. It has been observed that, regardless of age, first language background, and learning conditions, language learners appear to pass through the same phases in the acquisition of the English possessive, negative sentences, and questions. Krashen (1987, 1988) makes a distinction between acquisition (implicit learning based on comprehensible input and interaction) and learning (explicit learning resulting in declarative knowledge about the

Natural Order of Acquisition of Questions

1. Single words or units: *Why? This? Scissors? A boy? What color?*
2. SVO word order: *This is picture? They stay oceans?*
3. Preposing: *Why he is stopped the car? Does he going home?*
4a. Yes/no questions: *Is she mad about that?*
4b. Wh-questions: *What is this lady? Where are this place?*
5a. Inversions with do: *What does she hold in her hand?*
5b. Inversion with modal: *Where will she take this?*
6a. Tag question: *You can't, can you?*
6b. Negative question: **Can't she come in?*
6c. Embedded question: **Can you tell me who he is?*

(Adapted from Tarone and Swierzbin (2009, p. 48). Examples marked with an asterisk are hypothetical examples they created.)

language). Krashen believes that second languages can be learned implicitly just as the first language and that explicit grammatical instruction is not helpful. Learners will progress along the natural order if given sufficient comprehensible input and interaction at a level just beyond their current level of proficiency.

However, most second language learners do not receive enough comprehensible input or interaction to proceed through the natural order implicitly. Instead, explicit methods of instruction may be shortcuts to acquisition, if they accompany sufficient exposure and practice. This is because, with practice, declarative knowledge can become proceduralized and automatized into a system that may be indistinguishable from a linguistic system acquired through implicit learning. The implication of the natural order of acquisition is that grammatical patterns should not be taught in a lockstep sequence, as they are in many textbooks, because learners may not learn structures that are beyond their level of proficiency even if exposed to them. Grammar instruction should be tied to the needs and questions of learners because these indicate when learners are at the point where they can take advantage of explicit learning.

Priming and Automatization

At present, researchers are just beginning to study the effect of priming on implicit or explicit learning. McDonough (2006, p. 186) reports this sequence where Speaker 1 produced a more advanced question in response to a recast. He or she may have already been exposed to the more advanced question form in the past, and the priming in the recast simply activated the more advanced but incomplete knowledge. If priming takes place with forms that are near the learner's stage in the natural order of acquisition, it facilitates the production of a more advanced form, leading to more practice of that form. Priming might lead to acquisition of syntax because it activates and strengthens pattern-based

S1: *Where where where you break it?*
S2: *Where did you break it? Mae Sot.*
    (Recast)
S1: *Mae Sot in Tak?*
S2: *Yeah.*
S1: *Why why why did you go there?*
    (Modified output)

(McDonough, 2006, p. 186)

constructions, so they can facilitate later production even with different lexical items. McDonough (2006) explored whether recasts might be models for learning if they cause syntactic priming.

Syntactic priming studies have shown that speakers use constructions that they had just heard from others, or produced themselves, even when the constructions used different words. Priming occurs even when there is intervening material of quite a few sentences and with several seconds delay. McDonough (2006, p. 184) suggests that "the persistence of syntactic priming across intervening material and time has led some researchers to suggest that it might represent a form of implicit learning." While priming studies are still in their infancy in second language acquisition research, priming holds promise as an important factor leading to success in language learning.

Explicit learning can become automatic through continued exposure and usage in practice. When explicit knowledge becomes fully automatic, it is indistinguishable from implicit knowledge. For many second language learners, learning relies heavily on automatization of explicitly learned constructions and patterns, and not implicit learning, because there is not enough usage and exposure for implicit learning to take place. Crucially, the results of automatization of declarative knowledge may not be very different from the results of implicit learning. In the end, a linguistic architecture developed through slow implicit learning (e.g. native speakers) and a linguistic architecture developed through explicit learning and automatization (e.g. fluent non-native speakers) may be essentially the same.

DeKeyser (2007, p. 3) defines the term automatization as what happens in the learner's mind between the initial presentation of a construction and the final stage of spontaneous and accurate use of that construction. As a result of automatization, learners can use language faster with fewer errors. It may be easier to understand this process with an analogy to reading in English. At first, children learn to read by applying the letter-to-sound rules that they learn in school, so reading is cumbersome, slow, and error-prone. However, with time and continued practice, children improve quickly and, at a certain point, their reading speed and accuracy reaches a peak, and any improvements are hardly noticed. For most people, learning to read is not an implicit process in English; instead it involves the proceduralization and automatization of declarative knowledge of letters and sounds.

Practice

Practice improves priming associations among item- and pattern-based constructions for greater fluency and accuracy. Each time a linguistic feature is noticed or produced, its representation and associations with other constructions grow stronger until it becomes proceduralized and automatized. Construction Grammar supports the traditional three-stage approach to grammatical instruction. The first stage is awareness/presentation, to draw attention to the linguistic feature to be learned. The middle stage, the one related to automatization, is practice. The final stage is feedback. However, even something as obviously useful as practice is controversial.

> Practice gets a raw deal in the field of applied linguistics . . . For some, the word conjures up images of mind-numbing drills in the sweatshops of foreign language learning, while for others it means fun and games to appease students on Friday afternoons. *Practice* is by no means a dirty word in other domains of human endeavor, however. Parents dutifully take their kids to soccer practice, and professional athletes dutifully show up for team practice, sometimes even with recent injuries. Parents make their kids practice their piano skills at home, and the world's most famous performers of classical music often practice for many hours a day, even if it makes their fingers hurt. If even idolized, spoiled, and highly paid celebrities are willing to put up with practice, why not language learners, teachers, or researchers?
>
> (DeKeyser, 2007, p. 1)

It is not overstating to hypothesize that explicit learning and automatization may create a second linguistic system that is cognitively indistinguishable from a first linguistic system created through implicit learning. Both implicit and explicit learning must be factored into classroom activities through negotiated interaction, deliberate focus on form and meaning, practice, and feedback for maximal uptake.

But the language classroom is also a place where learners have opportunities to grow cognitively, socially, interpersonally, and intrapersonally, where they examine their identity and their situation in local and global society as well as acquire language skills and metalinguistic awareness. This more comprehensive approach to language learning is called the Language Awareness Approach (LAA).

The Language Awareness Approach

- Context
- Description
- Usage

The LAA is an instructional perspective which places grammatical description and focus on form in the context of genre and text types (essays, reports, emails) as well as stories, poetry, novels. Grammatical description includes linguistic variation, cross-linguistic comparisons and contrasts, metalanguage, and the appropriate alternatives for different genres and texts. Consciousness-raising activities (e.g. activities that combine a deliberate focus on form with analysis) help learners become aware of the lexical, grammatical, and discursive choices available in different texts.

Consciousness-raising is linguistic analysis: sound, word formation, vocabulary, phrases, sentences, and above. It is both bottom-up (data and detail driven) and top-down (pattern and rule driven). Absolute judgments of accuracy and correctness are discarded in favor of flexible ideas of structural appropriateness or naturalness of expressions within contexts. The goal of instruction in language awareness and standardized usage is to facilitate rapid decision-making in analytical and holistic processing, and more accurate editing abilities of written work.

The LAA demands an explicit focus on activities designed to foster and expand metalinguistic awareness. Malakoff (1992, p. 518) suggests that "a metalinguistic task is one that requires the individual to think about the linguistic nature of the message: to attend to and reflect on the structural features of language." In order to create or teach using metalinguistic tasks, teachers themselves may need to develop or expand their own awareness of language and metalanguage. For instance, Thornbury (1997, p. xii) suggests that teachers' own lack of metalinguistic awareness may contribute to devastating consequences in the classroom, among them:

Metalinguistic Awareness Development Activities

- Relate language, thinking, knowledge, and skill.
- Use authentic language or languages in socioculturally grounded spoken and written texts.
- Problematize sociocultural concepts such as standard or non-standard language, correct or incorrect grammar, accuracy, fluency, native speaker, and so on.
- Focus on both meaning and message (What is the meaning? How do the structure and vocabulary contribute to meaning?).
- Analyze abstract structure and relationships among lexis for analytical colligation and holistic collocation.
- Encourage learners to develop a personal subjective response to language through notice and reflection.
- Lead to improvement in personally identified language skills (accuracy, fluency, extent of vocabulary).

a failure on the part of the teacher to anticipate learners' learning problems and a consequent inability to plan lessons that are pitched at the right level; an inability to interpret course book syllabuses and materials and to adapt these to the specific needs of the learners; an inability to deal satisfactorily with errors, or to field learners' queries; and a general failure to earn the confidence of the learners due to a lack of basic terminology and ability to present new language clearly and efficiently.

Before I address this topic again in Part II, the next chapter discusses some new trends in English grammar pedagogy.

Study, Discussion, and Essay Questions

Write the answers to these questions in your Language Notebook.

1. Add these terms to your glossary and define them according to their usage in this chapter: language awareness, implicit learning, explicit learning, declarative metalinguistic knowledge, multicompetence, multilinguality, negotiated interaction, focus on form, clarification request, uptake, scaffolding, automatization.

2. Discuss Derewianka's point of view about grammar cited at the beginning of this chapter. Based on your own experience, what do you think "text-forming choices relevant to the students' communicative needs" refers to specifically?

3. Comment on the Kazmi quote.

4. What examples of implicit language awareness do you remember from your own childhood or from children that you know? Ask some children what they think of some "funny" sentences.

5. What is the difference between implicit and explicit knowledge?

6. What are some of the benefits of metalinguistic awareness? How would you rate your own metalinguistic awareness? What is the relationship between bilingualism and metalinguistic awareness?

7. Do you know any people who might be described as multicompetent?

8. Make a list of the types of feedback a teacher could give a learner. What kinds of feedback do you think is most useful to a learner?

9. Do you know any learners like Zoila? Do you know any learners like W? What is the difference between students like Zoila and students like W? What characteristics make Zoila a good language learner? What characteristics might make W a good language learner?

10. Look at the list of the stages of acquisition for questions and the examples that accompany them. What is SVO word order? What is preposing? What is inversion? What are tag questions? What is a negative question? What is an embedded question?

11. How is priming related to interaction, feedback, uptake, scaffolding, and natural order?

12. What are proceduralization and automatization? Why do you think that practice "gets a raw deal" in the field of applied linguistics?

13. What are the three dimensions of the LAA? Can you think of ways to make consciousness-raising activities interesting to learners?

14. What is a metalinguistic task? Can you find or make up an example of a metalinguistic task?

Activities

1. Do you agree with Thornbury (1997) that lack of metalinguistic awareness is a handicap for teachers? Before you write your essay, consider the following also. An article by Truscott (1999) is a critique of grammar correction and editing in L2 writing classes for a number of reasons, but one problem is that teachers may lack preparation for the task. He says:

First, the teacher must realize that a mistake has been made. The well-known problems involved in proof-reading show that this step cannot be taken for granted . . . If teachers do recognize an error, they still may not have a good understanding of the correct use—questions regarding grammar can be very difficult, even for experts, and someone who writes or speaks English well does not necessarily understand the principles involved . . . Thus, teachers may well know that an error has occurred but not know exactly why it is an error. If they do understand it well, they might be unable to give a good explanation; problems that need explaining are often very complex.

(Truscott, 1999, pp. 350–351)

Write an introspective paragraph that explores your personal reaction to the Thornbury and the Truscott quotes as far as you see any relevance to you or your situation. If you wish, share your essay with others.

2. Read this case history and write a paragraph about how it meets the three subject areas of the LAA, especially the criteria for activities that encourage metalinguistic awareness.

Ms. Moreno encourages academic writing proficiency

Besides her other language goals, Ms. Moreno wants to make sure her ninth graders understand and write academic essays. Her specific focus on language for this lesson is complex noun phrases. After some introductory pre-reading activities, she has assigned her class to read an economic essay from the newspaper for homework. Students begin by reading the article and discussing the points that it makes and its relevance to their families and their town.

The next day, she gives her class a few minutes to look over the article and ask questions. Then she begins her class with a short quiz to test for comprehension of the meaning of the article. She collects the quiz as an assessment, but she immediately goes over the quiz as a way of reviewing the main points from the reading. Learners are motivated to listen because they want to know if they got the answers right or wrong. After ten minutes, Ms. Moreno is confident that they have grasped the main ideas from the selection. She now turns to focusing on language issues, in particular their comprehension of and ability to use complex noun phrases.

She directs the learners' attention to the term *discount outlet merchandise* in the text. She asks them what it means and they are able to give her an answer easily. She points out its structure of three nouns in a row and asks which noun is the most important and which are descriptive. One young man is able to answer that the most important word is *merchandise* since that is what it is about. Ms. Moreno then asks learners to find one other example that is like this one on the first page of the article. The other example also has three nouns in a row and the last one is the most important. After some looking and a few mistaken guesses, a young woman comes up with *consumer power initiative*. They discuss what the complex noun phrase means.

Ms. Moreno invites her learners to come up with a generalization about the complex noun phrases. Some suggest that if there are three nouns in a row, the last one is the most important. Ms. Moreno asks class members to note the generalization in their Language Notebooks and to write down any similar constructions on page 2, which contains one example, "employee parking space." Everyone agreed that the example followed the generalization. A couple of learners find these also: *fast food franchise* and *major attraction*. They discuss these expressions, pointing out the similarities and differences between them and the others. These examples are also complex noun phrases, although their structure is different. The generalization evolved into the idea that in a complex noun phrase there could be any number of nouns and adjectives, but the last and most important word was always a noun. Ms. Moreno called that noun the **head noun**. The learners made a list of the expressions in their Language Notebooks and made up some original ones.

Ms. Moreno asked her students to translate their original expressions into their native language because the grammar of complex noun phrases is very different from English. Once the phrases were in their L1, and written in their Language Notebooks, she asked them to translate them back to English without looking at the original expressions. Ms. Moreno has prepared some follow-up exercises for tomorrow, so she leaves the topic for now and goes onto something else. However, at the end of the class period, she tells her class they can leave as soon as they tell her the complex noun phrases they studied that day. When a couple of learners volunteer "consumer power initiative" and others say "discount outlet merchandise," they are allowed to leave.

3. Find three other examples of complex noun phrases such as those in Activity 2 from the quotes in Chapters 1 and 2 of this textbook. List them in your Language Notebook. Can you analyze them in terms of the generalizations Ms. Moreno discussed?

New Trends in Post-method Grammar Pedagogy

4

The disjunction between method as conceptualized by theorists and method as conducted by teachers is the direct consequence of the inherent limitations of the concept of method itself. First and foremost, methods are based on idealized concepts geared toward idealized contexts. Since language learning and teaching needs, wants, and situations are unpredictably numerous, no idealized method can visualize all the variables in advance in order to provide situation-specific suggestions that practicing teachers sorely need to tackle the challenges they confront every day of their professional lives. As a predominately top-down exercise, the conception and construction of methods have been largely guided by a one-size-fits-all, cookie cutter approach that assumes a common clientele with common goals.

(Kumaravadivelu, 2003, p. 28)

A methodology is a system of guidelines for accomplishing a goal (e.g. learning a language) with specific techniques, tools, and activities. Kumaravadivelu (2003) argues that there is a gap between methodology as advocated by researchers and theorists and the practical methods put into practice by teachers because methodologies are based on idealized theories for idealized classroom settings. Globally, the stakeholders (teachers, learners, families, societies, etc.) and settings (culture, society, political system, school system) for learning are different, and no methodology stretches to cover local needs, wants, and situations. Further, methodologies are top-down and outside-in in that professional experts tell classroom teachers the best way to teach, as if there were just one best way for all teachers, learners, and classrooms.

In contrast, Kumaravadivelu (2003) describes **post-method** language teaching based on more general strategies that teachers can adapt to their own settings. What Kumaravadivelu discards is the idea of a one-size-fits-all methodology, but he still provides teachers with a set of principles for evaluating techniques and activities, so post-method pedagogy is bottom-up and inside-out. Many of Kumaravadivelu's strategies (e.g. maximizing learning opportunities, facilitating negotiated interaction, promoting learner autonomy, fostering language awareness, contextualizing linguistic input, integrating language skills, ensuring social relevance, and raising cultural consciousness) are compatible with the Language Awareness Approach described in the last chapter. In some cases, in post-method pedagogy, what is old is new again.

Holism and Analysis in Methodologies

Many English language teaching methodologies are based on language acquisition theories that do not sufficiently address holistic and analytical processing because until recently these processes have not been understood. Grammarians focus on what they can see and verbalize more easily: structural forms and rules, and thus so do language instructors. Some methodologies directly favor the analytical processing of grammar based on open choice because it is easier for teachers to teach rules and applications of rules than to spend time teaching vocabulary items and collocations. The problem is that language that is the result of purely open choice principles is often unnatural and unfluent.

Other methodologies favor holistic processing in that they value naturalness in language production over the learning of rules. The Audio-Lingual Method (ALM) focuses heavily on language structures and skills as behavior learned by habit formation, and not through learning rules explicitly. Teachers create an environment in which students form good language habits by not making mistakes; hence, the methods are rote memorization of dialogues and pattern practice drills. Learners become fluent and accurate through this methodology, although their linguistic repertoires can be rigid and limited.

At present, there is a focus on communicative methodologies in which the goal of instruction is communicative competence, or the accurate use of correctly chosen forms, meanings, and functions in a socially appropriate way. The classroom tasks are purposeful and interactive with authentic materials and cooperative learning. They involve as much real communication as possible using activities that promote negotiation of meanings and different communicative functions. However, some teachers have been uncomfortable with a lack of balance between direct instruction favoring accuracy and communicative activities for fluency.

Communicative activities don't always go as the teacher intends; they don't always provide the practice that the teacher has in mind. In the example from Kumaravadivelu, the students were supposed to discuss some pictures of wedding dresses and decide which would be best for the bride to buy. However, the learners in this case do not compare and contrast the cost, sizes, and appearance of the dresses in detail. Instead, they settle on the best answer using an abbreviated form of communication used for fast problem-solving. In these post-methodological times, teachers are both liberated from using methodologies that may not work very well in their setting, but they are also challenged to make curricular and pedagogical decisions that may go against the mainstream. They need to know what old methods to discard and what time-honored effective methods to keep.

S1: *First, one hundred ten dollars. This is costly.*
S2: *Yeah.*
S1: *Second, uh . . . size.*
S2: *Small.*
S1: *This one . . . size big.*
S2: *Which one . . . (laughs) . . . oh . . . yeah, that's right. No.*
S1: *This . . . she has only seven . . .*
S2: *Seventy dollars.*
S1: *Seventy-seven.*
S2: *Oh . . . yeah . . . Seventy-seven dollars.*
S1: *It's expensive.*
S2: *Yah . . . number five.*
S1: *Yeah.*

(Kumaravadivelu, 2003, p. 85)

Presentation/Awareness

Earlier discussions of metalinguistic awareness and explicit learning posited a relationship between declarative knowledge and procedural knowledge of grammar. The relationship could be that declarative knowledge develops through formal presentations and increases notice and uptake. Awareness, notice, and uptake restructure learners' linguistic system, improve their ability to create and test hypotheses about the system, and allow them to take greater advantage of scaffolding, feedback, and practice. Presentation is supposed to lead to awareness, but the linkage between the two can be problematic.

Kumaravadivelu cites this "interactive" presentation based on a textbook grammar exercise. This exercise is an assessment of the students' understanding of the differences between dependent clauses and main sentences, so it is declarative and explicit grammar instruction about the system of English grammar. The activity is not individualized; it is not clear if the students all need to spend their time this way—some may not be at the point where they can take advantage of this information.

1. T: *Who wants to try number one?*
2. S: (reads from the text) *A clause is a group of words containing a subject and a verb.*
3. T: *All right. Does everybody agree? Is that all right? Hmmm . . . All right. Look at number two and fill in the blanks. Who wants to try number two? . . . Yes . . .*
4. S: (reads from the text) *A dependent . . . independent clause is a complete sentence. It contains the main subject and verb of sentence. It is also called a main clause.*
5. T: *Right, everybody agrees? Let's try to do number three.*
6. S: *A dependent clause is not a complete sentence.*
7. T: *All right.*
8. S: *The dependent clause?*
9. T: *The dependent clause . . . right.*
10. S: *must be connected to the independent clause.*
11. T: *All right. Is that clear? . . . OK, eh . . . let's see now . . . number four. What would be your answer, S1?*
12. S: *Yah . . . main clause . . .*
13. T: *Eh . . . mmm. Now, let's go to the dependent clause. Same question. Does it have a subject and a verb?*
14. S: *No.*
15. S: *Yah.*
16. S: *Yah.*
17. S: *No.*
18. T: (in a very authoritative tone) *Who said no?*
19. S: *Yes.*
20. T: *A . . . ah . . .* (showing strong disapproval)
21. S: *Yes.*
22. T: *Right. Now . . .*

(Kumaravadivelu, 2003, pp. 179–180)

There is little notice and uptake; there is no scaffolding or actual language use. The teacher talks and the learners indicate yes or no. By asking questions like "Does everybody agree?" the teacher thinks that the exercise is interactive, but it isn't. The teacher's authority is threatened by a student's incorrect answer. The teacher may choose to do this classroom activity out of insecurity with grammatical forms and descriptions. Sometimes teachers lack the metalinguistic awareness to explain grammatical patterns, find examples that follow the patterns, and engage learners in dynamic learning activities.

Spontaneity

The sequencing of grammar instruction should be secondary to the subject matter and tasks in the classroom. Grammatical terms and explanations occur in response to something in a reading or writing assignment and to meet the needs and questions of the learner. This example shows how negotiated interaction about language emerges from a learner's notice of a linguistic structure, but this is a missed opportunity. The teacher is unable to raise the learners' awareness at the moment when they seem ready to take advantage of the information.[1] Even veteran teachers sometimes need to say "I'll find out more about it and get back to you tomorrow." And the next time the question comes up, they are better prepared to answer spontaneously.

> S: Why three bed, er, three bedroom? Why don't we say three bedrooms?
> T: Ahhm, oh, I don't know.
> S: Is not right.
> T: We don't say it. We don't say it. There's no explanation. But we often do that in English. Three bedroom house.
>
> (Nunan, 1989, pp. 181–182)

---

1. The explanation for this is in a later chapter, but lest I myself be guilty of missing an opportunity, I will explain. The fact is that 99 percent of the time, any logically plural noun modifiers like *three bedroom* that are used to modify another noun, *house*, are singular in form, to follow the generalization in English that modifiers in general (e.g. adjectives) cannot show any plural markings. Compare "three-ring circus" or "ten district councilman." There is some variation with adjectives in measurement: "She is three feet tall" or "She is three foot tall," but "The three-foot-tall spelling bee winner." There is also variation in the use of hyphens.

Mini-lectures

If the teacher prepares a mini-lecture beforehand to have it ready for when a grammar point "comes up" during a lesson, then grammar instruction only has the appearance of spontaneity. The more teachers prepare mini-lectures, the more they learn and the more they are able to take advantage of spontaneous opportunities for consciousness-raising. As teachers seek out grammar explanations from resource materials, their metalinguistic awareness grows. Mini-lectures should take place within a social and functional context about how the linguistic feature functions in a text with a specific writing purpose and context.

Teachers begin their mini-lecture by relating the grammar point to something that has been already learned, something relevant to the learner, and/or something in the lesson plan. In a deductive presentation, the teacher gives the grammar generalization first, followed by examples and applications. In an inductive presentation, the examples and applications precede the generalization. Novice learners and older, academically oriented learners prefer deductive presentations, but others like the sense of discovery that an inductive presentation gives and appreciate the opportunity to formulate a rule based on what they observe about sentences. Inductive mini-lectures are more time-consuming than deductive mini-lectures. When a grammar point comes up in class that needs to be covered quickly, it's best to choose a deductive explanation that begins with the generalization and follows with examples that fit the generalization.

Inductive Presentations

1. Draw learners' attention to the grammatical point and show its connection to already-learned material. Give at least one reason why this issue is important or relevant to them.
2. Give a series of examples taken from a reading or writing assignment, and then invite learners to say what consistent patterns they notice. Always be encouraging, giving learners the benefit of the doubt for unclear answers.
3. Once learners have identified the patterns as well as they can, rephrase the generalization correctly and ask for other examples that follow the generalization. Have learners write the generalization in their notebooks.
4. Discuss the most common exceptions to the generalization, if any.

Inductive mini-lectures are meant to "induce" learning by motivating students to notice and represent a grammatical pattern or structure themselves. Their sense of excitement at discovering a pattern themselves can lead to better recollection of the material. In more modern terminology, inductive learning is "data-driven." Referring to the use of linguistic databases or corpora as a means for learning, Johns (1991, p. 30) defines data-driven learning (DDL) as "the attempt to cut out the middleman as far as possible and to give the learner direct access to the data."

After the presentation, any important exceptions are given. One way to handle exceptions is called the **garden path method**, in which teachers cause learners to create errors and then correct them. The garden path method is effective because it helps learners notice the exception and remember it (Tomasello and Herron, 1988, 1989). For instance, after learning a number of regular past tense forms (*study–studied*, *want–wanted*), learners induce the "regular" past tense form *digged*, at which point the correct irregular form, *dug*, is presented. The garden path method encourages learners to compare their own utterances and the correct target utterances actively. During the comparison, learners mentally self-correct their original response; they modify their output.

Language Resources

Butzkamm and Caldwell (2009, p. 33) make some suggestions for using the first language as a resource, if it is the same for all class members. They suggest the "sandwich" technique, in which a bilingual teacher sandwiches a translation between uses of a L2 expression, often in a "tone of an aside, as a kind of whispered interpreting." For example, a teacher might say "environment (ambiente) environment."

Butzkamm and Caldwell (2009, p. 34) also suggest that learners use their first language for words they don't know, but continue to use the second language. The teacher provides the equivalent expression in L2 and learners note the word down in a notebook to study later. However, if teachers don't know some of the equivalents, they can look them up later and then provide a list of words for learners. With modern technology in the classroom, equivalent expressions can be accessed quickly on-line.

Interestingly, Butzkamm and Caldwell (2009, p. 52) believe that two types of translation activities benefit students' grammar learning and hence their metalinguistic awareness. One type is a literal, formal, or structural translation or a morpheme by morpheme gloss. For instance, students might work with sentences like this: *Language is a dynamic system* → lenguaje es un dinámico sistema. This gloss emphasizes a contrast in the use of articles with the subject noun *language* but a similarity in usage with *a system*. It also shows the position of the modifier with respect to the word modified. The other type of translation is meaning-to-meaning, producing translation equivalents that are accurate and fluent in both languages: *Language is a dynamic system* → El lenguaje es un sistema dinámico. Interpretation and translation are valued skills that rely heavily on metalinguistic awareness, and they may lead to better monitoring abilities and editing abilities for writing.

Practice/Automatization

Practice is valuable for holistic processing of inflectional endings, prepositions, or collocations because it increases priming at the level of words and their close associates. Practice is useful for analytic processing because it increases priming at more abstract levels of the linguistic system, like verb or sentence structures, where priming operates over pattern-based constructions. This may be why the Audio-Lingual Method, with its intensive practice, was successful in promoting fluency and accuracy. Nevertheless, ALM was ultimately disregarded because learners were not always able to use the constructions they learned productively. Possibly, in discarding the pattern practice drills, the good features of intensive practice were eliminated along with the bad.

Individualization

Individualization means that learners practice only what they need to practice. Teachers need files of worksheets, flash cards, and games to give to learners as they need them and can benefit from them. However, individualized grammar practice takes a lot of monitoring. One benefit of computer-assisted language learning (CALL) materials is that they require less monitoring because the learner receives feedback, the right answer, and explanations immediately. Working with a computer can make otherwise dull grammar exercises more interesting, and it is a good way to practice writing and spelling. A computer is patient and doesn't mind going over the same point again and again.

Drills

Oral practice should be mindful and not mind-numbing. Teachers use different types of drills to vary the routine of the classroom activities; drills can be mechanical, somewhat meaningful, or communicative. Mechanical drilling is pure practice for priming; no meaning is necessary. In meaningful drilling, learners pay attention to grammar and meaning, so it is more directed to notice and uptake. Communicative drills bridge the gap between the classroom activity and real communication because they require fluency and accuracy while learners say something that makes sense in a social context.

Choral drills are for fluency and accuracy in priming. They involve simple repetition of sentences or phrases for pronunciation, morphological, or grammatical work. Learners listen and repeat exactly what is heard so they must understand the sentence through prior study or reading. Long sentences are built up slowly in a process called "backwards build-up." In backwards build-up, the sentence is composed from the end by adding phrases one by one.

Substitution drills are oral exercises where one or more words (the cues) are inserted to substitute for another word and learners receive immediate feedback as the teachers repeat the correct answer. The drill starts with simple substitutions, then moves to combinations that result in new

Backwards Build-up

If it is raining, we won't go to the picnic in the park.
(Teacher) in the park →
(Class) *in the park*
to the picnic in the park →
to the picnic in the park
we won't go to the picnic in the park → *we won't go to the picnic in the park*
if it is raining we won't go to the picnic in the park → *if it is raining we won't go to the picnic in the park*

Substitution Drills

(Teacher) I study linguistics/you →
(Class) *you study linguistics*
You study linguistics (feedback)/he →
he studies linguistics
He studies linguistics/she
. . .
(Teacher) I study linguistics/he→
(Class) *he studies linguistics*
he studies linguistics/math → *he studies math*
he studies math/like → *he likes math.*

sentences. Substitution drills are done as choral work first and then by calling on individuals to make the substitutions.

A transformation drill changes something about the sentence. For example, a past sentence is transformed into present progressive or vice versa, an affirmative sentence is changed to negative or a question, and so on.

Chain drills are often questions and answers or comments and responses. The teacher models the first question and cues the type of answer needed. The answers and responses are relatively free but they must be accurate. The chain drill goes around the class with less teacher control. As a game, the answers can be provided and the learner provides the proper question.

Transformation Drill

(Teacher) You are eating a tofu burrito now/and yesterday →
And yesterday you ate a tofu burrito.
You are eating a tofu burrito now/no →
No, you aren't. You aren't eating a tofu burrito right now.

Chain Drill

(Teacher) Where is your ____?/location →
(S1) *Where is your book?* →
(S2) *On the table*
(S2) *Where is your pencil?*
→ (S3) *Over there . . .*

Creative Automatization

Gatbonton and Segalowitz (1988) offer some promising ideas for practice within a communicative context, to bridge the gap between drilling and real communication. Gatbonton and Segalowitz believe that automaticity can only be the result of much practice. With sufficient practice, learners can use formulaic speech and pay attention to learning while being engaged in communication. Repetition is the key to automatization, and teachers do activities several times with a slightly different focus each time. Teachers first identify common utterances (the target utterances) that are useful as collocations. Then they devise a main activity with a real and appropriate goal that creates a need for the learners to use the target utterances. In the main activity, learners notice and practice a set of utterances that are useful in accomplishing that goal. The follow-up is a more focused activity that reinforces the use of the target utterances. The combination of the two activities is meant to "provide students with the kind of consistent speaking practice with the selected utterances that leads to their automatization" (p. 482).

For example, the teacher informs the learners that they will be taking photographs of the class. The students must tell each other where to stand and what pose to adopt, after the teacher models common statements like: *Carlos, please stand up. Please walk to the front of the class. Move a little to the left. Stand between Helga and Bee. Please sit on the chair.* Learners must see to it that everyone is placed in the proper position without using gestures or pointing, with the teacher intervening to offer correct collocations. This activity takes quite a while, because people try out different positions. Finally, pictures are taken. The follow-up activity consists of looking at the pictures (or other pictures with poorly placed people) and discussing the placement and poses of the people. Drilling and creative automatization techniques can also be applied to writing through the use of dictations, summaries, retelling of stories, and other compositions.

Correction/Feedback

Teachers spend a lot of time making corrections and giving feedback. The more natural forms of form-focused feedback occur in response to what others say, so they are called reactive feedback: repetition, indications of misunderstanding, or recasts. Repetition means that listeners repeat what speakers say, perhaps with a questioning intonation. This gives speakers a chance to hear what they said and perhaps correct it. Listeners can indicate that they have not understood something by saying things like *What?* or *Pardon me?* Listeners can ask directly for clarification. This gives speakers feedback on their comprehensibility so that they can try to find different words or make a correction in their usage. A recast occurs when listeners restate speakers' utterances in a corrected form, but a recast doesn't always demand that learners try to correct their utterances.

Real-life teachers, however, have always known that students' errors are troublesome, that students themselves are very concerned about accuracy, and that responding effectively to students' grammatical and lexical problems is a challenging endeavor fraught with uncertainty about its long term effectiveness.

(Ferris, 1999, p. 1)

In the classroom setting, there are other forms of corrective feedback. Teachers give learners explicit linguistic feedback by saying, for example, *Has. It's supposed to be "has", not "have".* Teachers can give learners metalinguistic feedback by saying things like *Remember, it's third person singular present tense.* Teachers can elicit a correction: *What is the verb form that goes with that subject?* Feedback can also be pre-emptive, as when a teacher or learner makes a prediction about a potential problem in the interaction and asks a question or supplies an explanation, as in the example that Zhao and Bitchener provide.

> L: *What is the name for the flower, that is white, you put it before the tomb.*
> T: *It is Christianise.*
> L: *Christianise.*
>
> (Zhao and Bitchener, 2007, p. 436)

All of these methods of giving oral reactive or pre-emptive feedback are positive in that they may increase priming for the correct form if uptake takes place, but, as has already been established, uptake is a variable. Zhao and Bitchener found that it was fairly common for a teacher to give the learner no opportunity for modified output or even acknowledgement.

> L: *Het* (should be "hat")
> T: *Hat. How many of you have hats? Anything else?*
> L: *Blanket*
>
> (Zhao and Bitchener, 2007, p. 439)

One factor that makes measurement of improvement in accuracy difficult is that there are different types of errors. Feedback on pattern-based grammatical constructions may be more successful than feedback on idiosyncratic item-based constructions.

Ferris (1999, p. 7) argues for grammatical instruction and corrective feedback in writing because:

> it is critical that students become more self-sufficient in editing their own writing. Though it is arguable whether grammar feedback and instruction will be consistently effective for all L2 student writers, it seems clear that the absence of any feedback or strategy training will ensure that many students never take seriously the need to improve their editing skills and that they will not have the knowledge or strategies to edit even when they do perceive its importance.

Written feedback can be direct or indirect. Direct feedback occurs when the instructor identifies the error and supplies the correction. Indirect feedback means that the instructor identifies that an error has occurred but does not supply the correct form. A number of studies show that direct and indirect feedback on first drafts improves the learners' second drafts, when compared to learners who received no feedback at all. This outcome is hardly surprising because it is harder for students to revise their writing if they don't receive any feedback. In studying writing improvement over time, Bitchener et al. (2005) report that although both learners and teachers prefer direct and explicit feedback rather than indirect feedback, there is research that supports the idea that indirect feedback leads to greater accuracy. Learners who pay attention to feedback and make corrections on their own may become better at producing correct forms and self editing than learners who receive their correction from the instructor.

Bitchener et al. (2005, p. 201) also report that different types of feedback seem to have significant long-term effects. When instructors give learners full, explicit metalinguistic feedback on their writing along with oral feedback given during a five minute individual conference for each writing assignment, the feedback results in much greater accuracy in both simple past tense and the definite article but not in the use of prepositions. In the conference, the instructor and the learner go over the errors and the rules, and extend the rules to new examples. Using the term "treatable" to refer to pattern-based constructions, Bitchener et al. (2005, p. 201) suggest that:

> [C]lassroom L2 writing teachers provide their learners with both oral feedback as well as written feedback on the more "treatable" types of linguistic error on a regular basis. So that learners buy into this learning process, we would suggest that teachers discuss with their learners which linguistic errors should be focused on.

Chandler (2003, p. 280) reports that another important factor is what learners do with the corrections, finding that if they were not required to revise their writing based on feedback, their writing did not improve over one semester, but if they made corrections, their subsequent writing was more accurate and equally fluent. The types of correction Chandler studied were: (A) making the correction directly in the learner's text, (B) underlining the site

>   lay
> A. I crawled back to my sleeping bag and ~~lied~~ △ down again.
> B. *wrong form* I crawled back to my sleeping bag and <u>lied</u> down again.
> C. *wrong form* I crawled back to my sleeping bag and lied down again.
> D. I crawled back to my sleeping bag and <u>lied</u> down again.

of the error in the text and using descriptors in the margin, (C) writing the descriptors in the margin with no indication of the location of the error, and (D) underlining only.

Chandler (2003, p. 286) found that both correction (A) and underlining (D) led to more accurate writing on the next assignment, but the others (B and C) did not. In general, the use of the descriptors confuse students because descriptors like "wrong form" or "sentence structure" are too vague to provide much help. Chandler (2003, p. 290) notes that the fastest way to respond to student errors on one draft is to underline them, with correction as the second fastest way. So although corrective feedback is time-consuming, it is a good investment of time if learners revise their work and improve over several drafts and several assignments.

If teachers know the local L1 language and have experience with teaching, they can predict what English constructions cause difficulty, provide a mini-lecture about them, opportunities for practice, and then a follow-up writing assignment to assess mastery. Errors that have been covered in class become the focus for error correction. Another rule of thumb about error correction rests on a distinction between local errors and global errors[2]. Local errors do not impede comprehension but global errors cause a reader to misunderstand what the author is trying to say. It is important for student writers to correct global errors and less important to correct local errors. On the other hand, local errors like subject–verb agreement or verb tense problems might be things that subject matter teachers find annoying so that they affect their grading of students.

> **Global error:** I went to the library to get a book (meaning *bookstore*).
> **Local error:** I going to the bookstore to buy a book (meaning *am going*).

Self Editing Strategies

Ferris (1999, p. 5) suggests that there are alternatives to teacher correction of each draft during the process of writing a paper. She believes that students can learn to self edit their texts if they undergo training to identify and correct their frequent errors and are instructed explicitly about the patterns of their errors.

---

2. Another type of error that must be corrected immediately is a stigmatizing error, which is any type of pronunciation or lexical error that might cause laughter or embarrassment.

It takes several steps for learners to become confident enough to edit their own or another learner's writing without teacher intervention. The first step is to assess the writing using a diagnostic essay and then give learners feedback about what problems they have.

Ferris then suggests an editing workshop in several stages. In the first stage, the learners read their diagnostic essay and take 20 minutes to find as many errors as they can. In the second stage, the teacher highlights any remaining problems that were not found by the learners. In the third stage, the learners try to correct the errors and return the paper to the teacher. Finally, the teacher analyzes the students' success in finding and correcting errors, gives the learners an editing report, and explains any remaining problems or grammatical issues.

Although this process is labor intensive, it makes student writers feel more confident about what they know. There are also more specific strategies to develop the metalinguistic awareness crucial for self editing and improving. One strategy is the creation of a grammar log or notebook, which must be part of the classroom procedures (e.g. explanation of residual errors, discussion of progress, evaluation and grading for credit). In the grammar log, students become aware of their own errors and the correct forms, and they keep track of their numbers of errors, trying to make the number go down.

Peer Editing

Many student writers benefit from peer editing workshops, but only with proper preparation and monitoring. Ferris (2002, pp. 102–103) suggests that the primary purpose for peer editing is not to fix the problems in the writer's text, but to improve the reader's proofreading and editing abilities. Proofreading and editing are very useful metalinguistic skills. Simply asking learners to pass their papers to their neighbors and to correct any mistakes does not yield good results. Ferris proposes a three stage process in which students receive training in peer editing in carefully structured workshops under the close supervision of teachers.

Training takes place through modeling. Looking at a sample text from another class as individuals, small groups, and as a whole class, learners identify errors, correct them, explain errors, and consult reference books. In a series of mini-workshops, learners practice identifying specific errors on a classmate's text, as instructed on a worksheet (e.g. noun ending errors or verb tense errors), and tracking them on a report. During these workshops, learners interact about what they are doing, discuss questions or concerns, articulate patterns and rules, and weigh alternatives and choices. The teacher serves as a resource consultant and makes a note of unresolved questions for future mini-lectures. After a series of workshops on the same text, the student writers return the reports and the texts to the authors to make the corrections. To increase accountability, the peer editing reports are handed in with the final draft of the text so that the teachers can assess the whole process.

Ferris embeds self and peer editing into a system of error treatment following a specific sequence. First, teachers assess the class and individual needs with writing samples, objective tests, and surveys. Based on the needs assessment, the teacher develops mini-lectures, other materials, and metalinguistic awareness activities for use in the class. At this point, self and peer editing mini-workshops take place with students' drafts, with teacher feedback on selected student errors. Students keep track of errors in their grammar log. Finally, the teacher assesses progress and learning by examining the final drafts. The various activities in this sequence can be repeated as needed throughout the course, but the focus of the writing class is always on writing.

Not all teachers are prepared for process writing and editing at the academic level. For instance, Hinkel (2002, pp. 258–260) makes a strong case for more vigorous teacher training so that teachers can give feedback and assistance to their academically bound students:

> [T]eachers can't teach what they don't know . . . the training of teachers of English as a second language needs to provide a greater focus on language—beyond conversational discourse. In the end, teacher trainers and teachers may need to be reminded that the academic skills they themselves require in teaching and learning are not far removed from those of their NNS students.

That is the subject of the next part of this book.

Study, Discussion, and Essay Questions

Write the answers to these questions in your Language Notebook.

1. Add these terms to your glossary and define them according to their usage in this chapter: methodology, holism, analysis, inductive presentation, deductive presentation, garden path method, recast.
2. Based on your experience as a language learner or teacher, what are some of the problems associated with English language teaching methodologies? What do you think "post-method" language teaching is?

3. What exactly is the problem with the activity about the wedding dresses cited by Kumaravadivelu (2003, p. 85)? What do you think the teacher intended for the students to do?

4. What is the difference between meaning-oriented work and message-oriented work in the classroom?

5. Discuss the various examples of English language teaching in this chapter. What is your reaction to these examples?

6. Butzkamm and Caldwell (2009, p. 33) suggest using other languages for metalinguistic activities in the presentation of grammatical structures, but this is controversial. What are the pros and cons of this practice?

7. Drills are also controversial in English language teaching. What are the potential benefits and the potential problems?

8. Gatbonton and Segalowitz (1988) make suggestions about making practice more communicative on the basis of repetition. What is the relationship between repetition and the Usage/Exposure Hypothesis? Can you think of some activities that allow for repetition?

9. Some kinds of oral feedback seem "natural" but they may not be the most effective. Do you think teachers should train themselves to give another kind of feedback? What kind? Give an example of what you mean.

10. When you get feedback on your writing, what kind is it? What would you do with feedback on your usage errors? If you are a teacher, what kind of feedback do you give and why? Do you think your comments are effective?

11. How good are you at self editing? Have you participated in peer editing activities? Was your experience positive or negative? What would you do if you wanted learners to edit their peers' work?

Activities

1. This excerpt is from Ellis (1992, p. 212). In a paragraph in your Language Notebook, evaluate its effectiveness as a drill. Is any learning or practice happening? Is the student ready to be successful with this drill? What should the teacher do about S's performance?

T: *Now, Tasleem, what is this?* (T holds up a pen.)
S: *This is a pen.*
T: *What are these?* (T holds up two pens.)
S: *This are a pen.*
T: *These are _____?*

S: *Are pens.*
T: *What is this?* (T holds up a ruler.)
S: *This is a ruler.*
T: *What are these?* (T holds up two rulers.)
S: *This is a . . . are . . . This are a rulers.*
T: *These are rulers. What are these?*
S: *This are a rulers.*
T: *Not "a." These are _____?*
S: *Rulers.*
T: *Rulers.*
S: *Rulers.*

2. Data-driven learning is inductive learning by using software designed to search a document or a corpus. Go to the website http://www.lextutor. ca/concordancers/ (retrieved 10/31/12) and experiment with searching the different corpora to see how words are used in contexts. Start with this question: what do you think the most common usage of the word "kind" is? Is it the adjective for "friendly" or the synonym for "type"? Or something else? Enter the word **kind** and choose the Brown corpus, then click on "get concordance." What do you find out?

3. Here are two case histories of teachers. What approach does each one seem to be following, the LAA or a traditional writing approach? What seem to be the beliefs of each teacher about learning?

Mr. Green wants his students to write fluently. His long-term goal is to have the students write a research paper at the end of the term. Last week, he had learners practice writing direct quotes and he gave a short lecture about how they are incorporated into a paragraph, and the norms of punctuation.

Now he is having his class learn how to paraphrase what different authors say. After looking at the first draft of the students' paraphrases, he notices that some students have problems with verb

Mr. Brown wants his students to write fluently. He gives his students a variety of writing assignments throughout the term that are coded to different grammar points, called "mechanics lessons," which he follows in sequence throughout each school year. For instance, in the first assignment, after going over the formation of the present tense as an example of language mechanics, he asks the students to write about a city they know well in order to practice the present tense.

tenses. He decides that the typical verb forms for paraphrasing an author are the third person singular present and past tense.

Smith says that . . . Smith said that . . .

Garcia claims . . . Garcia claimed . . .

Lew proves that . . . Lew proved that . . .

Mr. Green prepares a mini-lecture to review these verb forms and a set of examples for students to use as models as they are writing their paraphrases.

The following week he goes over the past tense using the textbook materials and worksheets, and asks the learners to write about what they did over the weekend in order to practice the past tense.

Mr. Brown doesn't believe direct grammar corrections are effective, because he doesn't think that learners look at them, so he gives the papers back with a letter grade on the top and no feedback.

3. If these were spoken errors, what kind of oral feedback would you give? Would you expect modified output?

Global Errors= **No comprehension or miscommunication**

Wrong word
I have twenty. Intended meaning: I am twenty.

Wrong pronoun
She brought his baby son. Intended meaning: He brought his baby son.

Missing words/Wrong word
Heddy in the cook. Intended meaning: Heddy is in the kitchen.

Garbled word order
saw the man the policeman. Intended meaning: The man saw the policeman.

Stigmatizing Errors = **Ridicule or profiling (often pronunciation or lexical problems, not grammar)**

Wrong word
She is embarrassed. Intended meaning: She is pregnant.

Inappropriate slang (this usage is not appropriate everywhere)
Please don't <u>knock</u> me up. Intended meaning: Please don't <u>wake</u> me up.

Formality
It's <u>a turn on</u>. Intended meaning: It's <u>very nice</u>.

Local Errors =   **Do not interfere with communication**

Wrong word
She studies in the <u>bookstore</u>.

Missing article
She studies in library.

Missing subject
studies in the library.

Wrong verb form
The student <u>study</u> every night.

Part II

Consensus Grammatical Features

There is a general consensus about the more formal and stable norms of the spoken and written English used in education, politics, law, and business correspondence. Called Academic English (AE), these consensus features comprise a largely learned second or third dialect for most people, and are both the cause and the result of diglossia that has emerged in World Englishes. In Part II, the chapters are about the consensus features of AE that people use because they are unlikely to result in misunderstanding. Regionalisms and ELF usages are not proscribed at all costs, but they are discouraged. People in the academic or professional community often choose impersonal writing that avoids personal identification for the sake of highlighting the ideas, theories, and research in their texts.

Each chapter discusses the constructions at a certain level of grammatical analysis: morphology, words and word formation, phrases (noun, adjective, adverb, verb, and preposition), sentences, complex sentences, and discourse. Part III of this book will be about the grammatical features that seem more fluid, flexible, and potentially unstable.

Morphemes 5

The relationship of morphemes to words is therefore the hardest thing in language to analyze. Asking what morphemes a word contains and what they mean is asking what the coiner of the word had in mind when he coined it and possibly what unforeseen associations it may have built up since. It is less an analytical question than a question about history. The morpheme at best continues to live a parasitic life within the word. It remains half alive for one speaker and dies for the next; or it may be revived by education.

(Bolinger, 1975, p. 110)

Morphemes are the lexical bits and pieces from which words are formed, but the relationship between morphemes and words is sometimes hard to analyze. For instance, the word *handsome* means physically attractive and is most often said of men; the two morphemes composing it are *hand* and *some* but they do not relate obviously to the meaning. What most people don't realize is that the original meaning of the word was more like *handy, useful,* or *convenient,* and it was applied to things and people. The original structure of the word was the freely occurring noun *hand* plus an old suffix *-some* used to form adjectives from nouns (compare *troublesome* or *awesome*). It appears that over time a man who was able to do things became a man who was attractive to others. This association between word and meaning overshadowed the morphological structure of the word and overcame any other usages over the course of centuries. A word that was fairly broad in meaning became more specific; a word whose morphology was transparent became opaque.

In the first line in Figure 5.1, the phonological properties of the word *handsome* show a common deletion of the [d] sound between [n __ s] in pronunciation. The second line shows the morphological structure with two possibilities because some people do not break *handsome* down into two morphemes but some people do because they know something about the original story of the word. That is what Bolinger was trying to get at in the quote above; morphological analysis is complex because people's knowledge of morphemes is variable and changes over time. The third line shows the spelling.

The fourth line gives the syntactic information for the word. Any adjective can fill the variable X so the expression $[X]_{ADJ}$ stands for any word that is an adjective. This knowledge may be implicit; there are many people who can't say explicitly what part of speech the word *handsome* is. The adjective *handsome* can fit into an adjective slot X in a mixed construction, such as $[a\ [X]_{ADJ}\ man]_{NP}$, to yield the lexical construction $[a\ handsome\ man]_{NP}$. In the lower box, the conventional meaning of the word is as shown. Pragmatically, the word *handsome* has a more specialized meaning if applied to a woman; she may be attractive in a masculine way. The word is used mainly in conversation and perhaps fictional or popular writing, and it would be uncommon in academic or administrative writing.

There is another mixed construction associated with the word *handsome* because it is part of a pattern, as shown in the box. This pattern has a variable for a noun to be inserted in order to be converted to an associated adjective by

Word Formation by Derivation

$[[X]_N\ \text{-}some]_{ADJ}$

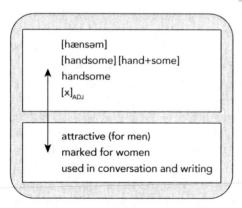

Figure 5.1 A Construction that Pairs the Form and Meaning/Function for the Word *Handsome*

adding the suffix *-some*. Nouns like *awe, quarrel,* or *trouble* can be applied to X to produce the words *awesome, quarrelsome,* or *troublesome,* but this particular word formation process is now mostly **unproductive** in modern English. Unproductive word formation processes are no longer used to produce new words but the pattern remains in the background of people's awareness of morphology, while **productive** ones (like adding *-tion* to a noun) are still used actively. Thus, morphemes and words have stories attached to them and knowing the stories can help people analyze the morphemes inside of words. The knowledge of different types of morphemes, their histories, and how they are used to compose words and meanings is called **morphological awareness**. Some people have a lot of morphological awareness and some don't, but the education needed to "revive" it or to awaken it is the topic of this chapter.

English morphology is complex because any analysis reveals several different types of morphemes that function in very different ways as they join together to form or create words and meanings. To begin with, a morpheme is a minimal construction, that is, a minimal form / meaning pairing. A morpheme can be **free** (*you, study, grammar, word, thing, in, what, of, half, one*) or **bound**, like *-ary* in *sanitary, -tion* in *communication,* or *re-* as in *redo* or *rethink.* This chapter is about bound morphemes, of which there are three types: prefixes, suffixes, and bound roots. **Prefixes** are morphemes added to the beginning of a word, **suffixes** are added to the end of a word, and **bound roots** are morphemes that occur mainly in English words derived or borrowed from Latin or Greek words. One complexity with morphology, as with words in general (discussed in the next chapter), is that there is a fundamental distinction between morphemes that are linguistic resources and morphemes that are part of the grammatical architecture.

Resource morphemes form an inventory of prefixes (*un-, pro-, sub-*), bound roots (*-ject-, -scrib-, -mit*), and suffixes (*-tion, -ive, -ity*) used in combinations together or with words, to derive words such as *project, submit, progressive.* Derivation is sometimes productive and sometimes

Morphemes

Free: *umbrella, eat, open, fast, for, up, which, the, book, sun, a, in, who, quick*

Bound:
Prefixes: *redo, untie, misspell, progress, subject, confine*

Suffixes: *doing, played, taller, happily, progressive, subjection, confinement*

Bound roots: *progress, subject, confinement, sanitary, communication*

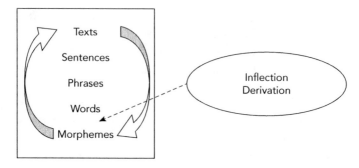

Figure 5.2 Two Primary Word Formation Processes Involving Resource and System Morphemes

unproductive, as in the word formation process that produced the word *handsome*. Derivational morphemes are relatively infrequent in normal usage and exposure so their priming associations are not predictable or regular. Derivation is partially pattern-based, and it may involve analytical processing like the mixed construction $[re + V]_V$ that results in verbs like *reanalyze* or *retile*.

System morphemes form a small inventory of inflectional suffixes added to words to indicate plurality (-*s*), tense (-*s* or -*ed*), and the like. Inflections are closely related to the grammatical system of English. Inflections are frequent in normal usage and exposure among expert speakers of English and thus they tend to be syntactically fixed with strong priming associations. Inflection is more holistic than analytical, and more productive than unproductive. High frequency makes inflectional morphology relatively regular and predictable when compared to derivational morphology. Inflection and derivation are the word formation processes that operate between morphemes and words.

Inflectional Morphology

System suffixes supply grammatical nuances that are important for understanding the meaning of a word or sentence. They do not change the part of speech when compared to the base they are added to, and they can be added to almost any word of a certain part of speech. They cause a predictable change in meaning when added to a word, but they do not result in a new word, just a different form of the same word. The full inventory of regular functional or inflectional suffixes in English is in Figure 5.3.

Nouns:		
Regular plural	-s	He needed two books.
Possessive	-s	The professor's books are old.
Verbs:		
III singular present tense:	-s	He donates the books.
Regular past tense	-ed	He donated the books.
Regular past participle	-ed	The books were donated.
Present participle	-ing	He is giving away his books.
Adjectives and Adverbs:		
Comparative	-er	His books are older than mine.
Superlative	-est	In fact, his are the oldest of all.

Figure 5.3 Inventory of Inflectional Suffixes in English

Figure 5.3 reveals a paradox: the same form [-s] is associated with three different constructions: the regular plural and the possessive for nouns and the regular third person singular for verbs. In pronunciation, all of the morphemes have the same three different pronunciations: [s], [z], [əz]. Even expert English speakers may have a hard time with inflectional morphology in English. Inflectional morphemes are not salient in speech. They are unstressed and not pronounced fully in many cases, so people have a hard time learning to use them in speaking and writing. While it doesn't seem to be difficult to grasp what the inflections mean if the learner comes from a language that also has inflections, it seems difficult to achieve automaticity with them. Some languages have few or no inflectional markings on words, and for students of those languages it may be difficult to notice the inflectional ending, to grasp what it is for, and to use it in speaking and writing with automaticity. The suffix -ing seems to be easier to learn than the third person singular present tense, -s, probably because it is more regular, more salient, and more grammatically meaningful.

Third Person Singular Present Tense

Figure 5.4 is an example of the form and function / meaning pairing for the third person singular present tense inflection -s. From top to bottom, the properties

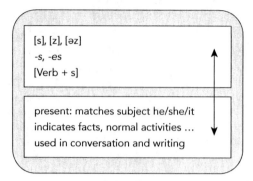

Figure 5.4   A Construction (Sound–Meaning Pairing) for the Third Person Singular Present Tense

of the morpheme have to do with form (phonology, morphology, orthography, and syntax) and meaning (semantics, pragmatics, and discourse). Phonologically, this morpheme has the three **allomorphs** (different forms) [s], [z], [əz], depending on the final sound of the verb it is added to. There are two different spellings, depending on whether its base verb ends with a non-sibilant consonant (*needs, represents, spells*) or a vowel or sibilant sound (*goes, studies, switches*). Syntactically, the morpheme is added to verbs to signal agreement with a third person subject.

The third person singular present tense is not very salient and it is the only inflection used in the present tense, but at the same time its high frequency in expert English usage makes it very robust and likely to continue. Nevertheless, it is an unstable feature. The third person singular is an area where ELF and other varieties of English diverge and go their own way, but standard varieties of inner circle English are unlikely to change. Breiteneder (2009, p. 258) says: "It is the idiosyncratic nature of the '3rd person -*s*', together with the social importance it seems to carry in some communities and its disappearance in others, that makes it so intriguing, suggesting that this feature has a symptomatic significance beyond its apparent triviality." This topic will be discussed further in Chapter 14.

Possessive 's

The possessive inflection is different from other inflections because it operates at the level of noun phrases (NPs), not individual words, as shown by examples like *the queen of England's press conference*. No other language has the preposed possessive noun phrase with an apostrophe -*s*, so learners need to be encouraged to use it. The possessive is distinguished with an apostrophe in writing. A singular noun or an irregular plural like *children* is marked as possessive with *'s*, and a plural noun is marked with an *'*, so these are ambiguous in speech unless clarified by something in the context of the situation. The singular example below is from the corpus made up of the quotes in this book; the plural example is a hypothetical example similar to one in the corpus.

> *[The learner's] ability to produce the form or construction with linguistic accuracy is only part of the overall production task.*

> *There is a growing body of evidence that [individuals'] parsing decisions are influenced in some way by their prior contact with comparable strings or structures.*

The possessive *'s* also appears somewhat commonly with time expressions, *tomorrow's meeting, today's agenda*. Sometimes there is variation in the use of the apostrophe, as in place names like *St. John's Academy* or *Pikes Peak* or with proper names that end with s or an s-like sound: *Mr. Gomes' office* or *Mr. Gomes's office*.

Regular and Irregular Plurals

Regular plurals are formed by adding the inflection *-s* to nouns. Irregular plurals are formed in a number of ways depending on whether they are old words from English or academic words borrowed from classical languages like Greek or Latin. English words show three possibilities: a vowel change in the stem (*mouse–mice, foot–feet, tooth–teeth, man–men, woman–women*); an ending (*child–children, ox–oxen*); or the same form (*deer–deer, sheep–sheep, fish–fish*). In addition, with some words ending in [f], the [f] changes to [v] (*wife–wives, leaf–leaves, life–lives*), but this change does not occur with all words (*roof–roofs, belief–beliefs*), and sometimes both plurals are possible (*scarves/scarfs, hooves/hoofs*).

Borrowed academic words maintain an ending reminiscent of their origins, such as *stimulus–stimuli, cactus–cacti, octopus–octopi, syllabus–syllabi, datum–data, memorandum–memoranda, larva–larvae, crisis–crises, phenomenon–phenomena, matrix–matrices*. However, these forms are not very frequent and, therefore, not very robust, so regular plural forms can also be seen: *octopuses, cactuses, syllabuses, matrixes*. For the word *antenna*, there are two plural forms: *antennas* for car receivers and *antennae* for insects. There are also some plural nouns without an -s: *people* or *cattle*, and nouns that are usually or always plural such as fields of study like *mathematics* or *physics*, or *clothes, goods, scissors, pants, trousers*.

There are some spelling issues with plurals as well. Nouns that end in s or an s-like sound add an extra vowel syllable: *wish–wishes, church–churches, press–presses*. This is the most salient or distinctive of the allomorphs for plural discussed above. In nouns that end in a consonant followed by a -y, the y changes to -i- as in *lady–ladies, city–cities, country–countries*. Finally, there are nouns that end with a consonant and a final -o: *tomato–tomatoes, potato–potatoes*, but see *studios, zoos, pianos*, and the like.

Comparative and Superlative Adjectives

Some adjectives form their comparative with the inflection *-er* and their superlative with the inflection *-est* (*taller, tallest*). Some adjectives occur with *more* and *most* (*more beautiful, most beautiful*). The rules are not hard and fast, but there are some trends, as shown in Figure 5.5.

Adjectives that end in *-y* or *-ly* undergo a spelling change, *pretty* → *prettier*, *early* → *earlier*. English learners benefit from learning these common adjectives in their inflected forms: *better, best, earlier, earliest, greater, greatest, higher, highest, larger, largest, lower, lowest, older, oldest, smaller, smallest, wider, widest*. In general, comparative and superlative adjectives tend to be used with rather generic nouns. These are the only examples from the corpus of quotes used in this book:

> *greater or less detail*
> *wider variety of associations*
> *a better material life*
> *a greater focus*
> *the best ways.*

Very few superlative adjectives are common in academic prose; these were the only ones found in the corpus:

> *the greatest effects*
> *the largest structural unit*
> *the smallest independent units*
> *the biggest stumbling block*
> *the hardest thing*
> *the highest and subtlest aspects.*

Taking -*er*/-*est* (and *less*/*least*):
Adjectives of one syllable except for *right, wrong,* and *real.*

Two-syllable adjectives that end in -*y* as in *angry, busy, crazy, dirty, pretty* . . .

Taking *more*/*most* (and *less*/*least*):
Two-syllable adjectives with no apparent morphology such as *common.*

Adjectives longer than two syllables.

Adjectives that end in -*ful*, -*less*, -*al*, -*ive*, -*ous* (*useful, mindless, musical, effective, zealous*).

Participial adjectives (*excited, exciting*).

Variable use of -*er*/-*est* and *more*/*most*:
Some monosyllabic adjectives like *fair, full, fierce, proud,* and *rude.*

Adjectives that end in -*ly*, e.g. *earlier, more likely* (*costly, deadly, friendly, lively, lonely, lovely, lowly, ugly*).

Adjectives that have unstressed endings: -*ow*, (*mellow, narrow*), -*er* (*bitter, clever*), -*le* or -*el* (*able, cruel*), -*ere* (*severe, sincere*), -*ure* (*secure, obscure*).

Figure 5.5 Comparatives and Superlatives

Inflectional Variation

Although inflectional morphology is regular, productive, and pattern-based, within the English-speaking inner and outer circles not all speakers use the same inflectional system as that found in Standard English. Some English users do not use the plural morpheme or the third person singular present tense consistently (*He have two book; He don't have three book*). There may also be different past participles or auxiliaries (*he had went* instead of *he had gone; he done froze the meat* instead of *he has frozen the meat*). These are examples of the problems with the diglossia in the transition from speech to writing. Indeed, even expert writers have problems with **subject/verb agreement**; the subject of the sentence must match the right verb form that goes with it. Plural subjects must have plural verb forms and singular subjects must have singular verb forms. In speech, people don't always notice subject/verb agreement errors, but in writing they do. Employers and professors sometimes form their opinion about someone's writing ability based on superficial details like subject/verb agreement errors, different past participles, or missing inflections. There is some subject/verb agreement and other inflectional practice in the Activities at the end of the chapter.

Derivational Morphology

A word formation process in which a new word is formed from combining free morphemes or bound roots and resource prefixes and suffixes is **derivation**. Bound roots are of Latin or Greek origin, and are quite common in

Word Families

subject	*reject*	*inject*
subvert	*revert*	*invert*
support	*report*	*import*
suppress	*repress*	*impress*

Academic English. They are bound because they require a prefix or a suffix to form a word. The underlined parts of *prescriptive* and *projection* are bound roots. Derivation results in word families, sets of words with related roots but different prefixes and suffixes. In these examples, the prefixes have different forms because the sounds assimilate, or become more similar phonologically to each other: *subport* → *support* or *inport* → *import*.

From the noun *clue* (not a bound root, a free morpheme), the adjective *clueless* is formed, which has a different part of speech and a different meaning. Derivation can apply to form new words almost indefinitely. For instance, to the word *clueless*, another suffix can be added to form an abstract noun: *clueless__ness__*. (The word *clueful* hasn't been derived yet, even though it might be a very useful word. This demonstrates the quirky item-based nature of derivational morphemes.) The complex word *cluelessness* is an example of an abstract lexical construction, which also applies to words like *lawlessness, useless-ness*, or *carelessness*. This construction simply means that a noun can be the base word for an adjective by adding the

$$[[N + less]_{ADJ} + ness]_{ABSTRACT\ N}$$

suffix *-less*, and that an adjective base can be converted into an abstract noun by adding the suffix *-ness*.

In this way, English derivational morphology is used to create new words from existing roots or words, prefixes, and/or suffixes. Derivation can change both the part of speech and the meaning of a derived word. In particular, suffixes (-*hood*, -*ship*, -*tion*) often change the part of speech of a word, as well as the meaning: *mother* → *motherhood*, *scholar* → *scholarship*, *rate* → *ration*. Prefixes (*un-*, *re-*, *mis-*) usually change the meaning but not the part of speech, as in *do* → *undo*, *make* → *remake*, *take* → *mistake*. The more frequent a prefix or suffix is, the more productive and regular its behavior is. The noun suffix -*tion* is much more common than is -*hood* or -*ship* and it can be added to many

Derivation

[**bound root + tion**]$_{\text{ABSTRACT N}}$
Examples: *friction, caption, tradition*

[**V + tion**]$_{\text{ABSTRACT N}}$
Examples: *attraction, reaction, refrigeration*

different verbs that are free roots or bound roots. Sometimes the spelling is adjusted by allowing for one -*t*-, although there could be two. There are also some pronunciation adjustments.

Back formation is a word formation process that is the opposite of derivation, but it is much less common. In back formation, new words are formed by subtracting derivational morphemes or what appear to be derivational morphemes. Examples are the formation of the verb *enthuse* (from the noun *enthusiasm*), the verb *intuit* (from the noun *intuition*), the verb *laze around* (from the adjective *lazy*), or the adjective *couth* (from the adjective *uncouth*). Back formations vary in acceptability and formality and differ from **clipping**, a very common procedure in which a word is simply shortened, often informally or as slang: *pro* (from *professional*), *math* (from *mathematics*), *prez* (from *president*).

Some Derivational Morphemes

Prefixes:

a-	on	afoot, aboard
ambi-	both	ambiguous, ambivalent
anti-	against	antiwar, antisocial
auto-	self	automatic, automobile
bi-, bin-	two	biweekly, binary
cent-	hundred	centennial, century
de-	from/down	degenerate, declaim
inter-	between	intersect, interdependence
micro-	small	micromanage, microscope
neo-	new	neonate, neoclassical

poly-	many	polyglot, polychrome
post-	after	postdate, postpone
pre-	before	predate, prefix
prot-/proto-	first	protein, prototype
re-	again	reexamine, rethink
semi-	half	semicircle, semiconscious
sub-	under	subordinate, subdivision
tele-	far	television, telephone
trans-	across	translate, transport
un-	not	unkind, unpleasant
un-	reverse	undo, unzip
under-	below	underfund, underestimate

Suffixes:
Classical

-arian	one who	librarian, humanitarian, agrarian
-ate	state/quality	desperate, candidate
-ation	action/process	refrigeration, electrification
-cy	state/quality	diplomacy, accuracy
-ian	relating to	simian, authoritarian
-ism	doctrine of	socialism, anarchism
-ist	one who	artist, linguist
-ize	make	standardize, euthanize
-ment	action/process	judgment, development
-mony	product	hegemony, matrimony
-oid	relating to	paranoid, humanoid
-ology	study of	biology, chronology, morphology
-ous	full of	nebulous, nervous
-tion	state/quality	intention, attraction
-tude	state/quality	certitude, attitude
-ure	action/process	nurture, nature

Native

-dom	state of	kingdom, wisdom
-en	made of	golden, wooden
-en	make	whiten, blacken
-er/-ar/-or	one who	baker, beggar, actor
-ful	full of	careful, colorful
-hood	state of	womanhood, boyhood
-ish	like/from	childish, Spanish

-less	without	childless, careless
-like	like	childlike, houselike
-ling	small	inkling, duckling
-ly	manner	happily, clearly
-ship	quality of	friendship, penmanship
-some	quality of	handsome, awesome
-th	order	fourth, thirtieth
-ward	direction	toward, homeward
-y	quality of	salty, cloudy

Greek and Latin bound roots:

-andr- / -anthr-	man	polyandry, anthropology
-ang-	bend	angle, triangle, angular
-arch-	chief	archcriminal, patriarch
-ast-	star	astronomy, asterisk, disaster
-chron-	time	synchronize, chronic, chronology
-crat-	rule	aristocrat, autocratic, democracy
-cycl-	circle / ring	cycle, Cyclops, encyclopedia
-dict-	speak	dictate, prediction, interdict
-doc- / -dox-	belief	doctrine, orthodox, heterodox
-log-	word	apology, monologue, catalogue
-mit- / -miss-	send	mission, permit, remit
-morph-	shape / form	morphology, metamorphosis
-path-	feeling	empathy, sympathy, pathology
-poli-	city	police, metropolis, policy
-pop-	people	populate, popular, repopulate
-the-	god	theology, atheist, theosophy
-tract-	pull / drag	tractable, attractive, tractor
-volv-	roll	involve, revolve, evolve

Discovery Procedures

There are some cases of overlap in the appearance but not the behavior of derivational and inflectional suffixes, as shown in the examples in the box on p. 94. These cases, -er and -ing, are morpheme homonym pairs. They look the same and they sound the same, but they are not the same. In such cases, grammarians don't guess. They arrive at an answer by using the characteristics and behavior of different morphemes and the co-texts they appear in as a **discovery procedure** to decide whether they are inflectional or derivational. For instance,

> **-er**
> . . . a great*er* focus on language . . .
> . . . the carri*er* of Anglo-American cultural imperialism . . .
>
> **-ing**
> I had been read*ing* about formulaic language . . .
> . . . less capable of draw*ing* support and gett*ing* guidance . . .

the discovery procedure takes meaning into account. The adjective *greater* shows comparison; the *-er* is added to *great* to produce the comparative form which has the same part of speech. In contrast, the noun *carrier* is derived from the verb *carry*; it is a different word meaning "that which carries."

To analyze these words, a grammarian looks at the syntactic co-text and function for each morpheme and word in question. In *I had been reading about formulaic language . . .*, *reading* is an inflected form, a present participle occurring with the primary auxiliaries *had been*. *Reading* functions as the main verb in the sentence. In the other excerpt, *less capable of drawing support and getting guidance . . .*, *drawing* and *getting* function as the object of the preposition *of*. Because they are objects, they must be nouns derived from the verbs *draw* and *get*. Since there is a change in the part of speech from verb to noun, this *-ing* suffix is a derivational morpheme. Nouns that are derived from verbs by adding *-ing* are called **gerunds**.

In grammatical analysis, meaning, syntax, and function are used as diagnostic tools to distinguish between different hypotheses about constructions. In both of these cases, the inflectional *-er/-ing* and the derivational *-er/ -ing* morphemes seem equally productive; they can be added to many different words. However, in general, derivational morphemes vary in productivity, while inflectional morphemes do not.

Derivational morphemes:

- are bound roots, prefixes, or suffixes
- often result in a change in the part of speech (suffixes)
- vary in productivity and meaning (*-tion*, *-hood*, *-ling*)
- make a substantial unpredictable change in the meaning of the derived word
- result in a new and different word

Inflectional morphemes:

- – are always suffixes and never roots or prefixes
- – do not change the part of speech when added to a word
- – are very productive and consistent (-ed, -s)
- – cause a predictable grammatical change in meaning
- – result in a different form of the same word

Morphological Awareness

Prior knowledge of morphemes (prefixes, suffixes, bound roots) aids in the application of discovery procedures like those described earlier, but the reverse is also true in that attempts to apply the procedures to analyze morphological structure improve knowledge of morphemes and strategies for morphemic analysis. In this circular fashion, morphological awareness grows. The citation from Bolinger (1975) at the beginning of this chapter links different degrees of morphological awareness with different language users and potentially with different educational experiences. Morphological awareness is part of the more general metalinguistic awareness that has an important impact on cognitive abilities and language learning. Morphological awareness is important in the acquisition of vocabulary because it gives learners an entry point into the meaning of words.

Morphological awareness allows the English learner to posit information about the meanings and grammar of newly encountered words, so that they can get started on forming a word-level construction to store in memory. After all, derivational prefixes and suffixes show evidence of repetition priming, that is, facilitation in processing linguistic forms due to language users' prior exposure to these forms (Grainger and Carreiras, 2009, p. 935). Thus, morphological awareness may facilitate vocabulary acquisition because words can be learned more quickly or with less overall effort. In a study of Japanese-speaking English learners, Zhang and Koda (2012, p. 1211) found that "those learners who possessed better morphological awareness tended to learn words better, and in turn, held a larger vocabulary."

However, while studying knowledge of derivational morphology, Ramirez et al. (2011, p. 514) found that morphological awareness was related to better word reading, but that English language learners (ELLs) had different morphological awareness due to transfer from the predominant word formation processes in their first language.

With respect to derivational awareness, the Spanish-speaking ELLs performed similarly to the native speakers of English after controlling for maternal education, whereas the Chinese-speaking ELLs performed significantly lower than either group. The syntactic and distributional properties of derivational morphology are similar in English and Spanish, which may explain why the Spanish-speaking ELLs performed on the same level as the monolinguals. In contrast, Chinese-speaking ELLs have fewer opportunities to develop these derivational morphological skills in their L1 due to the limited role that derivational morphemes play in the word formation process in Chinese.

If English learners are unfamiliar with English derivational morphemes and how they function, they cannot use them to form words or to understand unfamiliar words they come across in their reading or on tests. This is a disadvantage because academic language is often made up of Greek/Latin-derived words.

Most learners, non-native- or native-speaking, need to increase their academic vocabulary. In the Language Awareness Approach, there is a dual focus on linguistic forms and meanings in the classroom. The focus on form begins with the forms and meanings of morphemes in the context of different words and texts, and word formation processes like derivation. Learners who speak languages where there are cognate prefixes, suffixes, and bound roots can take advantage of the overlap. Learners from languages where there is little overlap in morphology can learn to look at words for cues to meaning and grammar as one of a series of vocabulary acquisition strategies. These learners especially benefit from practice with different prefixes, suffixes, bound roots, and free morphemes in a variety of ways, including decontextualized word lists and word families and more contextualized study of words in texts. Some learners like to keep a vocabulary journal in which they keep track of different morphemes they notice and the word families they belong to. In addition, the use of on-line dictionaries makes it very easy and even entertaining to find out more about the stories of words.

Study, Discussion, and Essay Questions

Write the answers to these questions in your Language Notebook. Create your notebook as a word processing document because you will be using the "find" command to analyze your writing.

1. Define these terms and add them to your glossary: morpheme, productive word formation processes, unproductive word formation processes, free morpheme, bound morpheme, derivational morpheme, inflectional morpheme, bound root, allomorph, resource morpheme, system morpheme.

2. Explain the term morphological awareness. What is your level of morphological awareness? What are some ways you might improve your morphological awareness?

3. These constructions are written with bracketed notation. With a partner, discuss what these formalisms mean and create some examples that follow them.

   a. $[[X]_N \text{-}some]_{ADJ}$
   b. $[a\ [X]_{ADJ}\ man]_{NP}$
   c. $[a\ handsome\ man]_{NP}$
   d. $[[[X]_N \text{-}less]_{ADJ} \text{-}ness]_{ABSTRACT\ N}$

4. What is the difference between resource morphemes and system morphemes? Give examples of each.

5. What are word families? Based on the examples in this chapter, can you find two other word families by looking in the dictionary? What is their basic bound root? What does the root mean or what is its origin?

6. What is back formation? What is clipping? What is the difference between the two? (Remember that clipping is much more common than back formation.) Using your own morphological awareness, a dictionary, or online resources, identify these words as examples of back formation or clipping:

   to burgle (from burglar)
   phys ed (from physical education)
   mike (from microphone)
   pea (from pease)
   stats (from statistics)
   to opine (from opinion)
   "tamale" (from Spanish "tamales")
   typo (from typographical error)

7. Imagine you are tutoring an English learner who makes these mistakes in speaking and writing. How would you explain the standard use of the third person singular present tense to your tutee?

I puts the eraser on the shelf for you.
He go into the office after class.
The drugstore close at 10 Monday through Friday.
They wants to speak English very well.

8. Look up these words from the corpus of this book in a dictionary: *co-texts,*
    coherent, collocation, co-occurs. What do you find? Do you encounter any
    problems in your search for information? Is this the same prefix *co-* in each
    case? What do the words mean? What is the morphological structure of
    each?

Activities

1. Choose five of the following words to analyse in your Language Notebook.
    Divide the words into their component morphemes. You will probably
    need a dictionary for some words. Write what the derivation or origin of
    these words is. Share your information with the class.

    multiple
    moustache
    carpet
    catsup
    tawdry
    glamour
    worship
    smog
    lynch
    candy
    perish
    grammar

2. Have you used any words with these bound roots in your essays in your
    Language Notebook? Make a list of several words that have these roots.
    What is the common meaning for the bound root? Consult a dictionary
    while doing this activity to see if you are correct.

    -aud-
    -cap-
    -cert-
    -cogn-

-cred-

-fac- or -fact-

-fig-

-mob-

-pos-

-rect-

-vac-

3. Examine each of the three sentences and decide what type of morpheme
    the underlined form is, using discovery procedures in this chapter. The
    three possibilities are inflectional morpheme, derivational morpheme, or
    a piece of a word that is not a morpheme. Once you have decided,
    articulate how you made your decision.

    i.   a. *Silver is beautiful.*
         b. *My employer is nice.*
         c. *Those puppies are cuter*
    ii. a. *I woke up after sleeping.*
         b. *They are eating again.*
         c. *I don't like that thing.*
    iii. a. *The report disturbed the viewers.*
         b. *The disturbed viewers called the TV station.*
         c. *You need to embed the announcement in the text of your speech.*

4. The three morphemes *-s* (possessive, plural for nouns, and singular for
    present tense verbs) each have three pronunciations (called allomorphs).
    The distribution of the allomorphs follow this pattern, based on the
    pronunciation of the final sound in the word the morpheme is added to:

    a. The voiceless sound $/s/$ is added to words that end in a voiceless
        sound (no vibration in the vocal cords).

Plural	Possessive	3rd singular of verbs
cats, maps, tents	*Brett's, Mr. Wick's*	*eats, walks, traps*

    b. The voiced sound $/z/$ is added to words that end in a voiced sound
        (vibration present).

Plural	Possessive	3rd singular of verbs
dogs, rules, ribs	*Bill's, Ms. Green's*	*spells, adds, says*

c.   The extra syllable /əz/ is added to words that end in a sibilant sound (a hissing sound like /s/).

Plural	Possessive	3rd singular of verbs
wishes, judges, ditches	*Mitch's, Dr. Gomez's*	*teaches, messes, buzzes*

Put these words in the proper category (a, b, or c) based on the pronunciation of the final sound. Say the words out loud.

Plurals: *cans, books, students, needs, bus, dishes*
Possessives: *Bee's, Mr. Birch's, Kathy's, Chris's*
Verbs: *loves, puts, fishes, fusses, writes*

Words   6

Most fluent speakers of English seem to know what a word is. They know, for example, that words are listed in dictionaries, that they are separated in writing by spaces, and that they may be separated in speech by pauses. But it is one thing to identify words and another to suggest a definition that will apply to all types of word in English . . . We shall consider the word as an uninterruptible unit of structure consisting of one or more morphemes and which typically occurs in the structure of phrases.

(Jackson and Amvela, 2000, p. 50)

The intuition that allows people to distinguish between words and non-words is a metalinguistic ability, yet linguists have struggled to find a scientific way of defining what essential quality makes a word. Jackson and Amvela suggest that the essential characteristics are twofold: that a word is a unit of linguistic structure more freely occurring than a morpheme and that a word is an element in a larger grammatical construction like a phrase. Jackson and Amvela's definition places the word at the middle of inflection/derivation and collocation/colligation in a linguistic architecture where priming goes from bottom up and from top down, as shown in Figure 6.1.

This model illustrates a linguistic architecture in a simplistic way but it is misleading. For one thing, as noted in the last chapter, possessive *'s* is an inflectional process that operates at the level of phrases, not words. For another, the priming in collocations can operate over larger constructions than phrases.

Hulstijn (2003, p. 204) defines words as linguistic units that have a "special status" because they are available for people's conscious, metalinguistic reflection, unlike smaller lexical units like morphemes or larger units like

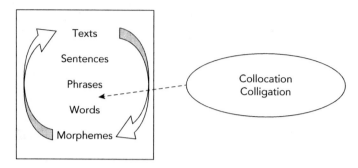

Figure 6.1 Words Are Intermediate between Morphemes and Phrases and Take Part in Collocations and Colligations

phrases. Words are the constructions that have the most salience in the neural architecture of language, because long-term usage and exposure to language causes memory traces to coalesce into important linguistic symbols. Words are stable mappings between form and function/meaning; this stability allows them to occur freely on their own and in collocations and colligations.

Types of Words

The free morpheme is a simple mapping from a phonological form to its meanings. Free morphemes are words like *this, pick, up, from, the, of,* and *free.* This definition also applies to a type of word called an **insert**. Inserts are words like *yeah, huh, bye,* and *uh-oh.* Inserts are common in conversation but they are rare in writing, except in written conversations. Inserts don't participate in larger grammatical constructions like phrases or sentences.

Some words are more complex than single free morphemes. They are multi-morphemic derived words built on bound roots (*subject, morpheme*) or free word roots (*handsome, player, swimming*). Some words are multi-word lexical units because even though people often think of them as composed of separate words, they function as single words, especially in speech (*a lot of* or *alotta, sort of* or *sorta, going to* or *gonna*).

Languages have a primary distinction between two types of word-level constructions, resource elements and system elements (Bolinger, 1975). In the sentence *The girl planted a small tree carefully,* the resource words are the nouns, verbs, adjectives, and adverbs: *girl, planted, small, tree,* and *carefully.* Resource words are creative and longer, and they receive more stress and emphasis in speech. The system word in this sentence is the determiner *a,* which tells the listener that *girl* and *tree* each refer to a specific identifiable girl and tree. Just as resource and system morphemes interact to form words, resource and system words interact with each other to compose phrases.

The difference between resource and system words seems to arise from frequency and priming effects. Resource elements are less frequent, so their priming associations are weaker, more flexible, and more open to change and variation. However, their strong associations with concrete meanings make them highly symbolic. System elements are frequent, and their priming effects are robust, rigid, and more impervious to change through time and variation across speakers. They tend to be shorter and less prominent in speech. They are less connected to specific meanings, so they operate less as stand-alone symbols and more as interdependent symbols in a system, gaining their meaning from their purpose or function.

Resource elements are derivational morphemes (prefixes, suffixes, and bound roots), as well as words that carry the weight of meaning in a sentence, permit free invention or borrowing from another language, and are nouns, verbs, adjectives, and adverbs.

System elements are inflectional morphemes and words that supply grammatical details about words and meaning, form a syntactic frame for resource elements, are resistant to invention or borrowing, and are prepositions, pronouns, conjunctions, modals, determiners, and the like.

Structure and Meaning

Grammar exists to convey meanings and meanings stem from perceptions and imagination. For instance, the utterance *The girl planted a small tree carefully* could be about a real girl, tree, and planting incident in immediate perception or in long-term memory. Alternatively, it could be about an imaginary planting incident. In either case, the words refer to entities and relationships in a mental situation, which may or may not reflect what is in the world accurately. The mental situation is called the focal situation, as exemplified in Figure 6.2.

Spoken and written sentences refer to focal situations. Resource elements refer to aspects of focal situations: nouns refer to mental entities (*the girl* and *a tree*), adjectives describe the entities (*small*), verbs refer to actions and relationships among the entities (*planted*), and adverbs (prototypically) describe the actions or relationships (*carefully*). Based on their correspondence to a focal

Figure 6.2 Utterances and Sentences Relate to Focal Situations

situation, resource and system words arrange themselves into typical constructions like noun phrases (*the girl*) or verb phrases (*planted a small tree carefully*).

System Elements

The meaning of the sentence *The girl planted a small tree carefully* can be understood from the words *girl, planted, small, tree, carefully* alone. Because system elements are not essential to the meaning of a sentence, their importance in the comprehension of discourse is underestimated. Discourse refers to texts longer than one sentence. In discourse, people comprehend the meaning of each phrase and sentence, and the overall meaning, more easily and rapidly if there are typical constructions made up of recognizable resource and system elements that prime each other and set up expectations about structure and meaning. Contrast the experience of reading the first "paragraph" in the box with the experience of reading the second.

In the first, readers encounter a list of words and must infer the relationships among them based on prior experience with the world. Holding all this uncertainty in working memory causes readers to find this text quite difficult to understand and remember. In the second, the system elements clarify the entities and their relationships so they can be stored in memory easily. There is little uncertainty, so there is less cognitive work. If readers cannot use system elements as cues to discourse meaning, everything they read is like the first selection. This may be the case with readers who lack syntactic awareness or learners with low proficiency in English.

1. newspaper carry big story man bit dog false people believe illogical silly people believe call talk show radio discuss host egg make fool when find out story untrue want sue talk show host.

2. The newspaper carried a big story about a man who bit a dog. It was false, but many people believed it even though it was illogical and silly. The people who believed it called into a talk show on the radio to discuss it and the host egged them on to make fools of themselves. When they found out that the story was untrue, they wanted to sue the talk show host.

System words are associated with particular sentential or phrasal structures and meanings, as shown in the examples from the corpus of quotes from this book (Figure 6.3).

Associated with Sentences (situations)	Conjunctions	*grammar and discourse* *the knowledge <u>or</u> strategies*
	Subordinators	*multilingual people <u>who</u> can* *communicate <u>though</u> it is arguable*

Associated with Noun Phrases (entities)	Determiners	<u>*the*</u> *position* <u>*this*</u> *system*
	Pronouns	<u>*they*</u> *mean* <u>*he*</u> *coined <u>it</u>*
	Prepositions	<u>*for*</u> *this view* <u>*about*</u> *grammatical forms*

Associated with Verb Phrases (relationships)	Primary Auxiliaries	<u>*has*</u> *never been* <u>*is*</u> *meant*
	Modal Auxiliaries	<u>*may*</u> *be further divided* <u>*will*</u> *ensure*
	Particles	*conjures <u>up</u> images*

Associated with with Adjective/ Adverb Phrases (modifications)	Intensifiers	*a <u>very</u> recent decision*

Figure 6.3 System Words and Their Associated Resource Words

Resource Elements

If we break any sentence down into the smallest independent units, we end up with single words that, according to traditional practice, can be classified into various types of word classes called *parts of speech* . . . Once we learn to recognize parts of speech, we can begin to explore how particular types of words interact with certain other types within the sentence, that is, how they function together to convey overall meaning . . . Individual words do not simply occur as unrelated strings in sentences. Rather, they occur as parts of particular units, and these units in turn play particular roles within the sentence.

(DeCarrico, 2000, pp. 2–4)

At the word level, resource elements divide themselves into four main word classes, also known as parts of speech or syntactic categories. They are nouns, verbs, adjectives, and adverbs. In English, these word classes do not have inflectional markings, but they have typical meanings, purposes/functions, morphological behavior, and syntactic contexts. Nouns **refer** to objects or people in a focal situation, so they are subjects and stand in contrast to verbs. Verbs state or declare, that is, **predicate**, actions or relationships among the objects or people in a focal situation. Adjectives **modify**; they describe objects or people in the focal situation. Adverbs also modify; they describe the manner in which an action is performed.

Word Class	Prototypical Meaning	Prototypical Function
Noun	object/people	reference
Verb	action/relationship	predication
Adjective/Adverb	property/manner	modification

Word classes can also be defined by their morphological behavior. The class of words that fills the variable in $[X + hood]_{\text{ABSTRACT N}}$ is the noun, as in *brotherhood* or *motherhood*. The verb is the class of words that takes the third person singular present tense inflection. Adjectives and adverbs are the classes of words that can be used with comparative system morphemes like $[X\text{-}er]$ or $[more\ X]$.

In a similar fashion, word classes can be distinguished by their syntactic behavior in collocations and colligations, that is, by the variables that they typically fill in phrasal constructions. A resource word like *small* fills the variable in the construction $[X]_{ADJ}$, and the resource words *tree* and *girl* fill the variable in $[Y]_N$. A syntactic category can thus be defined as the class of words that fill a

> Resource word classes are distinguished from each other by four criteria:
>
> – meaning
> – function
> – morphology
> – syntactic behavior

variable in a particular construction, or the class of words that fill similar variables/roles in a number of constructions. Syntactic categories with some corresponding resource words from the corpus are:

Nouns:	*forms, partners, languages, people*
	world, system, classroom
	globalism, prevalence, centrality
	English
Verbs:	*is, represent, places, steers*
	flaunt, expose
	been, attached
Adjectives:	*real, equal*
	economic, global, cultural
	American, British
Adverbs:	*proudly, creatively, actually*

System/Resource Continuum

The distinction between system and resource elements is not rigid. Prepositions are considered system words, and some prepositions, like *of* or *to*, seem to mark grammatical relationships, as in this sentence: *The retiring professor of English gave the old books to the students.* However, other prepositions make an important contribution to meaning, as in the sentence: *He donated the books after his last class and before his last department meeting.*

Also, system words can be used as resource words and vice versa. Prepositions have been converted into verb or noun forms (in a process of **lexification**) as in usages like *They went along on the class* *outing*. Intensifiers are considered system words in this book, but elsewhere they are often considered adverbs. Over time some intensifiers have become so frequent, and their priming effects so strong, that they are in the process of changing from resource words to system words. This process is called grammaticalization or delexification. Intensifiers occur before adjectives, other adverbs, noun phrases, and prepositional phrases to indicate the degree or intensity of the modified expression, but they are rare in academic writing. Here is one of the few examples from the corpus:

> . . . *the discourse competence [so vital] for developing effective reading and writing skills.*

Compounding and Other Word Formation Processes

Compounding is a word formation process where new English words are formed by combining two or more free morphemes or words. In compounds, the second (or rightmost) word is the head of the compound, except for phrasal verbs. That means that English compounds are "right-headed." In this sentence from the corpus, there are a number of clear examples of compounds:

> *The word conjures up images of mind-numbing drills in the sweatshops of foreign language learning . . .*

In pronunciation, compounds (except for phrasal verbs like *conjures up*) are typically stressed more heavily on the first word than on the second. In fact, the stress pattern is usually taken as a defining characteristic of a compound because the writing system doesn't treat compounds uniformly. In writing, compounds are sometimes treated as one word, and sometimes they are written with hyphens: *well-known*, *self-initiated*, or *mind-numbing*. Sometimes compound words are written with no obvious marking at all, as in the compound *language learning*. Examples like these are considered compounds mainly because of their stress pattern and the fact that they can be paraphrased

Phrasal verbs: *Conjure up* is a compound made up of a verb plus a particle, which means "to make something appear by magic." Note that the verb is the "head" of the compound.

Adjectival compounds: *Mind-numbing* is a participial adjective formed from a participle *numbing* and its object (*mind*) placed before it. Adjective compounds are right-headed. [*numbing* (*the*) *mind*]$_{VP}$ [*mind-numbing*]$_{PARTICIPIAL\ ADJ}$

Noun–noun compounds: The first noun describes the second noun, which is the head word. *Sweatshops* are factories where people work in inhumane conditions, where they "sweat." In this case, describing a classroom as a sweatshop is a metaphor.

with the word *for* or *of*. Most compounds are resource words, but there are also some system word compounds. These words are written as one word: *already, altogether, anymore, maybe* (to mean *perhaps*), and *whatever*. These are written as two separate words: *a lot, all ready, all right, every time, in spite of, may be* (*He may be here*), *no one.*

Compound System Elements

prepositions:	*out of, into, within*
pronouns:	*something, everyone, himself, themselves . . .*
determiners:	*another*
auxiliaries:	*cannot*

Besides derivation and compounding, **functional shift** is a very productive word formation process in English. In functional shift, a word with one part of speech is derived from a word with a different part of speech, simply by changing its function but with no accompanying morphological change. Noun-to-verb conversions are common, sometimes despite obvious noun morphology: *to author a book, to conference with a student, to transition to another phase, to mainstream a student.*

In **blending**, new words are formed by taking part of one word and blending it seamlessly with another word: *chocoholic* (from chocolate and alcoholic), *reaganomics* (to refer to former President Reagan's brand of economics), *brunch* (from breakfast and lunch). Blending can also push the envelope of word combinations: *prideandjoyography* (seemingly a word coined by an advertiser to draw parents to take pictures of their children, their "pride and joy"). **Coinage** refers to a process by which new words or names can be invented out of the blue for new products or concepts: *xerox, kleenex, google*. Coined brand names are then often generalized as common nouns or verbs, a word formation procedure called **generalization.**

Word Formation

Derivation	*define → definite → definitive*
Back formation	*editor → edit*
Compounding	*never + land → neverland*
Functional shift	*[egg] → to egg someone on*
Blending	*cybernetic organism → cyborg*
Coinage	*Kleenex* (brand name)
Generalization	*kleenex* (for tissue)

Discovery Procedures

Just as a doctor uses diagnostics to determine a patient's illness, a grammarian uses diagnostics to discover information about a word in question. The diagnostics are the meanings, morphology and word formation, syntactic co-texts, and functions of a focal word.

> *It is critical that students become more self-sufficient in editing their own <u>writing</u>.*

Discovery Procedure Example 1

Meaning: *Writing* is an activity.

Morphology: *Writing* could be derived from *write* by adding the inflectional morpheme *-ing*, so it could be a verb. Alternatively, it could be a noun derived from the verb *write* by adding the derivational (gerundive) suffix *-ing*.

Co-text: The word *writing* is the head word in the phrase [*their own* ____], e.g. with the determiner *their* and the word *own*, and both of these words are possessive. Words that occur with possessives are nouns.

Function: The phrase [*their own writing*] is the direct object of [*editing* ____]. Direct objects are nouns.

Example 1: The question is "What part of speech is the word *writing?*" The answer to the question begins with the properties of the focal word, as shown in the box. There is conflicting information, such as the two morphological possibilities (inflection or derivation). In that case, the alternatives must be weighed carefully, and the weight of all of the evidence determines the best analysis. After using the diagnostics, the grammarian knows that *writing* is an activity noun, a gerund, in this context.

> *It is critical that students become more <u>self-sufficient</u> in editing their own writing.*

Discovery Procedure Example 2

Meaning: *Self-sufficient* describes students.

Morphology: *Self-sufficient* is comparative: [*more self-sufficient*]. Comparatives are adjectives.

Co-text: The construction [*more self-sufficient*] occurs after a linking verb *become*. Linking verbs are usually followed by nouns or adjectives.

Function: *Self-sufficient* is a subject complement. Subject complements are either nouns or adjectives.

Example 2 starts with a question about the part of speech of the word *self-sufficient*. To answer the question, it is necessary to look at the properties of the focal word, as shown in the box. Some evidence points to either a noun or a verb as answers, but most of the evidence is consistent with the answer of adjective. It describes, it occurs after a linking verb as a subject complement, and it is comparative.

Discovery procedures are circular in that they are highly dependent on each other and on the grammarian's syntactic awareness as a starting point. There is no way to identify a focal word's part of speech without knowing something about meaning, morphology, word formation, syntactic behavior, and function, and that makes the discovery procedure difficult at first. However, lexical and syntactic awareness grows from practice and experience. Students soon see the diagnostics as useful tools or strategies to follow when they are perplexed about a word. At some point, they do not need to guess the part of speech of a word, because they have strategies to figure it out.

Lexical Awareness

The quote from Jackson and Amvela (2000, p. 50) at the beginning of this chapter is about lexical awareness, or what people know about words. Language users differ in the size and scope of their vocabulary, their active knowledge about words that permits easy usage, their receptive knowledge about words that allows comprehension of words in contexts, and their ability to distinguish different classes of words as system or resource, or noun, verb, or adjective. Their ability to verbalize what they know in metalanguage is also variable.

First, there is implicit knowledge about words, or priming associations. The more vocabulary language users know, the more elaborated the meaning and syntactic associations, and the more primings and nested primings they have accumulated, the more quickly, fluently, and accurately they can understand and use language.

Lexical awareness is also explicit knowledge of words. In the quote from Shapira (1978, p. 254) cited in Chapter 3, Zoila shows that she can distinguish resource words (big words) from system words (little words) and she realizes that resource words are crucial for meaning but system words are less important in conversations. She is also aware of an important comprehension strategy that she relies on: she takes advantage of resource words over system words for comprehension, and she uses them to guess what the meaning of the sentence is. Nevertheless, when Zoila speaks, she uses system words like *the, for, my* as the framework for her resource words, like *words, continue, conversation*. Two more examples reveal that, despite her lexical awareness, Zoila isn't interested in noticing, representing, and storing English words and morphology in long-term memory for later retrieval.

> Shapira: *It makes no difference.*
> Zoila: *Anyway, it making no difference.*
>
> Zoila: *. . . very /sɛnsər/.*
> Shapira: *Sincere?*
> Zoila: *Sincero, sincero.*
> Shapira: *Sincere.*
> Zoila: *Yeah.*

Richards (2002, pp. 35–50) suggests that, in interaction, language users rely on broad communicative strategies linked to cognition (world knowledge, expectations) to maximize their communication, but, as seen with Zoila, these strategies don't always lead to improved ability to use new linguistic constructions to communicate. Learners need to be encouraged and shown how to become active word learners.

Lexical awareness transfers from the first language to later languages. Recall from the last chapter that Spanish-speaking English language learners (ELLs) are better at derivational morphology than are Chinese learners because Spanish and English have similar derivational word formation, but Chinese doesn't. However, for compounds, Ramirez et al. (2011, p. 514) found some evidence that Spanish learners had problems understanding compounds because they tended to think that the first or leftmost word was the head of the compound:

> A different pattern was observed for compound awareness. After controlling for age, maternal education, and nonverbal ability, there was no difference between the Chinese-speaking ELLs and the English-speaking monolinguals on the compound awareness test, but the Spanish-speaking ELLs performed significantly lower than the English-speaking monolinguals. These results confirm our hypothesis that ELLs' compound awareness in English is also influenced by their L1 background. Chinese-speaking ELLs are exposed to similar compounding rules in Chinese and English. Spanish-speaking ELLs, by contrast, have less experience with compounds in their L1, and have to overcome left-headedness when learning English compounds.

The importance of lexical awareness and priming, and the fact that learners have uneven and meager knowledge of words and word meanings, make vocabulary acquisition a high priority in the Language Awareness Approach.

Vocabulary Acquisition

According to Hinkel (2002) English L2 writers often overuse vague nouns like *human, girl, man, society, stuff,* and *world* instead of common academic vocabulary. Academic vocabulary falls into sets based on elements of their meaning or their purpose in discourse, as shown in the box. Hinkel (2002, p. 95) concludes that the vocabulary that learners have and can use in productive oral communication may not be sufficient for writing:

Thus it seems clear that L2 instruction needs to focus on expanding the vocabulary range of NNS students, as well as identifying lexical features of formal academic texts that are distinct from those employed in spoken registers . . . familiarity with L2 conversational lexicon does not necessarily lead to the expansion of vocabulary employed in academic texts.

To reinforce uptake and retrieval of words, active vocabulary learners practice vocabulary through rote memorization techniques such as flashcards, practice sentences, recording words in a vocabulary notebook, as well as extensive reading and writing. As a learner's lexicon grows, the linkages and primings among words, concepts, meanings, and grammatical patterns grow denser and stronger. Learners begin to restructure their knowledge, form hypotheses, and experiment with constructions. Finally, modified output means that learners move beyond tried and true communicative strategies, to communicate using new words and structures.

Sets of Nouns Based on Purposes

Enumeratives: *advantage, aspect, attempt, branch, reason, stage, term*

Advance/retrospective stance: *accident, approach, background, contingency, difficulty*

Language activity: *account, consensus, contrast, controversy, formula, summary*

Interpretives: *belief, cause, idea, mistake, opinion, point*

Resultatives: *effect, outcome, result*

In the Language Awareness Approach, the context for vocabulary acquisition is negotiated meaning and message-oriented interaction with a focus on form and feedback for learners. Classroom activities are creative and innovative to encourage lexical awareness and more general metalinguistic awareness. Teachers try to connect words to previously learned material but also to new concepts and meanings in order for learners to internalize words as well as elaborated (not specific) meanings. This means that learners can use words in many contexts, not just a single one. There are inductive and deductive word study activities with practice and feedback. Naturally, collocation is also important and will be discussed in Chapter 15, but, crucially, although words can be learned in isolation, word study also takes place within the context of frequent colligations.

Data-driven applications of word study can be enlightening. For instance, a search of the database of the quotes in this book using just a hyphen (-) revealed several types of compound adjectives found in academic prose. Some of these compounds are ordinary, like *old-fashioned* or *well-known*, formed by combining an adjective or adverb and a participial adjective. Others are academic compounds formed from a noun and an adjective, like *self-sufficient* or *situation-specific*. This last example is part of a more general pattern-based construction $[[X]_N\text{-}specific]_{ADJ}$ that permits coinage of new expressions like *register-specific*, *culture-specific*, and *language-specific*. There is another type of compound commonly found in academic writing. These compounds are formed from Latin and Greek bound roots: *psycholinguistic, morphosyntactic, Judaeo-Christian, neurosynchronic, ontogenetic*.

Another type of adjective is formed with a head adjective derived from a past participle and combined with a noun that is in some sense an object of a preposition:

usage-based approaches	approaches based on usage
meaning-focused communication	communication focused on meaning
the *frequency-biased abstraction*	abstractions biased by frequency
a *self-initiated searching mode*	searching mode initiated by the self

In the Language Awareness Approach, learners also begin to understand that English words are flexible, not just in meaning but also in their syntactic category membership. For instance, Lewis (2002, p. 42) says:

It may seem that this abstract question of categorization is a long way from the classroom, but it does have important pedagogical implications. Words in English are exceptionally mobile, able to move from word category to word category very freely; in particular nouns can readily be used in adjectival or verbal (to do with the verb) functions . . . Pedagogically, if students learn words as belonging to a particular category, they may well not see, and be unwilling to experiment with, the kind of flexible categorization which maximizes communicative power.

Study, Discussion, and Essay Questions

Write the answers to these questions in your Language Notebook. Create your notebook as a word processing document because you will be using the "find" command to analyze your writing.

1. Add these terms to your glossary and define them: free morpheme, inserts, multi-word lexical units, resource words, system words, focal situation, reference, predication, modification, compound words, gerund, lexical awareness.

2. What are some of the problems with defining the word "word"? Referencing both Jackson and Amvela and Hultstijn, write your own definition of "word" in your glossary.

3. What are the four parts of speech that are resource elements? What is the communicative function of each?

4. Why isn't the distinction between system and resource elements clear? What are some unclear cases?

5. a. What are some words that exemplify these word formation processes: derivation, inflection, back formation, clipping, compounding, functional shift, generalization, and blending?

    b. Invent your own compound word based on the model $[[X]_N$ -specific$]_{ADJ}$ for *culture-specific* or *language-specific*. What does your word mean? Use your word in a sentence.

6. Use the diagnostic methods from the discovery procedure to answer these questions about the sentence *Professional athletes dutifully show up for team practice.* Remember, do not guess! Make a note of any questions you have as you go through the process because these are important.

    What part of speech is the word *professional*? What is the evidence?
    What part of speech is the word *team*? What is the evidence?
    What part of speech is the word *show up*? What is the evidence?

7. What other words will fit logically and syntactically into the empty slot to make a similar sentence with a different meaning? Are all of your words the same part of speech? What part(s) of speech are they?

    Teachers may know that an error   *Teachers ____ know that an error has*
    has occurred.   *occurred.*

    The sentence with the blank is called a **substitution frame** and it is another type of diagnostic to identify parts of speech.

8. How do you like to learn new words?

9. Using one of your paragraphs in your Language Notebook, apply a message-oriented approach to your answer:

a. Delete all of the system words, leaving only resource words. How does this affect understanding?

b. Choose four words and discuss their morphology, using terms like free morpheme, derivational morpheme, prefix, suffix, etc.

c. Make three columns in your Language Notebook, then find as many examples of each as you can.

NOUNS	VERBS	ADJECTIVES

Activities

1. Make up a set of flashcards with the system parts of speech (conjunctions, subordinators, determiners, pronouns, prepositions, auxiliaries, particles, and intensifiers). On the one side put an example from the chapter or your own example, and on the other identify its part of speech. Add to your stock of flashcards throughout this book.

Conjunctions (side 1)	grammar _and_ discourse the knowledge _or_ strategies (side 2)

Prepositions (side 1)	_for_ this view _about_ grammatical forms (side 2)

2. Capitalization is relevant to nouns and adjectives, and is the source of problems in writing. Some rules are fairly rigid; others are more variable. Capitalize the first word of a sentence, proper names, subject matters, days

and months, nationalities, cultures, religions, and languages. The initials used in abbreviations are capitalized. Proper adjectives show some variability if they are used to refer to a type or category: roman numerals, arabic numbers or Roman numerals, Arabic numbers? Why are the following examples in capital letters?

> *To begin with, there is little question that English is . . . the carrier of Anglo-American cultural imperialism, neo-colonialism, commercialism.*

> *English ceases to be an exponent of only one culture—the Western Judaeo-Christian culture.*

> *Our learners will produce discourse reminiscent of Kroll's (1990) college-level ESL composition students.*

Some of the following sentences (but not all) have errors in capitalization norms. If there is an error, with your partner, take turns explaining the error and the correction, imagining that your partner made the errors in a composition.

a. Edward decided that he wanted to become an English Teacher because he loved shakespeare.
b. The most commonly spoken languages in the world are chinese and english.
c. I bought a book about mexican food for aunt Giselle.
d. When was the roman calendar invented?
e. We learned that thursday is named after thor and wednesday is named after woden; thor and woden are both ancient northern european gods.
f. The general development fund lost some money last year.
g. I think he's a physical education major.
h. Compounding is a common english word formation process.

3. Grammar logs. When teachers individualize their curriculum, it is more relevant to the learner. The best way to individualize learning and increase individual autonomy is to put the learner in charge of his or her own learning. Grammar logs are intended to improve the English users' ability to proofread and self-edit. Teachers collect grammar logs and make comments on them. They are interactive journals with minimal grading.

Begin keeping a grammar log in your Language Notebook. Make a note of any usages that are signaled by grammar or spelling checkers, marked by your instructors, or that you are not sure of. Make three columns. Label the first column MY USAGE, the second column STANDARD (global or local), and the third EXPLANATION. Go through the paragraphs you wrote in previous chapters or other written work you have done. Make additions to your grammar log throughout the semester.

MY USAGE	STANDARD	EXPLANATION
This problem effects me.	*This problem affects me.*	The verb is *affect*; the noun is *effect*.
I speak english.	*I speak English.*	Capitalize the names of languages.
I use to study at night.	*I used to study at night.*	*Used to* is a past construction.
We are suppose to drive.	*We are supposed to drive.*	Past participle.

Major Phrases 7

PHRASE . . . In general usage, any small group of words within a sentence . . . such as "in general usage", "small groups", and "a clause". Such a group is usually recognized as having a syntactic structure: groups like *usage any* and *or a* would not normally qualify as phrases . . . There are five types of phrases, named after their main word: noun phrase (*a very bright light*); verb phrase (*may be eating*); adjective phrase (*extraordinarily happy*); adverb phrase or adverbial phrase (*quite casually*); prepositional phrase (*in our city*).

(McArthur, 1992, p. 776)

Phrases are an important syntactic level in the linguistic system, but one that is not as stable or salient as individual words are. Phrases are smaller than sentences but they are the pieces of which sentences are composed analytically or holistically. They form a layer of grammatical structure higher than the word level and are a locus of priming, colligation, and collocation, so they cannot be random sequences of words. Four types of phrases (NP, VP, ADJP, ADVP) correspond to resource word classes, and one type of phrase (PP) corresponds to a system word class. This chapter is an overview of these phrases and their principal colligational requirements, as shown in Figure 7.1.

NP	noun phrase
VP	verb phrase
ADJP	adjective phrase
ADVP	adverb phrase
PP	prepositional phrase

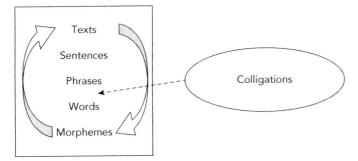

Figure 7.1 Colligations Are the Structural and Functional Requirements Inherited from the Main Word in the Phrase

Colligational requirements are the most probable constructions and functions associated with a head word of a certain word class.

Colligations encode the grammatical preferences associated with a part of speech derived from usage and exposure. Colligations are abstract grammatical structures closely related to the open choice principle. Colligational processes allow language users to compose innovative phrases and sentences that sound natural by making lexical choices at crucial moments based on weak priming. For example, once a speaker chooses the word *put*, the required verbal construction for the accompanying words becomes available to express the ideas "something" and "somewhere." Colligations are different from collocations, which are the result of strong priming associations among specific words.

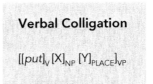

Verbal Colligation

$$[[put]_V [X]_{NP} [Y]_{PLACE}]_{VP}$$

Nouns and Noun Phrases

Prototypically, nouns refer to people and things. A noun can refer to a physical thing like a *chair* or a *mountain*, or an abstract emotional entity like *happiness* or *grief*. It can refer to a concrete countable thing like a *finger* or a *bottle*, or a non-countable mass like *sand* or *air*. It can even refer to a situation or event like a *meeting* or a *financial collapse*, or to a very complex set of facts like *language-specific properties*. There are some other words used as nouns as well. For instance, adjectives are usually descriptive words, yet they occur as nouns in constructions that have a definite article (*the*): *She helps out the sick and the injured.* The descriptive properties *sick* and *injured* refer to the category of people who have those properties. That explains the fact that these nouns can't be plural (*the sicks, *the injureds*). Verbs can also be used as nouns, through the word formation process of functional shift: *They transitioned slowly to a new corporate organization* or *The teacher and the student conferenced together about the essay.*

Types of Nouns

English has two prototypical types of nouns, common nouns and proper names, because humans perceive at least two types of entities, classes of things (common nouns) and very specific individuals (proper names). Proper names allow people to identify and talk about particular things, especially other people and pets, exclusively: Aunt Geraldine, Dr. Geraldine Page, Buster, Page Veterinary Hospital, Golden Retriever.

In English, proper names are capitalized to make them stand out in a text. Some proper names are composed of common nouns with the definite article *the*, as in *the Hospital Advisory Committee, the Veterinary Complaints Board*, or *the National Animal Lovers Foundation*. These names are called **definite descriptions**, and the fact that these are capitalized symbolizes that they are the proper names of specific entities and not common nouns, as in *the committee, the board*, or *the foundation*.

Common nouns, which are usually not capitalized, are *hair, veterinarian, woman, dog, fur, tail*. Common nouns refer to categories, classes, types, and materials or "stuff." For example, the common noun *woman* refers to a class of people, *veterinarian* refers to one type of profession, *hair* and *fur* refer to materials.

There are various kinds of common nouns. **Abstract nouns** refer to entities that have a conceptual reality, that is, a reality in our minds: *concern, grief,*

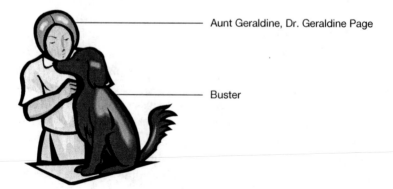

Aunt Geraldine, Dr. Geraldine Page

Buster

Figure 7.2   Proper Names Refer to Specific Individuals

hair

veterinarian

woman

dog

fur

tail

Figure 7.3 Common Nouns Refer to Classes or Categories of Individuals

intelligence. **Concrete nouns** refer to entities that have a physical reality: *woman, dog, balloon, finger, air*. **Count nouns** refer to concrete things that can be counted: *dog, tail, finger, toe, words*. **Mass nouns** refer to concrete entities that are non-countable, that is, "*stuff*": *hair, fur, air, wine*. However, these terms are very flexible. An abstract noun can be used very concretely, as in this example:

Abstract: <u>*Love*</u> *is a wonderful emotion.*
Concrete: *The great <u>love</u> of her life is wagging her tail.*

Similarly, count nouns can appear as mass nouns and vice versa.

Count: *She gave the dog <u>a tofuburger</u>.*
Mass: *There was <u>tofuburger</u> in the dog food.*

As usual, morphology, syntax, function, and meaning are used to determine if a word is a noun or not, and what type of noun it is. For instance, nouns often have specific derivational prefixes and suffixes, such as <u>*bi*</u>*cycle*, <u>*mega*</u>*phone*, *program*, <u>*pre*</u>*fix*, *presenta<u>tion</u>, judg<u>ment</u>, pres<u>sure</u>, sani<u>ty</u>, bus<u>iness</u>, intelli<u>gence</u>, brother<u>hood</u>, scholar<u>ship</u>, social<u>ism</u>*. **Gerunds** are nouns derived from verbs by adding -*ing*, as in *ski/skiing, work/working*. Gerunds are very common in academic prose. Countable nouns take the plural inflection, -*s*, as in *fingers, chairs, apples*. Proper names, abstract nouns, and mass nouns occasionally take the plural inflection (*the Browns, the wines of France, intelligences*) too.

NP Colligation

In the most typical NP colligation, syntactic category names like Determiner or Adjective are variables which stand for the words of the class. The plus sign marks the fact that there can be more than one

$$[(\text{Determiner}) \ ([^+\text{Adjective}]_{\text{ADJP}}) \ \text{Noun}]_{\text{NP}}$$

an ideal speaker-listener
the ability
multilingual identity
the learner's ability
idolized, spoiled, and highly paid celebrities

adjective in a sequence within an adjective phrase, possibly with a conjunction *and* or *or*. This colligation is an abstract construction with a grammatical meaning: that the main word, the most essential word, is the noun, and that there are optional elements that limit or describe the noun: determiners and adjective phrases. The open choice principle means that different words, if their word classes and meanings are appropriate, can fill the variables in the colligation provided that they obey the colligational constraints.

Adjectives and Adjective Phrases

In the past, there was no sharp distinction between adjectives and adverbs in English, and the demarcation between them remains fuzzy to this day. That may be why adjective/adverb usage can be a source of insecurity for many English users. This section will discuss adjectives; adverbs will be discussed in the next section. Prototypical **descriptive adjectives** attribute qualities of color, size, shape, personal characteristics, value (and others) to nouns.

Adjectives are frequent but mostly optional resource words. Because they occur in complex noun phrases, they are more frequent in academic prose and news than in conversation. Descriptive adjectives often have opposing forms like *large/small*, *big/little*, *low/high*, *tall/short*, *general/particular*, *primary/secondary*, *long/short*, *first/last*, *final/initial*, *same/different*, *necessary/possible*, *young/old*, *previous/following*, *simple/complex*, and *positive/negative*.

In the example of Academic English prose below, the adjectives are underlined. All of the adjectives are **attributive adjectives**, that is, they occur before their nouns and attribute some quality to their following noun/entity. One instance (*special*) is a descriptive adjective, but the others (*economic*, *collective*) are **classifying adjectives**, which will be discussed in a later chapter.

Note that the word *network* is a **descriptive noun**, not an adjective. In Academic English, descriptive and classifying adjectives and descriptive nouns are quite common.

> *Languages represent a very <u>special</u> class of <u>economic</u> goods: they are not only <u>collective</u> goods but also display network effects.*

Common attributive adjectives in academic prose are: *simple, basic, common, following, higher, individual, lower, particular, similar, specific, total, various, local, natural, normal, physical,* and *public.*

Prototypical Adjectives

Prototypical adjectives have morphological characteristics that identify them. These derivational suffixes are frequent: *-al (final, social), -able (provable), -ent (different), -ive*

> **Prototypical Adjectives**
>
> Color: *black, white, bright, dark . . .*
> Size: *tall, short, wide, narrow . . .*
> Shape: *round, square, rectangular . . .*
> Personality: *intelligent, wise, kind, happy . . .*
> Value: *good, bad, useless, useful . . .*
> Others: *appropriate, complex, empty, practical . . .*

(active), -ous (serious), -ate (appropriate), -ful (beautiful), and *-less (endless).* In inflectional morphology, adjectives form their comparative with *-er* or *more,* and their superlative with *-est* or *most.*

These are the only inflected comparatives in the database: <u>greater or less</u> detail, <u>wider</u> variety, a <u>greater</u> focus; there are several examples of inflected superlatives but they seem to cluster around concepts of importance or quality: *the largest, the best, the smallest, the biggest, the hardest, the greatest, the highest, the subtlest.* In the database, there are far more comparatives and superlatives with *more* and *most: more self-sufficient, more effective, more varied, the most time-consuming and exhausting, the most general.* This uneven distribution of comparative / superlative morphology probably has to do with the types of adjectives most commonly found in academic prose, that is, multi-syllabic derived adjectives from Latinate roots or adjectives derived from participial verbs.

Predicate Adjectives

Some adjectives exhibit strong preferences to be either attributive or predicative but not both. Adjectives that tend to be attributive are *mere* and adjectives ending in *-al* like *general, industrial, local, national, social*. Adjectives that tend to be predicative are *glad, ill, impossible, ready, sure, anxious*, as well as *unable, aloof, able, aware, asleep, afraid, aghast* (Biber et al., 1999, pp. 511–516). Predicative adjectives common in academic prose are:

aware	*low*	*impossible*	*better*
common	*present*	*unable*	*hard*
dependent	*similar*	*important*	*right*
equal	*useful*	*necessary*	*sure*
equivalent	*able*	*clear*	*wrong*
essential	*true*	*small*	*possible*
greater	*different*	*available*	*ready*
large		*unlikely*	*likely*

ADJP Colligation

[(Intensifier) Adjective (Adverb)]$_{ADJP}$

In the prototypical colligation for adjectives there is an obligatory adjective (in bold, below), an optional intensifier before the adjective, and an optional and rare adverb (*indeed, enough*) after it.

Attributive adjectives occur before nouns as part of a NP colligation.

Languages represent a [very **special**] class of economic goods:

[**Explicit**] learning is the construction of [**explicit, verbalizable, meta-linguistic**] knowledge in the form of symbols (concepts) and rules, specifying relationships between concepts.

The [**present multicultural**] character of English is clearly revealed in its uses around the globe, especially in [**creative**] writing.

Predicate adjectives occur after linking verbs as subject complements.

As a complex system, the systematicities of language are [**emergent and adaptive**].

*[P]roblems that need explaining are often [very **complex**].*

*[Q]uestions regarding grammar can be [very **difficult**].*

Adverbs and Adverb Phrases

The most prototypical adverb is the adverb of manner, which is derived from an adjective by adding the suffix -*ly*, as in these examples: *obviously, rapidly, chemically, politically*. However, some common adverbs reflect a more ancient form of English, when there was no morphological difference between adjective and adverb usage: *fast, well, slow*.

ADVP Colligation

[(Intensifier) Adverb (Adverb)]$_{ADVP}$

Adverb phrase colligational constraints allow for a head adverb modified by an intensifier and with a possible but rare adverb behind it. In these examples from the database, the adverb phrase modifies a verb phrase.

> *We, the speakers of English, [should [**proudly**] flaunt] the banners of cultural imperialism . . .*

> *The present multicultural character of English [is [**clearly**] revealed] . . .*

> *Cognition . . . and history [are all [**inextricably**] intertwined] in rich, complex, and dynamic ways in language.*

In these examples, the adverb phrase modifies a following prepositional phrase:

> *we are [**scientifically and technologically**] in the lead . . .*

> *The present multicultural character of English is clearly revealed in its uses around the globe, [**especially** in creative writing].*

Verbals and Verb Phrases

A **verbal** identifies a relationship of some kind among the entities, the nouns, in a focal situation. The term "relationship" includes states of being, physical, mental, and emotional activities, and experiences. Most verbals are resource words, but two types, primary auxiliaries and modal auxiliaries, are system words. If verbal constructions indicate past or present tense, they are called **finite**. If they don't indicate tense, they are called **non-finite**. Finite and non-finite verbals interact in a complex verbal system that combines tense, aspect, voice, negation, and modality to express nuances of meaning:

> *Monolithic descriptions of English grammar **will be replaced** by register-specific descriptions.*

> *The input **has to be mapped** onto innate linguistic categories, but the categories or principles of core syntax **do not have to be learned** because they **are** there right from the beginning.*

> *If we **believe** that learning an L2 **is** a process of socialization where we **are learning to construct** new sociocultural identities and **to reshape** our subjectivity, then we **need** a theory of language that **enables us to understand** how grammar **is implicated** in such processes.*

Finite verbals are
main verbs: *go, goes, went; think, thinks, thought; need, needed*
primary auxiliaries: *be, have, do*
modal auxiliaries: *may, might, shall, should, will, would, can, etc.*

Non-finite verbals are
bare infinitives: *go, think, need*
infinitives: *to go, to think, to need*
present participles: *going, thinking, needing*
past participles: *gone, thought, needed*

Finite Main Verbs

Main verbs and primary auxiliaries have present and past tense forms, but modal auxiliaries do not have different forms. The terms **past** or **present** refer to verb forms, that is, what the verb looks like, and not the time it refers to, because verb forms in English are only indirectly related to time concepts. People talk about past, future, and present times, but there are only two tenses marked on the verbs by inflections: present and past. These two simple tenses account for the majority of all verb usages. Verbs have typical derivational endings like -ize (*cauterize*) or -ate (*mediate*), but, for main verbs, inflections are more informative. Regular English verbal inflectional morphology is important but meager when compared to some other languages.

> **Third person present tense -s**
> *he plays, she collects, he talks*
>
> **Present tense (other subjects)**
> *I play, you collect, we talk*
>
> **Past tense (all subjects) -ed**
> *I played, he collected, they talked*

Despite their simplicity, some English learners have trouble with English inflected verb forms because of interference from their first language. Some languages, like Chinese and Hmong, don't have verbal inflections at all, so learners from these languages have little awareness of inflections. Other languages have inflections (and often more than English) but learners still have difficulty choosing the correct inflection or using the third person singular form. The lack of salience of this morpheme makes it unstable in spoken forms of World Englishes. The main verbs *be*, *do*, and *have* (which are also primary auxiliaries) are common and have irregular verbal forms in the present and past.

Used to is a past tense verb that corresponds to the choice of *usually* in present tense. Learners sometimes leave off the past tense ending because they hear the sound of the "t" right after it:

	Present	Past
BE	am, is, are	was, were
DO	do, does	did
HAVE	have, has	had

He usually drinks tea now but he used to drink three cups of coffee a day.

He didn't use to jog around the block every day, but now he does.

Non-finite Verbals

Non-finite verb forms occur within verb phrases; they are the bare infinitive (*take*), the infinitive (*to take*), the present participle (*taking*), and the past participle (*taken*). Their contribution to the verb phrase, when paired with a primary auxiliary or a modal auxiliary, has to do with aspects or voice, and not time. They occur with main verbs also.

Non-finite Verbals

With auxiliaries: *can sit, is speaking, have written*

With main verbs: *let go, plan to do, remember seeing, got burned*

Verbal Colligations

Transitive verb phrases, intransitive verb phrases, and linking verb phrases are the three prototypical VP colligations.

Transitive verb phrases relate two entities (two NPs) directly in a situation. The first entity is the subject, the agent or experiencer of the action is not part of the verb phrase, but the second entity is the direct object, the receiver of the action. The variable (Z) stands for indirect objects, adverbs, and prepositional phrases that may appear in the sentence optionally.

$[V\ NP\ (Z)]_{TRANSITIVE\ VP}$

> We $[[need]_V$ $[a\ theory\ of\ language]_{NP}]_{VP}$

> He $[[proposed]_V$ $[a\ life\text{-}span\ practice\ model]_{NP}]_{VP}$

> Correct English language use $[[requires]_V\ [the\ possession\ of\ a\ competence]_{NP}]_{VP}$

Intransitive verb phrases have no direct object. If there are other nouns in the sentence besides the subject, they are usually in prepositional phrases.

$[V\ (Z)]_{INTRANSITIVE\ VP}$

> Professional athletes dutifully $[[show\ up]_V$ $[for\ team\ practice]_{PP}]_{VP}$

> Performers of classical music often $[[practice]_V$ $[for\ many\ hours\ a\ day]_{PP}]_{VP}$

Emphasis	*[[will shift]*$_V$	*[from structural accuracy . . .]*$_{PP}$*]*$_{VP}$

Linking verbs phrases with *be, seem, become,* or *turn into* are intransitive because they link the subject to a **subject complement**, either a noun phrase or an adjective phrase. NP subject complements

1. [V NP (Z)]$_{\text{LINKING VP}}$
2. [V ADJP (Z)]$_{\text{LINKING VP}}$

don't introduce a new entity into the situation and they don't refer to anyone. They merely describe the subject, and that is what makes linking verbs intransitive. There are two typical colligations, one (1) with a noun phrase in the predicate and one (2) with a predicate adjective.

Frequency	*is*	*[a key determinant of acquisition]*$_{NP}$
Rules of language	*are*	*[structural regularities]*$_{NP}$
The sentence	*is*	*[notoriously difficult to define]*$_{ADJP}$
The variation	*seems*	*[endless]*$_{ADJP}$

The linking verb colligation is common with impersonal expressions with the pronoun *it* in the subject position.

Though it [is arguable]$_{\text{VPLINKING VP}}$ *whether grammar feedback and instruction [will be consistently effective]*$_{\text{LINKING VP}}$ *for all L2 student writers, it [seems clear]*$_{\text{LINKING VP}}$ *that the absence of any feedback or strategy training [will ensure]*$_{VP}$ *that many students never take seriously the need to improve their editing skills.*

Prepositions and Prepositional Phrases

Prepositions are system words that take no inflections and have no consistent derivational or compounding patterns, but some of them are multi-word lexical units. Prototypical single word prepositions have to do with connecting entities and relationships or situating them in space and time. Multi-word prepositions, common in Academic English, have abstract meanings and express complex relationships. The NP can be of any type, including a gerund, a noun formed from a verb by adding *-ing*.

Biber et al. (1999, pp. 74–75) found that the most common single word prepositions are:

about	*for*	*round*
after	*from*	*since*
around	*in*	*than*
as	*into*	*through*
at	*like*	*to*
between	*of*	*toward*
by	*off*	*with*
down	*on*	*without*

The most common two word prepositions are compounds made up of a first word followed by *as, for, from, of, on, to,* or *with.*

such as	*away from*	*out of*	*due to*
but for	*ahead of*	*depending on*	*next to*
except for	*because of*	*according to*	*thanks to*
apart from	*instead of*	*close to*	*along with*
together with			

Three/four word prepositions usually have the form [P + (DET) + N + P]:

as far as	*in spite of*	*in relation to*
as well as	*in view of*	*with regard to*
in exchange for	*on account of*	*with reference to*
in return for	*on top of*	*with respect to*
by means of	*as a result of*	*in comparison with*
by way of	*for the sake of*	*in contact with*
for lack of	*in the case of*	*in line with*
in front of	*in the event of*	
in lieu of	*in addition to*	
in need of	*in contrast to*	
in place of		

The primary colligation for prepositional phrases has a preposition, where the preposition can be a one word, two word, or multi-word preposition, and a noun phrase. Here it is possible to see that colligations can be quite commonly

[P NP]_{PP}

nested within other colligations. In this case, because NP constructions can contain PPs and PP constructions contain NPs, PPs can be multiply nested inside of other PPs.

It is less an analytical question [than a question [about history]$_{PP}$]$_{PP}$

As [in other countries]$_{PP}$, increasing integration [with the rest [of Europe]$_{PP}$]$_{PP}$ has led [to general trends [in society [like globalization and individualization]$_{PP}$]$_{PP}$]$_{PP}$

A phrasal diagram can show how the multiple embedding in constructions occurs.

Conjoined Constructions

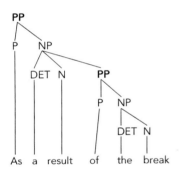

Figure 7.4
A Phrasal Diagram Illustrating Multiple Embedding or Nesting of Prepositional Phrases

The conjunctions *and*, *or*, and *but* conjoin lexical categories, phrasal categories, and sentences, which are called the **conjuncts**. Two different constructions [X] and [Y] can be conjoined if they have the same syntactic category represented by the subscript variable Z and the conjoined construction has the same Z syntactic category.[1]

Conjunction

$[[X]_Z$ conjunction $[Y]_Z]_Z$

1. Of course, very occasionally the two conjuncts are not the same syntactic category but they share some other characteristic, such as in these two examples. The first one is hypothetical, but natural. The second is a road sign in California about using seat belts while driving or riding in a car:
The temperature is [40 °C]$_{NP}$ or [over body temperature]$_{PP}$ (Shared semantic function.)
Click it or ticket (Shared phonology.)

And

In this sentence, the two conjoined NPs are each part of one larger NP construction that is the object of the preposition *of*, even though the preposition is only mentioned once.

> *Explicit learning is a conscious, deliberative process of* [[*concept formation*]$_{NP}$ *and* [*concept linking*]$_{NP}$]$_{NP}$

These examples show verbals and adjective phrases as conjuncts with *and*:

> *The sentence is notoriously difficult to define; numerous definitions have been* [<u>*offered*</u> *and* <u>*found wanting*</u>]$_{PAST\ PARTICIPLE\ CONJOINED}$

> *. . . they write* [<u>*logically organized*</u> *and* <u>*coherent*</u>]$_{ADJP\ CONJOINED}$ *texts but with such a high number of morphosyntactic errors that native speakers find it difficult, if not impossible,* [*to* <u>*read*</u> *and* <u>*understand*</u>]$_{TO-INFINITIVE\ CONJOINED}$ *their texts.* (Note only one *to* marker for the conjoined infinitives.)

> [<u>*Psycholinguistic*</u> *and* <u>*cognitive linguistic*</u>]$_{ADJP\ CONJOINED}$ *theories of language acquisition hold that all linguistic units are abstracted from language use.*

As well as[2] is a conjunction in academic writing, with this structure: [X]$_Z$ as well as [Y]$_Z$, where Z is a variable for any kind of word or phrase as long as they match each other. Here are some examples from the database:

> *Classroom L2 writing teachers provide their learners with both* [*oral feedback*]$_{NP}$ *as well as* [*written feedback*]$_{NP}$

> *A new model of multilingual identity is developing which is oriented* [*towards contemporary transcultural interaction*]$_{PP}$ *as well as* [*towards regional self-identification*]$_{PP}$

> *Correct English language use in speech and in writing requires the possession of a competence which includes* [*the knowledge of grammar rules and vocabulary items*]$_{NP}$, *as well as* [*the ability to use them in real-life contexts*]$_{NP}$

---

2.   *As well* is also used as a synonym of "also": *These mechanisms should suffice to learn the more general and predictable patterns of that language as well.*

But

The conjunction *but* is adversative; it conjoins two or more words, phrases, or sentences that contrast in meaning. The first example below shows an unusual use of *but* at the beginning of a sentence as a discourse organizer to relate it in contrast to the sentence before it. The second example conjoins two verb phrases and emphasizes the contrast with the adverb *rather*. The third example contrasts two *by*-phrases with the addition of the emphasizer adverb *instead*.

> *When you study grammar, you learn to analyze language by breaking sentences into separate pieces in order to focus on individual parts, to recognize what the parts are, and to understand how these parts function together to convey meaning.* **But** *the study of grammar . . . <u>does not end with learning about structures and functions within the sentence</u>* **but rather** *<u>uses the sentence as a starting point for exploring how grammar can be used in discourse to achieve more effective communication</u>. That is, when we speak or write, we do not communicate <u>by putting together lists of isolated sentences</u>* **but instead** *<u>by using sentences that are interrelated and woven together to form a coherent discourse</u>.*

Or

The conjunction *or* is meant to give two alternatives as the conjuncts, but sometimes they are in a cause / result relationship. The alternatives can be either inclusive or exclusive. **Inclusive** *or* means that both of the conjuncts are possible. **Exclusive** *or* means that only one of the conjuncts is possible. The expression *either . . . or . . .* is exclusive. This example is inclusive, in that *form* and *construction* are paraphrases of each other:

> *. . . the learner's ability to produce the <u>form</u>* **or** *<u>construction</u> with linguistic accuracy is only part of the overall production task.*

This example is exclusive, in that *random* and *characteristic* are opposites of each other:

> *Linguistic theory is concerned primarily with an ideal speaker-listener, in a completely homogeneous speech-community, who knows its language perfectly and is unaffected by such grammatically irrelevant conditions as memory limitations, distractions, shifts of attention and interest, and errors (<u>random</u>* **or** *<u>characteristic</u>) in applying his knowledge of the language in actual performance . . .*

This example uses both inclusive and exclusive *or*.

> *[Explicit learning] may **either** take place <u>when learners are being taught concepts and rules by an [instructor]</u> **or** <u>[textbook]</u>, **or** <u>when they operate in a self-initiated searching mode</u>, trying to develop concepts and rules themselves . . .*

Inclusive *or* is commonly used to offer an alternative or paraphrase as a definition, as in the first example above and in this example where the term *modal verbs* is offered as an alternative to *modal auxiliaries*.

> *Auxiliaries may be further divided into primary auxiliaries (be, have, do) and [modal auxiliaries] **or** [modal verbs] (may, can, will shall, must, ought to, need, dare).*

When expressions are conjoined with exclusive *or* and serve as the subject of sentences, the verb should be singular, as in this hypothetical example modeled on forms in the database.

> *A speaker's random mistake **or** habitual error <u>is</u> considered local if it doesn't impede comprehension.*

Correlative conjunctions operate at the word, phrasal, or sentence level. These examples from the corpus show conjoined verb phrases and conjoined noun phrases respectively:

> *Languages represent a very special class of economic goods: they are [<u>not only</u> collective goods <u>but also</u> display network effects].*

> *The noun phrase "that man" is thereby used as a referring expression whose referent is a specific man whose identity the addressee must [<u>either</u> know <u>or</u> be able to determine].*

Discovery Procedures

The **substitution frame** is a strategy that makes use of hypothetical examples to get more information about the syntactic categories in a construction, in addition to clues from meaning, morphology/word formation, co-text, and function. The substitution frame is a phrase or a sentence with an underlined slot or "fill in the blank" portion. Then, candidate words are introduced into

Substitution Frame

Category 1	Category 2	Category 3
	linguistic	*form*
___		
a		
the		
this		
its		
*clock		
*when		
*puppy		

the slot in the substitution frame to see if they will yield a natural or likely phrase (e.g. *its linguistic form, this linguistic form*) or not. Words that do not yield a good phrase are marked with an asterisk (e.g. **clock linguistic form*).

Grammarians then ask questions about the data in the substitution frame. What are the words in the first column? Recognizing that *a* and *the* are determiners, grammarians hypothesize that all of these words are determiners because their behavior in the colligation is the same. In a way, substitution frames are a form of data-driven analysis, but in this case the data are created by the grammarian.

Substitution frames must be used with care, but they are a useful strategy to gather more information about a grammatical structure and the parts of speech within it.

Substitution frames can also give information about semantic categories, such as those mental verbs that take a subordinate sentence like *that a mistake*

Substitution Frame

The teacher must	realize	that a mistake has been made.
	understand	
	know	
	comprehend	
	think	
	hypothesize	

has been made. These verbs have in common that they relate a person to an idea by describing a cognitive relationship.

However, one disadvantage of the substitution frame is that it requires fluency and expertise to know how to create plausible frames and how to evaluate the results. To avoid these problems, naturalistic substitution frames can be used. For instance, a search of the database created for this book revealed these examples of noun phrases with the noun *system.* The examples illustrate a range of different determiners, adjectives, and even conjoined adjectives that can be paired with the word *system(s).*

Naturalistic Substitution Frame with "System"

this		system
a	dynamic	system
a	complex	system
a	global	system
their	existing	system
the learner's	implicit or unconscious	system
these two	knowledge	systems
the	perceptual and motor	systems

In this example, a search on the word *seem* reveals its two major uses, either as a linking verb with adjective phrases, as in the first set of examples, or with a *to*-infinitive followed by a variety of different complements.

Substitution frames and data-driven learning like searching a database or a concordance for naturalistic colligations improve phrasal awareness, a subtype of metalinguistic awareness.

Two Naturalistic Substitution Frames with "Seem"

1.	the variation	seems	endless
	it	seems	clear
2.			
[ ]NP	seems to be	one such "third way"	
[ ]NP	seem to be	largely missing	
[ ]NP	seemed to fly	in the face	
[ ]NP	seem to know	what a word is	

Phrasal Awareness

There are two non-technical activities, chunking and sentence unscrambling, that improve implicit phrasal awareness and knowledge of Academic English usage without any metalanguage. Both activities help learners notice how sentence-level constructions are made up of five types of phrasal constructions. These activities are very controlled; very little creativity is allowed.

Chunking

Chunking involves dividing the text into meaningful phrasal units of around five to seven words, or fewer if the text is complex. The units are usually the five phrases, NP, VP, ADJP, ADVP, or PP. Reading in chunks facilitates comprehension of complex texts. In the example below, Hinkel and Fotos (2002, p. 6) point out that there has been quite a bit of research on the view that communicative interaction is one causative factor in the acquisition of grammar and direct instruction is another. They suggest that the two different types of grammatical knowledge (declarative or procedural) are actually connected through awareness or consciousness. The phrases can be chunked maintaining the paragraph structure or as a list or outline:

The psycholinguistic foundations / for this view / involve the distinction / between two types of grammatical knowledge: / explicit and/or declarative knowledge, / which is conscious knowledge / about grammatical rules and forms / developed through instruction; / and . . . procedural knowledge, / which is the ability to speak a language / unconsciously developed / through acts of meaning-focused communication. /

The psycholinguistic foundations
for this view
involve the distinction
between two types of grammatical knowledge:
explicit and/or declarative knowledge,
    which is conscious knowledge
    about grammatical rules and forms
    developed through instruction;
and . . . procedural knowledge,
    which is the ability to speak a language

unconsciously developed
through acts of meaning-focused communication.

Sentence Unscrambling

The second analytical activity, sentence unscrambling, requires that learners take scrambled phrases and reassemble them into coherent sentences in Academic English. Using a familiar text, learners are given the task of putting the phrases back into their coherent order. Naturally, the punctuation and capitalization are clues, so they are discarded.

1. for this view
    of grammatical knowledge
    involve the distinction
    the psycholinguistic foundations
    between two types

2. developed through instruction
    explicit and/or declarative knowledge
    about grammatical rules and forms
    which is conscious knowledge

3. through acts
    and . . . procedural knowledge
    unconsciously developed
    which is the ability to speak a language
    of meaning-focused communication

Study, Discussion, and Essay Questions

Write the answers to these questions in your Language Notebook. Create your notebook as a word processing document because you will be using the "find" command to analyze your writing later.

1. Review these terms and add them to your glossary with a definition and some examples: common noun, proper name, definite description, abstract noun, non-countable or mass noun, count noun, descriptive adjective, attributive adjective, predicative adjective, adverb of manner, finite verb,

non-finite verb, main verb, primary auxiliary, modal auxiliary, bare infinitive, *to*-infinitive, past participle, present participle, transitive verb phrase, intransitive verb phrase, linking verb phrase, conjunction, correlative conjunction.

2. What are the main characteristics of phrases? What are the five types of phrases described in this chapter? What is colligation?

3. The count/mass distinction for nouns is not always intuitive, and the meanings are subtly different. What different meaning do you understand with each of these? Who might drink more, Lanny or Lois?

   Lanny drank a wine each night before going to bed.
   Lois drank wine each night before going to bed.

4. What is the prototypical colligation for noun phrases? Using your own texts, find some examples of noun phrases that follow the pattern.

5. What is the prototypical colligation for adjective phrases? Find some examples from your own text. What is the prototypical colligation for adverb phrases?

6. What are the inflections for main verbs in all three persons singular and plural in the present tense? Past tense?

7. What are the three main colligations for verb phrases?

8. What is the prototypical colligation for prepositional phrases? Find some examples of prepositional phrases in your texts.

9. What are the three main conjunctions? Find some examples of conjoined words and phrases from your texts. Do you have any examples of inclusive *or* or exclusive *or*?

10. What are substitution frames? What is data-driven analysis?

Activities

1. Learners sometimes make mistakes matching present tense verbs with their subjects. They sometimes match the verb with the closest NP instead of the true subject of the sentence, which may be farther away. There is an intervening phrase that separates the verb from its real subject.

The condition of the roads ~~make~~ *makes drivers feel that their taxes are wasted.*

The cost of the supplies ~~are~~ *is too high for anyone to pay for right now.*

In formal writing, with the **existential expression** *there is/are*, the verb matches the NP after the expression; in informal and spoken varieties, there is variation in usage.

There'̶s̶ <u>are</u> too many detail<u>s</u> in this report.

Unfortunately, there'̶s̶ <u>are</u> too many garish color<u>s</u> in the painting.

Underline the true subject and choose the correct verb form to go with it:

a.   The information in his letters was/were interesting.
b.   The furniture in the rooms is/are arriving today.
c.   Basic knowledge of mathematics has/have been improving in that class.
d.   The cost of television ads rises/rise every year.
e.   There is/are a list of items that you need to buy for the party.
f.   There was/were some equipment in the garage.

2.   Find a paragraph in a subject matter textbook and chunk it into phrases. Then create some unscrambling exercises from the paragraph and try them out on classmates. Do the same with one of your paragraphs.

3.   Go to the website at http://www.lextutor.ca/concordancers/concord_e.html (retrieved 11/8/2012). This website gives access to a number of corpora in English. Enter a key word, select a corpus from the dropdown list, and click on "get concordance." The results will show the usage of the key word you selected. For example, these sentences were adapted from the result of a search on the word *seems* in the British National Corpus (Written). What do you notice about usage with the verb *seems*?

1.   at the customers, it **SEEMS so** most took themselves to the next village
2.   As a piece of poetry, it **SEEMS a** fairly conventional summoning
3.   In Britain, it **SEEMS a** recession is noted when national production
4.   It **SEEMS almost** self-evident that a subject catalogue should
5.   He arrived late yesterday afternoon, it **SEEMS, and** he has offered to
6.   when you reenter memory it **SEEMS as** if time is the dream.

In student pairs, select some words to search and report on what you find in a few sentences.

4. Look at the phrasal diagram (Figure 7.4) used to show the structure of embedded or nested prepositional phrases. Draw the diagram in your Language Notebook and see if the same diagram can be used to represent the embedding in these underlined prepositional phrases as well:

a. *Very few studies have focused on systematically collecting huge samples <u>of spontaneous speech in specific situations</u>.*
b. *The argument <u>in favour of</u> parsing is fourfold.*
c. *As in other countries, increasing integration <u>with the rest of Europe</u> has led to general trends <u>in society like globalization and individualization</u>.*

What did you find? Discuss.

Noun Phrases   **8**

> **Reference.** The relation between a part of an utterance and an individual or set of individuals that it identifies. Thus one might say, on some specific occasion, "That man is my brother"; the noun phrase *that man* is thereby used as a **referring expression** whose **referent** is a specific man whose identity the addressee must either know or be able to determine.
>
> (Matthews, 1997, p. 312)

People need to refer to people and things they know, so reference is a communicative function based on a perceived relationship of identity between the word or name and an individual, a thing, or groups. The identity relationship creates a link between NPs in the language system in the mind and focal situations described in sentences and texts. In sentences, referential NPs are the subjects, direct objects, indirect objects, and objects of preposition. In communication, people also need to describe people and things, so there are descriptive functions that involve NPs in sentence constructions: subject complements, object complements, adverbials, and appositives. This chapter also discusses pronouns which are used to refer to previously named or identifiable people and things relevant in a discourse.

Noun Phrase Roles

Noun phrases can either **refer** to specific individuals or they can **describe** individuals in sentences and texts. **Reference** means that a word in a sentence

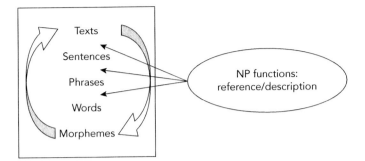

Figure 8.1   Noun Phrases Perform Referential and Descriptive Communicative Functions in Sentences and Texts

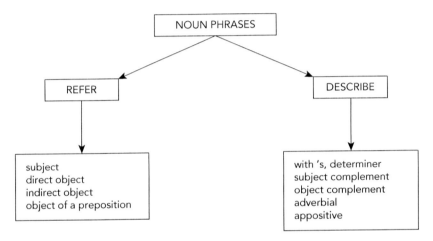

Figure 8.2   NPs' Roles Are either Referential or Descriptive

points to or identifies an entity in a focal situation. **Description** means that the word adds information about a person or thing in the focal situation.

Referential Roles

The order of the NPs in the sentence construction and their position with respect to the verb determine their different referential roles: subject, direct object, indirect object, or object of a preposition.

  The **subject** identifies the **agent,** or "doer," in the focal situation. The subject is placed just before the

Subject: *The optometrist gave Jennifer her new glasses.*

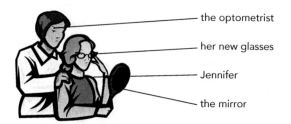

the optometrist

her new glasses

Jennifer

the mirror

Figure 8.3 NPs Are Subjects, Direct Objects, Indirect Objects, and Objects of a Preposition in the Sentence and Text Based on Their Role in the Focal Situation

main verb in the sentence. The subject determines what form the verb takes, whether it is singular or plural. Even when there is no real subject, a subject placeholder (*it, there*) must appear in the sentence (*It rains. There are too many people here.*)

The **direct object** refers to another entity in the focal situation, in this case the thing that is given, *the glasses*. The direct object occurs inside the VP but it is not always the second entity in the order of words in the sentence because its position also depends on the indirect object. Direct objects are most often inanimate or non-human entities.

> **Direct object:**
> *The optometrist gave Jennifer <u>her new glasses</u>.*

The **indirect object** refers to a third entity, the entity that "receives" the direct object in the focal situation. Jennifer receives the glasses and therefore her name is the indirect object in the sentence. Indirect objects are usually (but not always) animate entities. The direct and the indirect objects can reverse orders, so the inanimacy of the direct object and the animacy of the indirect object are important clues to the role the NPs take in the sentence.

> **Indirect object:**
> *The optometrist gave <u>Jennifer</u> her new glasses.*
> *The optometrist gave the new glasses to <u>Jennifer</u>.*

Finally, a noun phrase can be an **object of a preposition** in a prepositional phrase. Prepositional phrases often provide information about manner, location, destinations, or time. It is helpful to learn these common prepositions so that they can be identified quickly and easily: *across, at, after, around, before, between, by, down, for, from, in/into, like, near, of, opposite, over, to, under, up, with.*

> **Object of a preposition:**
> *Jennifer admired her glasses in <u>the mirror</u>.*

Descriptive Roles

Descriptive roles do not point out or introduce any additional entities in the focal situation. Descriptive NPs specify a characteristic of a person or thing that has already been mentioned with another noun. (Descriptive nouns like the underlined gerund in the example *their editing skills* will be discussed in Chapter 9.)

Determiners

When NPs take the possessive inflection *'s*, they don't refer. Instead they state a relationship of ownership or belonging together. Possessive NPs function like other determiners: *the*, *a*, or *my*, which are discussed further in Chapter 14 because they are unstable. In academic prose, the possessive is mainly used with non-concrete nouns, as in these examples from the database:

Determiner:
Dr. Page's beautiful dog
the girl's new classes

> *the world's most multicultural language*
> *the learner's ability*
> *the speaker-hearer's knowledge*
> *the person's history.*

Subject/Object Complements

A subject complement describes the subject by means of a linking verb. In the focal situation, the subject complement doesn't introduce a new entity. Subject complements are very common in academic prose (underlined below); object complements are less frequent because only a few verbal colligations permit them, so those examples are hypothetical.

Subject complement:
Grandma is an artist.

> . . . *the formulaic language was the biggest stumbling block*
>
> . . . *they are morphologically and syntactically a distinct word class*

Object complement:
Everyone considers Grandma an artist.

. . . all users of English are <u>equal partners in ELF (English as a Lingua Franca)</u>

*Ellis considered [language]*_{OBJ} *[a dynamic system]*_{OBJ COMP}

*Lack of practice makes [formulaic language]*_{OBJ} *[a stumbling block for learners]*_{OBJ COMP}

*Prodomou called [all users of English]*_{OBJ} *[equal partners in ELF]*_{OBJ COMP}

NP Adverbials

In this function, NPs provide additional information about the time or place that the focal situation takes place, without introducing any more entities into the situation. Given this highly explicit contextualized function, this use of NPs is not a frequent construction in academic prose.

Adverbial is a word that refers to a modifier **role** that a variety of constituents can have in the sentence. In the sentences in the box, the underlined NPs are modifiers, so they are called adverbials. However, they are not adverbs; their part of speech is still NP. The term adverb refers to a part of speech like *quickly, slowly, always, then, now*.

It is important to distinguish different types of grammatical information: the part of speech (in bold) and the role (capitalized) that the NP plays in the sentence.

> **NP Adverbials**
>
> <u>Tuesday</u> *Grandma will be painting a picture.* <u>Next year</u> *she'll have an exhibition.*

Tuesdays	*the artist*	*always*	*paints*	*portraits.*
NP	**NP**	**ADV**	**V**	**NP**
ADVERBIAL	SUBJECT	ADVERBIAL	PREDICATE	DIR OBJ

Appositives

A simple NP that renames and refers to a prior NP is called an appositive. The appositive is often separated from the rest of the sentence construction by commas,

> **Appositive NPs**
>
> *Aurelia Perez, <u>my grandmother</u>, is an artist.*

but in academic prose the appositive NP is sometimes in parentheses, as in these examples from the database:

> . . . *all users of English are equal partners in ELF (English as a Lingua Franca)*

> . . . *there are strong effects of word frequency on the speed and accuracy of lexical recognition processes (speech perception, reading, object naming, and sign perception) and lexical production processes (speaking, typing, writing, and signing)* . . .

> *The position of each language in this system may be characterized by its "communication value" (Q), the product of its prevalence and its centrality.*

In the last example, there are two appositives, one in parentheses and one separated with a comma. In speech, there are often pauses around appositives, and the pauses are represented in writing with punctuation. In sentences with a pronoun subject (*we*) or object (*us*) and an appositive, the choice of the correct pronoun form follows the function. Removing the appositive is a good way to know which pronoun is standard usage.

> *We, <u>the speakers of English</u>, should proudly flaunt the banners of cultural imperialism, neo-colonialism, and commercialism.*

Types of NPs

Proper names

Proper names can be subjects, indirect objects, objects of a preposition, and subject complements; more rarely, they are direct objects.

> **Colligation**
>
> [Proper Name]$_{NP}$

[The Smiths]$_{SUBJ}$ *gave [John]*$_{IO}$ *the book.*

[Ms. Crandall]$_{SUBJ}$ *spoke to [Mary]*$_{OBJ\ OF\ PREP}$ *about [John]*$_{OBJ\ OF\ PREP}$

My favorite teacher is [Ms. Crandall]$_{SUBJ\ COMP}$

Common Nouns

Common nouns optionally combine with determiners to form NPs which serve all of the various NP roles in sentences:

> **Colligation**
>
> [(Determiner) (ADJP) [N]$_{COMMON}$]$_{NP}$

subjects, objects, complements, and adverbials. Chapter 7 introduced the NP with a discussion of some classes of nouns: abstract, concrete, countable, non-countable, and gerunds. This discussion will continue in Chapter 14, because the interaction between nouns and determiners is a source of instability and diversity in World Englishes.

subject

[[Happiness]$_{ABSTRACT}$]$_{NP}$ *is*

subject complement

[[an emotion]$_{COUNTABLE N}$]$_{NP}$

subject

[People]$_{PLURAL}$]$_{NP}$ *usually like*

direct object

[[eat + ing]$_{GERUND}$]$_{NP}$

adverbial   **subject**

[Every year]$_{NP}$, [the students]$_{NP}$ *elect*

direct object   **obj complement**

[a classmate]$_{NP}$ [president]$_{NP}$

Pronouns

Pronouns refer to people and things in a focal situation, but because they are system words and not resource words, they are highly efficient and frequent, especially in conversation. With a

> **Colligation**
>
> [Pronoun]$_{NP}$

minimum of effort, they refer to anything. The word *it*, for instance, can refer to any inanimate or non-human entity (*the yeti*), any event (*your birthday party*), or any complex situation (*the populist agenda*) anywhere at any time. Pronouns have the same referential roles as NPs, but some of the roles are unlikely. For instance, they are rare or impossible as adverbials or object complements. There are also some pronominal usages that fulfill the subject role but do not refer to an entity or person in the focal situation. They are called "dummy" pronouns.

subject

[You]$_{PRONOUN}$ *saw*

direct object

[it]$_{PRONOUN}$ *on top of*

object of a preposition

[them]$_{PRONOUN}$

subject			indirect object
$[It]_{DUMMY}$ *is generous to give* $[the\ book]_{NP}$ *to*			$[her]_{PRONOUN}$

subject	subject complement	subject	subject complement
$[Who]_{QUESTION}$ *is*	$[it]_{DUMMY}$?	$[It]_{DUMMY}$ *is*	$[I/me]_{PRONOUN}$

In speech, most people use object pronouns for pronominal subject complements after the linking verb *be*. Biber et al. (1999, p. 335) gives these examples from conversation or fiction:

Hello gorgeous, it's me!
Carlo immediately thought it was me who had died.
Some people say it was him that wrote it.

There aren't any examples from academic prose because the construction is unusual. The prescriptive grammar rule that requires subject pronouns after *be* (*It is I*) is a rule imported from Latin, but it has affected only the speech of people most concerned with correctness. In formal speaking and writing, language purists prefer these:

Carlo immediately thought it was I who had died.
Some people say it was he who wrote it.

When writers are in doubt about which pronoun form to use, paraphrasing the sentence is a common resolution.

Carlo immediately thought that I had died.
Some people say that he was the person who wrote it.

Types of Pronouns

Personal Pronoun Forms

Function:			Subject	Object
1st	singular		*I*	*me*
	plural		*we*	*us*
2nd			*you*	*you*
3rd	singular	masculine	*he*	*him*
		feminine	*she*	*her*
		impersonal	*it*	*it*
	plural		*they*	*them*

Subject pronouns are in bold in the examples from the corpus below. In the last example, the pronoun *it* is a dummy pronoun to fill the subject slot in the sentence. *It* doesn't refer to anything in the focal situation; instead it gives the writer's stance toward the sentence X in the impersonal expression *it seems clear that X.*

> *Asking what morphemes a word contains and what* **they** *mean is asking what the coiner of the word had in mind when* **he** *coined it and possibly what unforeseen associations* **it** *may have built up since.*

> *When* **you** *study grammar,* **you** *learn to analyze language by breaking sentences into separate pieces in order to focus on individual parts . . .*

> *Once* **we** *learn to recognize parts of speech,* **we** *can begin to explore how particular types of words interact with certain other types within the sentence, that is, how* **they** *function together to convey overall meaning . . .*

> *. . .* **it** *seems clear that the absence of any feedback or strategy training will ensure that many students never take seriously the need to improve their editing skills.*

Object pronouns are also common in academic prose. In the last example, *it* is a placeholder or dummy that connects the discourse to the expression *to read and understand their texts.*

> *. . . in the classroom, we will expose learners to those forms and varieties of English which will empower* **them** *to meet the challenges of globalism . . .*

> *Our study of grammar, then, should help* **us** *gain insights into how grammar itself can be a means for packaging effective expressions in extended discourse of various kinds.*

> *In conceptualizing and researching ELF, we need "a third way," which steers clear of the extremes of fighting [the spread of English] for its linguistic imperialism, and accepting* **it** *in toto for its benefits.*

> *. . . they write logically organized and coherent texts but with such a high number of morphosyntactic errors that native speakers find* **it** *difficult, if not impossible, to read and understand their texts.*

However, subject and object pronouns are unstable and diverse in their usage in World Englishes. For instance, with conjoined subjects, some people use object pronoun forms instead of the expected subject pronouns. This occurs almost exclusively in conversation or reported conversations, as in these examples from Biber et al. (1999, p. 337):

> *Me and her mother split up about two years ago.*
> *And you and me nearly—nearly didn't get on the train.*
> *Him and Ed stink, both of them.*

This usage is not appropriate for academic writing, where subject and object pronouns are used conventionally. Generally, more formal varieties of English prefer the first person (I) to be the last one mentioned in any conjoined pronoun subject: *Her mother and I split up.*

Teachers have focused time and attention on this usage for years, and as a result many people have internalized the idea that it is always better to use subject pronouns, so they often use them in prepositional phrases, when it is correct to use object pronouns. A very common example is *between you and I* instead of *between you and me*. This is called **hypercorrection**. When people hypercorrect their speech or writing, it means that they feel insecure about their usage, have learned a usage rule incorrectly, and/or misapply the usage rule to instances it should not cover. These examples are from conversation or fiction (Biber et al., 1999, p. 338):

> *Well there's two left in there and that's not enough for you and I.*
> *Balthazar says that the natural traitors like you and I are really Caballi.*

When *as* and *than* are considered prepositions, it is standard to use the object pronouns. Otherwise they are subordinators and take a subject and a verb or auxiliary.

> *He has as many toys as me.*   *He has as many toys as I do.*
> *He has more toys than me.*   *He has more toys than I have.*

In Academic English prose, writers generally avoid referring to themselves or using the pronoun *I*, in order to make their statements seem more objective or scientific. However, this is not a hard and fast rule, as shown by these examples from the corpus for this book:

> *I consider explicit knowledge to be a worthwhile, sometimes indeed indispensable, form of knowledge to be used as a resource where and when implicit knowledge is not (yet) available.*

I refer to this property as nesting, where the product of a priming becomes itself primed in ways that do not apply to the individual words making up the combination.

Possessive and Reflexive Pronouns

Expressions like *He is a friend of mine* with a possessive pronoun are more indefinite than *He is my friend* with a possessive determiner. Possessive noun phrases with *'s* have a similar function to possessive pronouns in expressions like *He's a friend of Bill's*.

Reflexive pronouns often refer back to a noun phrase elsewhere in the sentence, often the subject, as in the first example from the database below. The noun phrase and the reflexive pronoun in object position are said to **co-refer**, because they both point to the same entity in the focal situation. Reflexive pronouns are also common as emphasis markers.

> *I refer to this property as nesting, where [the product of a priming] becomes [**itself**] primed in ways that do not apply to the individual words making up the combination.*

> *The disjunction between method as conceptualized by theorists and method as conducted by teachers is the direct consequence of the inherent limitations of [the concept of method **itself**].*

> *Our study of grammar, then, should help us gain insights into how [grammar **itself**] can be a means for packaging effective expressions in extended discourse of various kinds.*

> *In the end, teacher trainers and teachers may need to be reminded that the academic skills [they **themselves**] require in teaching and learning are not far removed from those of their NNS students.*

Reflexive pronouns are sometimes used in subject position in conversation and in reported conversations in fiction and news (Biber et al., 1999, p. 339). In these examples, there is no co-reference. The choice to use a reflexive pronoun as a subject in conjoined expressions might be a strategy to avoid having to distinguish between a subject pronoun and an object pronoun. That is, the speaker avoids saying either *Paul and I* or *Paul and me*.

Paul and myself went up there, didn't we?

My three associates and myself are willing to put big money into the club to get the best players for the team.

Person			Possessive	Reflexive
1st	singular		*mine*	*myself*
	plural		*ours*	*ourselves*
2nd			*yours*	*yourself/ves*
3rd	singular	masculine	*his*	*himself*
		feminine	*hers*	*herself*
		impersonal	*its*	*itself*
	plural		*theirs*	*themselves*

Note that *its* is a possible form, but it is rare. *This piece of meat is the dog's. It's its.* There is also a difficulty between two very similar forms: *its* and *it's*. The first is a possessive determiner, the second is an abbreviation for *it is*.

Demonstrative Pronouns

Demonstrative pronouns introduce or identify entities or they refer to a particular situation, fact, or event described in a previous or following sentence. This usage is very common in Academic English.

Demonstrative Pronouns

Singular	Near	*this*
	Distant	*that*
Plural	Near	*these*
	Distant	*those*

[*Explicit learning is a conscious, deliberative process of concept formation and concept linking*]. [*This*] *may either take place when learners are being taught concepts and rules by an instructor or textbook, or when they operate in a self-initiated searching mode, trying to develop concepts and rules themselves . . .*

[*This*] *means that the task of "learning a language" must be reconceived.*

In the end, teacher trainers and teachers may need to be reminded that [the academic skills they themselves require in teaching and learning] are not far removed from [those] of their NNS students.

The demonstrative pronoun *that* is often used in the collocation *that is*, that defines a concept or restates a complicated idea, as in this example:

> *The first was that native speakers seem to find formulaic (<u>that is</u>, prefabricated) language an easy option in their processing and/or communication.*

The following example shows a contrast between *these* used as a determiner within a NP and *these* used as a pronoun:

> *The same applies to word sequences built out of [<u>these</u> words]*$_{NP}$*; [<u>these</u>]*$_{NP}$ *too become loaded with the contexts and co-texts in which they occur.*

Those occurs very commonly with an expression that identifies a group:

> *English is now the language of [<u>those</u> who use it]; the users give it a distinct identity of their own in each region.*

> *In the end, teacher trainers and teachers may need to be reminded that [the academic skills they themselves require in teaching and learning] are not far removed from [<u>those</u> of their NNS students].*

Quantifying Pronouns

Quantifying pronouns are forms like *some, any, each, many, much, none*, but in the database there are few examples.

> *Connected speech is what we must hold before our inner ear as the true and foremost manifestation of language, if we are to be successful in [**any**] of our investigations into the living essence of language.*

Indefinite pronouns

Indefinite pronouns are not common in academic prose because most writers prefer a specific common noun with quantifying determiners (*every human,*

Indefinite Pronouns

Every: *everybody, everyone, everything*
Some: *somebody, someone, something*
Any: *anybody, anyone, anything*
No: *nobody, no one, nothing*

some details, any answer, no object). There are also some adverbs of place derived by compounding in a similar fashion: *everywhere, somewhere, anywhere,* and *nowhere.* The compounds with *-one* are more common than the compounds with *-body,* except in conversation. The quantifying determiner *every* is used with singular nouns, and the compound indefinites with *every* are singular in form and take singular forms of verbs. One way to make this clear is to equate *every* with *each.*

> *Everyone needs a backpack.*
> *Everyone needs his/her backpack.*
> *Each one needs a backpack.*

When writers use an indefinite NP, they sometimes are unsure about how to complete the sentence. With singular forms like *everyone* or *every student,* the traditional resolution was to use the masculine singular pronouns, as in these examples from Biber et al. (1999, p. 316):

> *Each novelist aims to make a single novel of the material he has been given.*

> *Each individual is thus the recipient of the accumulated culture of the generations which have preceded him.*

However, more recently style manuals for news and academic speech and writing prefer a gender-neutral resolution, as in this example from the database:

> *There is a growing body of evidence that [an individual's] parsing decisions are influenced in some way by [his or her] prior contact with comparable strings or structures.*

An alternative that is common in speech and informal writing, but not in formal writing, is the use of the third person plural forms. This alternative has resisted the best efforts of English teachers and language purists to stamp it out for years. Biber et al. (1999, p. 316) gives these examples from news reports:

> *[Everybody] remembers where [**they**] were when JFK was shot.*

> *[Nobody] likes to admit that [**they**] entertain very little or that [**they**] rarely enjoy it when [**they**] do.*

One way to avoid all of these problems is to use plural forms. In this example, the author switches from singular to plural reference:

*[A speaker's sensitivity] to previous encounters with language forms and meanings suggests that language use is sensitive to the occurrence of language forms and meanings in the environment. In other words, the exact forms and meanings that [speakers] use can be affected by the language that occurred in discourse [**they**] recently engaged in.*

Wh-Pronouns

Wh-pronouns are used in questions and some subordinate sentences like indirect questions or adjective clauses (to be discussed in a later chapter). In direct and indirect questions, the wh-pronouns are *who, whose (whom), what, which, when, where, why,* and *how.* In adjective clauses, they are *who, whom, which, whose,* and *that,* and they are commonly called relative pronouns.

*The languages of the world together constitute a global system held together by multilingual people [**who**] can communicate with several language groups.*

Very formal English has two competing forms: *who* and *whom.* In the sentence above, *who* takes the place of the subject in the subordinate clause. In the invented sentence below, *whom* marks the object of the verb *detested.*

He is the guide <u>whom</u> the elephant detested.

For animals or inanimate objects, *which* is a possibility in addition to *that.*

*. . . the growing respect for real examples led in the mid-1980s to a notion of textual well-formedness, [**which**] was dubbed naturalness.*

Word processing grammar checkers prefer *that* as a relative pronoun, and mark other relative pronouns with an underline; *that* is the most common relative pronoun in the corpus, with many examples like this:

*In other words, the exact forms and meanings [**that**] speakers use can be affected by the language [**that**] occurred in discourse they recently engaged in.*

Reciprocal Pronouns

Each other and one another express the
idea that an action is mutual. Each other
is more common than one another,
which some people reserve for those
contexts where there are more than two
entities.

Reciprocal Pronouns

They looked at each other.
(2 people)

They looked at one another.
(2 or more people)

One

The pronoun one (not the number) substitutes for a NP with a count noun. It
has a plural form, ones, which substitutes for plural nouns (not NPs), possessive
forms (one's or ones'), and a reflexive pronoun (oneself). These forms refer back
to indefinite entities that have been mentioned before or that can be inferred
from the context, as in these examples:

> . . . we must work toward [an interactive model of grammar and discourse],
> [one] that demonstrates the necessity and importance of both levels of language
> to the language learning process and to the attainment of communicative
> competence.

> Accepting hybridity and using English creatively for [one's own communicative
> purposes] seems to be one such "third way" . . .

One is also an impersonal pronoun for those situations when you might be used
in less formal conversation and writing.

> However . . . [one] might speculate that, in time, self-regulation might move
> toward less dependence on native norms so that these written modes also take
> on the kind of distinctive features that are evident in spoken ELF . . .

Discovery Procedures

In Chapter 1, the meaning and relevance of this paragraph were discussed; it
describes de Swaan's (1998) view on the organization and value of languages
of wider communication. Now this paragraph will be examined using a
message-oriented perspective.

The languages of the world together constitute a global system held together by multilingual people who can communicate with several language groups. The position of each language in this system may be characterized by its "communication value" (Q), the product of its prevalence and its centrality. Languages represent a very special class of economic goods: they are not only collective goods but also display network effects . . . The special characteristics of language, language groups and their accumulated textual capital help to explain the dynamics of language acquisition, conservation, and abandonment.

It is not always easy to determine the syntactic role that NPs occupy in a sentence, but practice with the diagnostics and substitution frames can help. The first step is to identify the noun phrases, and there are a lot of them in this excerpt of Academic English.

[*The languages of the world*] *together* **constitute** *a global system held together by multilingual people who can communicate with several language groups*.

The second step is to look at the relationship among the noun phrases, their co-texts, and their relationship to other constituents in the sentence, especially the main verb, in this case the verb *constitute*. The NP before the main verb is *the languages of the world*. Its location before the main verb makes it the prime candidate for subject because that is the default syntactic choice in English. In this case, the subject is not an agent, but it is the main topic in the discourse. There are two nouns with the determiner *the*, and the second noun *the world* is related to the noun *the languages* by means of the preposition *of*. The noun *languages* is called the simple subject because it is the head noun of the NP.
The NP *the world* is the object of the preposition *of*.

Diagnosis: languages→noun
Meaning: topic (not agent)
Morphology: plural inflection
Co-text: occurs with a determiner *the* and a PP; occurs before the main verb
Function: the subject of this sentence

The NP colligation, quite a common one, looks like this [*the* N [*of the* N]$_{PP}$]$_{NP}$. This colligation can be used as a substitution frame. It is also a good example for data-driven analysis of the corpus, because a search on the word *of* reveals a plethora of examples in which there is a relatively generic noun followed by a more specific prepositional phrase.

Substitution Frame: [the N [of the N]$_{PP}$]$_{NP}$

the languages	of	the world
the people	of	the earth
the woman	of	the year

Database Search on of:

a source of frustration and boredom
the structure of speech and writing
the formal discussion of syntax and function
the achievement of confidence

What is the role of the NP *a global system* that occurs after the main verb *constitute*? There is an indefinite (*a*) determiner, an adjective which ends with a common adjective suffix *-al*, and a noun *system*. The possibilities for its function in the sentence are **direct object** if *constitute* is a transitive verb or a **subject complement** if *constitute* is a linking verb. The indications are that it is a subject complement.

Diagnosis: system→noun
Meaning: gives another name to or restates the topic; does not refer to a new entity
Morphology: (none)
Co-text: occurs with a determiner *a*; occurs after a linking verb
Function: subject complement

[The languages of the world] constitute [a global system]

The following sentence has a direct object, although the structure is complicated with a series of NPs conjoined with the conjunction *and*. Without the conjoined structures, each NP is actually quite similar to the NP colligation above [the N [of the N]$_{PP}$]$_{NP}$.

[The special characteristics [of [language, language groups and their accumulated textual capital]$_{NP}$]$_{PP}$]$_{NP}$

help to explain

[the dynamics [of [language acquisition, conservation, and abandonment]$_{NP}$]$_{PP}$]$_{NP}$

The NP *the dynamics* after the main verb
help to explain is a direct object.

subject
↓
[The special characteristics] **help**

direct object
↓
to explain [the dynamics].

Noun Phrase Awareness

The examples above show that academic writing usually contains many complex NPs with conjoined elements and prepositional phrases. There are also many adjectives (e.g. *global system, multilingual people, special class*) and descriptive nouns (e.g. <u>communication</u> value, <u>network</u> effects, <u>language</u> groups), which will be discussed further in the next chapter. The texts cited above also show the value of repeating the same word *language* within diverse complex co-texts to accomplish two discourse purposes, continuity and coherence, but also variety and textual interest. Another way that NPs are used in discourse has to do with alternatives that paraphrase or substitute instead of repeating pronouns and the original noun, in order to create a more interesting text. Hinkel (2002, p. 88) gives this example from a NS undergraduate writer, in which the paraphrases or synonyms are underlined:

> <u>A job</u> is <u>a method of economic support</u>. Self-respect and self-esteem are the key to success in <u>one's work</u>. <u>Employment</u> represents <u>a way of paying bills or earning cash</u>.

This writer understands the value of paraphrase instead of repetition; in this case the paraphrases help to obscure the fact that there is very little content in the sentences.

In general, academic authors avoid the first person pronouns (*I/me* or *we/us*) except for specific emphatic uses that underscore the author's opinion or difference from other researchers. In contrast, Hinkel (2002) found that English learning undergraduates used first person pronouns twice as often as the native English undergraduate writers. This was related to the fact that their writing included personal narratives and accounts of their own experiences more than the academic writing of the native-speaking undergraduates. The writing of the NNS students also contained many generalizations, vague assertions, and accounts of third party experiences and narratives. Hinkel (2002, p. 87) points out that students often combine personal experience narratives with commentary about their educational value for the reader, who is directly urged to learn from the writer's mistakes or avoid them.

This kind of stylistic choice causes NNS essays "to resemble interpersonal narrative and increases the use of *I, we, you,* and imperative constructions." Hinkel cites this text as an example of typical pronominal usage of NNS undergraduate writing, which is overly conversational:

> *If you are an undergraduate student, you may have difficulty choosing a major field. You have to try to find jobs that have both your interests and can satisfy your living . . . Remember, this is your life, and you need to do what you need to do.*

The students that Hinkel studied also overused universal pronouns, which resulted in exaggeration and overstatements:

> *I believe <u>everyone</u> will choose the former because <u>everyone</u> wants happiness.*

Hinkel also found that the NNS writers avoided the use of impersonal or indirect expressions with the dummy subject *it,* although they are common in academic prose, as shown by these examples from the corpus for this book.

> *it is arguable/possible/impossible/better that . . .*
> *it seems clear/obvious/undeniable that . . .*
> *it is reasonable/unreasonable/possible to ask whether*
> *find it difficult/easy/impossible/better/worse*
> *It is a question of*
> *it has recently been suggested that . . .*

Study, Discussion, and Essay Questions

Write the answers to these questions in your Language Notebook. Create your notebook as a word processing document because you will be using the "find" command to analyze your writing later.

1. Review these terms and add them to your glossary with a definition and some examples if they are not already present: subject, direct object,

indirect object, object of a preposition, subject complement, object complement, adverbial, appositive.

2. What is reference? How does it differ from description? What roles do referential noun phrases play in the composition of a sentence? What are the descriptive uses of NPs?

3. What are the three types of NPs and their colligations? What makes pronouns highly efficient? What are "dummy" pronouns?

4. What are some problems people have with pronouns in speech or writing?

5. Make flashcards for the different pronouns: personal (subject and object), possessive, reflexive, demonstrative, quantifying, indefinite, interrogative, relative, reciprocal, dummy pronouns, and impersonal *one*. Use the flashcards to review the forms of the different pronouns so that you can recognize them easily in context.

6. What are some characteristics of nominalization in Academic English writing? What are the characteristics of NNS academic writing, according to Hinkel (2002)?

7. Underline the pronouns in this text from Prodomou cited in Chapter 1 and identify what type they are. What problems, if any, do you have in doing this task?

> *It goes without saying that, in the real world, all users of English are equal partners in ELF (English as a Lingua Franca); in the classroom, we will expose learners to those forms and varieties of English which will empower them to meet the challenges of globalism and to resist the hegemony of one culture over another.*

8. In the following text discussed in Chapter 1 (meaning) and this chapter (message), identify the functions or roles of the underlined NPs. Be sure to use the diagnostics and the discovery procedures.

> *The languages of the world together constitute a global system held together by <u>multilingual people</u> who can communicate with <u>several language groups</u>. <u>The position of each language in this system</u> may be characterized by <u>its "communication value"</u> (Q), the product of its prevalence and its centrality. <u>Languages</u> represent <u>a very special class of economic goods</u>: they are not only collective goods but also display <u>network effects</u> . . . The special characteristics of language, language groups and their accumulated textual capital help to explain the dynamics of language acquisition, conservation, and abandonment.*

> <u>multilingual people</u>
> <u>several language groups</u>

The position of each language in this system
its "communication value"
Languages
a very special class of economic goods
network effects

Activities

1. What would you say to your learners in order to improve their academic writing? In groups, take turns explaining what the problem in each sentence is and suggesting a more formal Academic English alternative. Make sure to identify what the problem is using metalinguistic terms.

    a. Everyone must remove their personal items from their lockers as soon as the semester is over.
    b. This math problem is too difficult for Sheila and I.
    c. In public speaking, you don't want to leave your audience without a clear idea of your conclusion.
    d. The three men saw each other as soon as the smoke cleared.
    e. Mario and me performed the chemistry experiment last week.
    f. Trisha and myself were the only ones who understood the question.
    g. Is very difficult to clarify the historical perspective.
    h. Each athlete should consult with his advisor once a week.
    i. Each student has an archeological dig in the making in their backpacks.
    j. A doctor should never make his patients wait more than 15 minutes.

2. There are three system words that are often confused. They are written differently but they are pronounced the same. They are:

    To = Preposition/infinitive marker: *I want [to$_{INF}$ take] the dog [to$_{PREP}$ the park] for a romp. Will you go with me?*

    Two = Determiner/pronoun: *It's more fun walking the dog with [two$_{DET}$ people], but only [two$_{PRO}$].*

    Too = Intensifier or Sentential Adverb: *I'd like my sister to go along [too]$_{SA}$. She's not [too$_{INT}$ busy] for a walk.*

Using the concordance software at http://www.lextutor.ca/concordancers/concord_e.html (retrieved 11/8/12), find several examples of *to*, *two*, and *too*. How is each one used?

3. Review: Taking turns with a partner and for each pair of sentences with homonyms below, label the underlined form as either a resource or a system word in the context of the sentence. Use diagnostics; do not guess.

   a. Yeng <u>will</u> study very hard for the English Placement Test.
   b. Where there's a <u>will</u>, there's a way.
   c. Sue hid the money in a coffee <u>can</u> in her freezer.
   d. Do you think anyone <u>can</u> find it?
   e. Those tomatoes don't taste <u>like</u> these.
   f. I <u>like</u> food diversity.
   g. <u>May</u> Lee enjoys reading the dictionary.
   h. She <u>may</u> have the biggest vocabulary of anyone I know.

   Then verbalize how you identified the word as such as best you can.

Modifiers

9

MODIFICATION [15c: through French from Latin *modificatio/ modificationis* setting limits] A term for the dependence of one grammatical unit on another, the less dependent unit being delimited or made more specific by the more dependent unit: the adjective *good* modifying the noun *weather* in the phrase *good weather*; the noun *diamond* modifying the noun *mines* in *diamond mines*; the adverb *strikingly* modifying the adjective *handsome* in *strikingly handsome*.

(McArthur, 1992, p. 667)

As McArthur says, the prototypical words that accomplish a modifying function in communication are adjectives, nouns, and adverbs of manner, all resource words. This chapter also discusses determiners as they are system words which depend on nouns, delimiting them and making them more specific. Like reference and description, discussed in the last chapter, modification is a communicative function which has an impact on words, phrases, sentences, and texts. (Predication, discussed in the next chapter, and indeed all further communicative functions are the same in this respect.)

Here are some examples of modification from the corpus that show its importance in creating dense academic text:

Determiner with Attributive Adjective Phrases
*If we break any sentence down into [**the smallest independent** units], we end up with [**single** words] that, according to [**traditional** practice], can be classified into [**various** types] of word classes called parts of speech . . .*

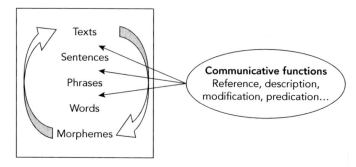

Figure 9.1   Communicative Functions Participate in Constructions at All Levels of the Grammatical System

Predicate Adjective Phrases (but note the underlined determiner and attributive adjectives)
*Because of <u>the perceived importance</u> of error correction and the amount of emphasis both teachers and students place on it, it is [**reasonable**] to ask whether <u>grammatical</u> correction is [**effective and appropriate**].*

Determiner with Descriptive Nouns
*. . . if we teach grammar without reference to discourse, our students will fail to acquire [**the discourse** competence] so vital for developing [effective **reading and writing skills**].*

Adverb Phrase of Manner (note the underlined predicate adjective and the conjoined attributive adjectives)
*Cognition, consciousness, experience, embodiment, brain, self, communication and human interaction, society, culture, and history are [[**inextricably**] <u>intertwined</u>] in <u>rich, complex, and dynamic</u> ways in language.*

> **Colligation**
>
> [(Determiner) (ADJP) [N]$_{COMMON}$]$_{NP}$

Determiners

Speakers and writers choose their determiners based on how they perceive or want to portray the entity pointed out by the noun. If the entity has not been

A List of Determiners

Definite:	*the*
Indefinite:	*a/an*
Possessive:	*my, your, his, her, its, our, their*
Demonstrative:	*this, that, these, those*
Quantifying:	*both, some, any, no, every . . .*
Numbers:	*one, two, second, eighth . . .*
Wh-words:	*which, whose, whatever . . .*
Possessive NPs:	*a speaker's, an individual's . . .*

discussed before or if it is a new entity that is being introduced, speakers and writers introduce the noun with the indefinite articles *a/an*.

*First, the teacher must realize that [**a** mistake]*$_{NP}$ *has been made.*

*Practice gets [**a** raw deal] in [**the** field of applied linguistics].*

Note that *the field of applied linguistics* uses the definite determiner *the*, presumably because the author realizes that readers would already be familiar with that concept. In the hypothetical sentence below, *the mistake* refers to a specific mistake or type of mistake familiar to the reader.

*First, the teacher must realize that [**the** mistake]*$_{NP}$ *has been made.*

The distribution of the determiners is similar to that of their close cousins, pronouns, discussed in the previous chapter. There is variation in determiner usage in World Englishes and in ELF, perhaps because many languages don't have determiners at all, or the determiners have different distributions, as in Spanish. For instance, English prefers an indefinite determiner in a subject complement construction having to do with professions: *I am a teacher.* The corresponding sentence in Spanish, *soy profesora*, doesn't have a determiner. In Spanish, abstract nouns take a definite determiner, *la felicidad*, but in English they don't, *happiness*. Spanish also avoids using possessive determiners in places where English has them. This is especially true with parts of the body.

English: *My hand hurts.*
Spanish: *Me duele la mano. (To me hurts the hand. The hand hurts me.)*

Although there are a few consistent and learnable patterns for determiners, the determiner system is far from pattern-based. Their standard usage depends on exposure to common colligations and collocations, but unfortunately determiners are unstressed in speech. They are spoken with little emphasis, loudness, and force, which makes learning through oral usage and exposure problematic. Therefore, an effective strategy is for teachers to raise their learners' awareness of determiners as they are used in written texts, asking them to focus attention on them as they are reading. It is easy for learners to skip over determiners and consider them unimportant. Unfortunately, if they do, they are ignoring the main source of exposure to accurate determiner usage.

In the NP colligation, only one determiner position has been specified, but in fact more than one determiner can occur. **Central determiners** are the most prototypical. **Predeterminers** occur before them and **postdeterminers** occur after them. The series of determiners in the following NPs shows pre-fabrication.

> . . . *no idealized method can visualize **all the variables** in advance.*

> *As more and more attention is given to English, **the first language** is marginalized.*

> *On **the other hand**, various advanced syntactic constructions that are commonly associated with academic texts seem to be largely missing from NNS essays.*

Predeterminers are words like *such, all* or *both*, fractions (*half, one quarter*), and multipliers (*double, three times, once*).

Central determiners are the **definite article** *the*, the **indefinite article** *a/an*, **demonstratives** (*this, that, these, those*), **possessives** (*my, your, his, her, its, our, their, Mary's, John's*), **Wh-determiners** (*which, whose, whatever*), and **quantifiers** (*no, some, any, neither, either, every, each, enough, little, less, few, fewer*).

Postdeterminers are ordinal numbers or similar (*first, last, third, next*) or a quantifier (*two, three, other*). There can be more than one postdeterminer in a NP.

Adjectives and Adjective Phrases

The examples from the beginning of the chapter show that adjective phrases are either **attributive**,

Prototypical ADJP Colligations

1.   [([Intensifier]) $^+$[Adjective] ([Adverb])^1]$_{ADJP}$
2.   [([Adverb]) $^+$[Adjective]]$_{ADJP}$

modifying a head noun in a NP, or **predicative**, modifying a NP by means of a linking verb. Adjectives may be conjoined or they can appear in a list. The plus sign superscript in the colligation is a reference to the fact that more than one adjective can occur. Prototypical adjectives are descriptive; they take normal comparative and superlative morphology (-*er*/-*est* or *more*/*most*) and intensifiers or adverbs of manner.

Attributive: *a [completely homogeneous] speech-community*
such [grammatically irrelevant] conditions
a [very special] class
the [biggest] stumbling block

Predicative: *are [very concerned]*
seems [clear]
was [so easy]
be [consistently effective]

Some attributive adjectives (*involved, available*) can optionally occur after their head nouns:

. . . *someone who writes or speaks English well does not necessarily understand [the principles **involved**].*

Attributive adjectives occur after indefinite pronouns:

*The third points the way to a better material life for [everyone **concerned**].*

Non-prototypical Adjective Phrases

Some adjectives do not meet all of the defining characteristics of prototypical adjectives. For example, classifying adjectives are usually incompatible with comparative/superlative or intensifiers, e.g. *the very chemical reaction* or *the chiefer reason*. Classifying adjectives are common in academic writing because they classify their head nouns in relationship to others of the same group, origin, subject area, and others.

> *Languages represent a very special class of [[economic] goods]: they are not only [[collective] goods] but also display network effects.*

Classifying Adjectives

relationships	*average, chief, internal, left, main, maximum, standard, previous . . .*
origin	*American, Catholic, British, Indian, Navajo . . .*
subject area	*chemical, commercial, social, environmental, legal . . .*

Non-gradable adjectives are absolute words; they refer to characteristics that an entity either has or

Non-gradable adjectives	*pregnant, unique perfect, dead, alive, lone*

doesn't have; there is no relativity or degree involved. If something is *unique*, then there is no other like it. If something is *perfect*, then it is logically impossible to be more perfect. However, in speech, people use absolute adjectives with intensifiers or degree words, sometimes to say something about appearance; if someone says a woman is *very pregnant*, then the speaker means that she is very advanced in her pregnancy. Absolute adjectives do not lend themselves to comparison or degrees in academic writing. The example below is an exception, perhaps because the style is literary:

> *The morpheme . . . remains [half alive] for one speaker and dies for the next.*

Participial adjectives come from present or past participles, verbs ending in *-ing* or *-ed* or with irregular forms, and they are not always easy to distinguish from the verbs they come from.

*Ideally one would like to have [a [rigorous [possibly [statistically **determined**]]] way] to define what is meant by a "common" or "frequent" expression.*

In the following example, the attributive participial adjectives are in bold and passive past participles are underlined. Other adjectives are classifying: *reciprocal, global, mutual,* and descriptive: *overt. Maintained* and *adhered to* are past participles used as part of a passive verbal construction.

Participal Adjectives

[V + -ed/en]$_{ADJ}$
[V + -ing]$_{ADJ}$

*It stands to reason that in [**written** language use], where there is no possibility of the overt reciprocal negotiation of meaning typical of [**spoken** interaction], there is more reliance on [**established** norms], and these are naturally maintained by a process of self-regulation whereby these norms are adhered to in the interest of maintaining global mutual intelligibility.*

The work has exhausted me.	Main verb past participle
I was exhausted by the work.	Main verb past participle
I was exhausted every day.	Participial adjective
The work was exhausting me.	Main verb present participle
The work is very exhausting.	Participial adjective

The meanings of participial adjectives depend on the participle they come from. The -ing adjectives (*boring, interesting, amazing, exciting, following*) have a progressive or active meaning. The -ed adjectives (*advanced, alleged, bored, complicated, excited, exhausted*) have a completed or passive meaning.

ADJP Constructions in Sentences

In sentences, there are two prototypical locations for an ADJP. Attributive adjectives occur inside NPs and predicative adjectives occur after linking verbs as subject complements. Object complements are relatively rare, but there is one example in the database with this colligation: [[Verb] [NP] [ADJP]]$_{VP}$.

To withdraw or abandon the language through which tradition speaks is to [[render]$_V$ [tradition]$_{NP}$ [mute]$_{ADJP}$]$_{VP}$

Very complex adjective phrases sometimes shift to a position after the noun. When a speaker or writer places the "heavy" adjective phrase after the noun, it makes it easier for the listener or reader to find the noun and connect it with the other constituents of the sentence. The heavy adjective phrase becomes more salient in the sentence, as shown in this example from the corpus:

> It stands to reason that in written language use, where there is no possibility of [the overt reciprocal negotiation of meaning *typical of spoken interaction*]$_{NP}$, there is more reliance on established norms,

Speakers or writers sometimes choose to place adjective phrases in a preposed position in a sentence so that it serves as a displaced modifier or discourse organizer, as in this hypothetical example composed from sentences in the corpus.

> *Typical of spoken interaction*, negotiations of meaning are rarely found in written language use.

Descriptive Nouns

Descriptive nouns are usually optional modifiers within noun phrases, but they are important. If they are present in a NP, they occur just before the head noun. These examples from the database show the range of descriptive nouns found in academic prose:

> **Descriptive Noun Colligation**
>
> [([DET]) (⁺[ADJP]) (⁺[N]) [N]]$_{NP}$

	Descriptive Noun	**Head Noun**
	learner	*awareness*
	memory	*limitations*
a	*target*	*feature*
the	*acquisition*	*problem*
these two	*knowledge*	*systems*

In this colligation, the first noun describes or classifies the type of the second noun. Descriptive nouns usually do not take plural or possessive inflections and often show regular noun-like derivational morphology like suffixes (e.g. *-er*, *-tion*). The phrase can often be paraphrased with "N *for/of* N," as in *awareness of the learner* or *limitations of memory*. It is not always easy to distinguish descriptive adjectives and nouns, because the two colligations are similar. People's intuitions have been shaped by the traditional grammatical notion that every word that modifies a noun must be an adjective, so naïve hypotheses are not reliable. This is a time when consistent use of diagnostics and discovery procedures will replace traditional but erroneous ideas. Derivation, inflection, intensifiers, and paraphrases are revealing clues:

> Inflection: An adjective usually takes -er/more or -est/most but nouns do not.

| the larger corpora | *the texter corpora |
| more powerful abilities | *more generalization abilities (where *more* modifies *generalization*, not *abilities*) |

> Intensifiers: An adjective can take *very* and other intensifiers.

| the very large corpora | *the very text corpora |
| the very powerful abilities | *the very generalization abilities |

> Paraphrase: A noun has the paraphrase with *for* or *of*, although these may be rare.

| *the corpora of large | the corpora of text(s) |

These diagnostics differentiate most descriptive nouns and adjectives, but in some cases not all the diagnostics will work. For instance, Biber et al. (1999, p. 68) list the following to contrast Noun–Noun combinations with Adjective–Noun combinations. In these examples the only diagnostic that works is paraphrase, possibly because both the adjectives and the nouns are derived from verbs. In some ways, the adjective retains more of a dynamic or active quality, while the noun (gerund) is static and fixed.

Noun	Noun	Adjective	Noun
living	*standards*	*living*	*creatures*
dancing	*classes*	*dancing*	*children*
working	*conditions*	*working*	*mother*

Applying the paraphrase diagnostic to some similar examples from the corpus is somewhat awkward, but helpful. In each case, the focal word is a noun, a gerund.

| *by general [learning] mechanisms* | Noun: by general mechanisms of learning |

the biggest [stumbling] block	Noun: the biggest block for stumbling over
an individual's [parsing] decisions	Noun: an individual's decisions for parsing

In fact, English learners sometimes substitute paraphrases with *for* or *of* for descriptive nouns in NPs in ways that are grammatical but non-conventional or unlikely, such as **the abilities of generalization* or **the differing events of language*, instead of the more conventional descriptive noun modifier colligation.

Descriptive nouns that modify head nouns through analytical colligational processes or holistic collocational processes are difficult to distinguish from prefabricated compound nouns like *teacup* or *housecoat*. Innovative combinations have little priming among the two words, and show no signs yet of fusion into one lexical unit. Noun–noun collocations have priming associations between both elements, making the construction the result of holistic processing. True compounds are fused together as multi-word lexical units; they have a pattern of stress on the first noun in speech. That stress pattern is not characteristic of collocations or free combinations. It seems that there is a continuum between these types of expressions and the more priming, the more they seem like compounds and are written as one word. The less priming, the more they are simply colligations that follow a pattern.

> Compounds: *clássroom, nétwork, tímescales*
>
> Noun–noun collocations: *language gróups, human interáction, school currículum, foreign languages*
>
> Innovative combinations: *symbol awareness, practice skills, method limitation, theory confrontation* (What could these mean?)

Lists of Adjectives

Celse-Murcia (1998, p. 688) suggests that, when there is a list of adjectives, "the more semantically peripheral of the two adjectives occurs first in the sequence or farther away from the head noun." Size adjectives often occur before more general (like color) or classifying adjectives, as in these examples:

[the **smallest independent** units]$_{NP}$
[the **largest structural** unit]$_{NP}$

When attributive adjectives and descriptive nouns occur in a series, the order is general adjectives, physical state adjectives, proper adjectives, descriptive nouns, and finally the head noun. Predicative adjectives have a weaker tendency to particular orders; some orders are more awkward than others. Different orders convey different meanings. Usually there are never more than three descriptive words together. The comma before *and* in a series of more than two adjectives is optional. These preferred orders are learned from usage and exposure to language, from which the probabilities of certain orders rather than others are acquired.

At a very beginning level, English learners may have problems placing adjectives before nouns and, for more advanced learners, the orders of adjectives and descriptive nouns can be a problem. They should notice the adjectives in their reading and attempt translation activities. They might translate the modifiers into their first language, first word for word and also by chunks that maintain the meanings the same.

	General/ Physical State	Proper Adjectives	Descriptive Nouns	Head Nouns
the		Western		culture
the	overt reciprocal			negotiation
the	more general			patterns
	differing		language	events
	large		text	corpora
	powerful		generalization	abilities

Adverbs and Adverb Phrases

There are three types of adverb phrases considered prototypical: adverbs of manner, time and place expressions, and adverbs of frequency.

Adverbs of Manner

Adverbs of manner are closely related to descriptive and classifying adjectives. Most descriptive adjectives (*obviously, rapidly*) and all classifying adjectives (*chemically, politically*) form their adverb of manner by adding the suffix *-ly*.

However, some common descriptive adverbs reflect a more ancient form of English, when there was no morphological difference between adjectives and adverbs (*fast, well, slow*). The colligation allows for a main adverb modified by an intensifier. Adverbs of manner derived from descriptive or classifying adjectives are quite common in academic prose, as shown by these examples from the database.

> *When a language point is noticed [frequently], learners develop awareness of it and [unconsciously] compare it with their existing system of linguistic knowledge, [unconsciously] constructing new hypotheses to accommodate the differences between the noticed information and their L2 competence.*

> *Linguistic theory is concerned [primarily] with an ideal speaker-listener, in a [completely] homogeneous speech-community, who knows its language [perfectly] and is unaffected by such [grammatically] irrelevant conditions as memory limitations, distractions, shifts of attention and interest, and errors (random or characteristic) in applying his knowledge of the language in actual performance . . .*

Adverb of Manner

$[([Intensifier])\ ^{+}[Adverb]]_{ADVP}$

Sentence Adverbs

Sentence adverbs and adverbs of frequency operate as single word constructions within a sentence. Sentence adverbs are quite free in terms of where they can occur in a sentence. Here are some examples from the corpus:

> *English is **now** the language of those who use it . . .*

> *__Then__ they test these new hypotheses . . .*

> *. . . they are **not only** collective goods but **also** display network effects . . .*

The location of the sentence adverb is important to meaning. In the examples below, the adverb *only* has scope over a

Sentence Adverbs

all, now, then, every day, today, yesterday, here, there, home, only, not, not only, therefore, also, too.

verb phrase, noun phrase, and a prepositional phrase. In the last example, the preposed sentence adverb triggers inversion in the main part of the sentence (underlined). Inversion is a change in the verbal construction, when the auxiliary is placed before the subject.

*English ceases to be an exponent of [**only** one culture]*$_{NP}$

*Beating it down into words and rules is [**only** a dead artifice of scientific analysis]*$_{NP}$

*This traditional notional definition, however, [**only** solves the problem by transferring it]*$_{VP}$

*We [can **only** account for collocation]*$_{VP}$ *if we assume that every word is mentally primed for collocational use.*

*. . . its true definition [can **therefore only** [be a genetic one]]*$_{VP}$

*[**Only** by adopting an integrative, dynamic framework]*$_{PP}$ <u>will we understand</u> *how they come about.*

Adverbs of Frequency

Adverbs of frequency like *always* and *sometimes* are single word constructions in sentences. They tend to be placed before a main verb in a sentence but immediately after auxiliaries or forms of *be*.

Adverbs of Frequency

always, sometimes, usually, often, rarely, never, seldom

*. . . the learner [**often** tends] to notice the feature in subsequent input . . .*

*. . . many students [**never** take] seriously the need to improve their editing skills.*

*The regularities of pattern [are **sometimes**] spectacular.*

*. . . these two knowledge systems [were **often** treated] as separate . . .*

*Such a group [is **usually** recognized] as having a syntactic structure.*

*Real-life teachers . . . [have **always** known] that students' errors are troublesome.*

As in the example with *only* above, some adverbs of frequency appear at the beginning of the sentence and trigger inversion in the verb phrase. These are hypothetical examples:

> [**Never** <u>have</u> *students taken*] *more seriously their need to improve their writing skills.*

> [**Seldom** <u>did</u> *learners notice*] *the feature unless it was salient.*

The negative adverbs (*seldom, never, rarely*, and *hardly*) do not occur with the negative sentential adverb *not* or negative forms of *do* (*don't, didn't*). This is part of the "double negative" problem of English that involves combinations of negative verbs, the negative quantifying determiner (*no*), and the indefinite pronouns (*nothing, no one, nobody*).

> *. . . the need to achieve an adequate proficiency in English language use [has* ***never*** *been] greater.*

Double negatives are common in many languages of the world and in many varieties of World Englishes and they are not illogical. As such, they are discussed further in Chapter 15.

Discovery Procedures

Sometimes English users are not sure whether to use an adjective or an adverb. Which of the sentences in the box is correct? The confusion lies in the distinction between a linking verb and a main verb. Linking verbs are *be, seem, feel, taste,* and other verbs of sensation. With linking verbs, a predicative adjective (or a noun) functions as a subject complement. With main verbs an adverb is used to modify the action of the verb. Because so many people have overgeneralized the idea that "adverbs modify verbs," they hypercorrect[1] *I feel bad* to *I feel badly.* The correct sentence is *I felt bad about the accident* because *feel* is a linking verb.

> **Adjective or Adverb?**
>
> I felt <u>bad</u> about the accident.
>
> I felt <u>badly</u> about the accident.

---

1. Hypercorrection is the activity of overusing a linguistic feature or using a feature incorrectly because of linguistic insecurity, overgeneralizing a pattern, or mislearning.

In general, *good* is an adjective and *well* is an adverb and they appear in this distribution:

I was in good health. I felt good. More colloquially US: *I am good.* (healthy)

I am in good health. I feel well. I am well. (healthy)

The blanket was soft and smooth. It felt good.

My car got a tune-up. It worked well.

The immigrants always did good and donated to charities. (good works)

The immigrants always did well at that company. (were successful; made money)

Participles, Adjectives, or Gerunds

There are three different ways to categorize forms that end in -*ing*. Sometimes differentiating a participial adjective or a gerund from verbal participles is very difficult.

Present participle of a verb:
Now they are <u>living</u> in Mumbai.

Participial adjective:
<u>Living</u> animals can be seen at the zoo.

Gerund:
<u>Living</u> in the city is necessary.

FORMS WITH -ING

Most of the examples with -*ing* in the database are a special type of nouns, called gerunds. These nouns are derived from verbs by adding the suffix -*ing*. In this quote, for example, there are five gerunds which display typical characteristics of nouns. They function as subjects of a sentence or objects of a preposition. On the other hand, they can also display verbal characteristics because they have a direct object, also indicated within the square brackets. The example which occurs with the determiner *the* in the final sentence requires that the direct object be expressed as a prepositional phrase with *of*.

This means that the task of "[learning a language]" must be reconceived. [Learning a language] is not a question of [acquiring grammatical structure]

*but of [expanding a repertoire of communicative contexts]. Consequently, there
is no date or age at which [the learning of a language] can be said to be complete.*

There are only a few examples of truly verbal present participles, as in this
sentence with a past perfect progressive form.

I [had been reading]$_{VP}$ *about formulaic language in the context of language
proficiency.*

There are some examples with participial adjectives ending in *-ing*. They are
clearly adjectives because they modify nouns and occur within the prototypical
colligation with determiners, but without intensifiers or adverbs. In the third
example, the participial adjective is conjoined with a word that is a descriptive
adjective, but there is also a classifying adjective modifying the noun *experience*.
Conjoined expressions are usually the same part of speech or, at the very least,
they perform the same function in the sentence.

As this [transmuting]$_{ADJP}$ *alchemy
of English takes effect . . .*

. . . the [growing]$_{ADJP}$ *respect for
real examples led in the mid-1980s
to a notion of textual well-
formedness.*

*A language is not a
[circumscribed]*$_{ADJP}$ *object but a
loose confederation of [available
and overlapping]*$_{ADJP}$ *[social]*$_{ADJP}$ *experiences.*

**Past participle of a verb
(passive):**
The theory has been
advanced by the researchers.

Participial adjective:
Advanced proficiency is a
requirement for the job.

In this last sentence, there is also a participial adjective ending in *-ed*.

FORMS WITH *-ED*

Participial adjectives end in *-ed* because they are derived from past participles
of verbs. In the first example below, the focal word *prefabricated* substitutes for
a word that is clearly an adjective (*formulaic*). Both of these words are meant to
modify the noun *language*. In the second case, the focal word *advanced* is
conjoined with a clear adjective (*intermediate*) and they both modify the noun
proficiency.

... *native speakers seem to find formulaic (that is, [prefabricated]$_{ADJP}$) language an easy option.*

[intermediate and advanced]$_{ADJP}$ proficiency

The following examples, and there are many of these in the corpus, are passive verbal constructions with *be* and the past participle because they are followed by a prepositional phrase with *by* that names the agent of the passive verb. These sentences have active paraphrases.

The morpheme . . . [may be revived]$_{V\ PASSIVE}$ [by education]$_{PP}$
Education [may revive]$_{V\ ACTIVE}$ the morpheme.

. . . established norms . . . [are naturally maintained]$_{V\ PASSIVE}$ [by a process of self-regulation]$_{PP}$
A process of self-regulation [naturally maintains]$_{V\ ACTIVE}$ established norms.

. . . these written modes [become increasingly used and appropriated]$_{V\ PASSIVE}$ [by non-native users]$_{PP}$ . . .
Non-native users [increasingly use and appropriate]$_{V\ ACTIVE}$ these written modes.

. . . the exact forms and meanings that speakers use [can be affected]$_{V\ PASSIVE}$ [by the language that occurred in discourse they recently engaged in]$_{PP}$
The language that occurred in discourse they recently engaged in [can affect]$_{V\ ACTIVE}$ the exact forms and meanings that speakers use.

However, the following examples show that, in the absence of a *by* phrase or some other diagnostic, it is impossible to distinguish passive verb forms from participial adjectives, so both of these analyses are possible.

. . . various [advanced]$_{ADJP}$ syntactic constructions that [are commonly associated]$_{V\ PASSIVE}$ with academic texts [seem to be largely missing]$_{V\ PROGRESSIVE}$ from NNS essays . . .

. . . various [advanced]$_{ADJP}$ syntactic constructions that are [commonly associated]$_{ADJP}$ with academic texts [seem to be largely missing]$_{V\ PROGRESSIVE}$ from NNS essays . . .

Syntactic ambiguity is the term for a case where a sequence of words corresponds to two different syntactic constructions. Sometimes meaning will disambiguate the two structures, as in this example caused by two different attachments of the prepositional phrase: *The man saw the woman [with binoculars]*$_{PP}$. In one meaning the man has the binoculars; in the other meaning, the woman does. However, in the cases indicated in the following paragraph it seems impossible and pointless to try to distinguish different structures, so this must be left as a "gray area" or overlapping area between two parts of speech, verbals and adjectives.

> *We can only account for collocation if we assume that every word is mentally [primed] for collocational use. As a word is [acquired] through encounters with it in speech and writing, it becomes cumulatively [loaded] with contexts and co-texts in which it is [encountered], and our knowledge of it includes the fact that it co-occurs with certain other words in certain kinds of context.*

Perhaps the important thing to note here is that the suffix *-ed* must occur; at times English users of all types omit the suffix. This is discussed in Chapter 14.

Awareness of Modification

Nowhere is the difference between conversation and academic prose more evident than in the use of adverbs. In conversation, over 60 percent of the adverbs are adverbs like *again, always, already, far, here, never, now, soon, still, then, yet, very, rather, quite,* and *pretty.* Only about 20 percent of the adverbs are *-ly* forms. In academic prose, it is the opposite; about 55 percent of the common adverbs are *-ly* forms like *generally, possibly, probably, certainly, obviously, rapidly, entirely, carefully, relatively, particularly, exactly, approximately,* and *slightly.* Only 30 percent of the adverbs are simple common adverbs (Biber et al., 1999, pp. 540–541).

Attributive descriptive and classifying adjectives and descriptive nouns contribute to the dense and complex structure of academic prose, because they add additional specificity or elaboration to the NPs.

> *In summary, [contemporary]*$_{ADJP}$ *approaches to [English language]*$_{NP}$ *teaching and learning emphasize the need for learners to engage in [purposeful]*$_{ADJP}$ *interaction using [spoken, written, and visual]*$_{ADJP}$ *modes. Learners are expected to be [critically literate]*$_{ADJP}$ *and able to create [accurate, contextually appropriate]*$_{ADJP}$ *texts.*

Modifiers are often used with generic nouns in academic prose. A search of the RAC academic corpus on the Lextutor website (http://www.lextutor.ca/concordancers/concord_e.html, retrieved 11/10/2012) on the key adjective *central* revealed these uses: *a central way, a central problem, a central role, a central issue, a central focus, a central component, a central factor, the central purpose, the central position, the central argument,* and *the central point.*

Predicative adjectives are less common in academic prose, unless they are of the participial type that look like passive verb forms.

In contrast, Hinkel (2002, p. 126) found that her English learning undergraduate writers used attributive adjectives significantly less than native-speaking undergraduates in their essays, but predicative adjectives were twice as common than they were in native-speaker essays. She explained these findings by pointing out the linking verb/predicative adjective colligation is fairly easy to construct, as shown in these examples from student papers:

In my country, farmers are poor, their work is hard, and nobody cares if they are happy with their lives.

The money-making is very important, of course.

Students who are loyal to their interests are happy in their study.

There are a number of ways to increase awareness of natural dense modification during students' writing assignments. **Sentence manipulation** activities involve learners in combining the information from two or more sentences using different types of modification. In **sentence combining** activities, learners are given two or more sentences to combine into one. Here are some examples in which NPs are made more complex with descriptive adjectives and nouns.

The cat was black. The cat lived in a barnyard. The cat liked to catch mice.

The black barnyard cat liked to catch mice.

Luna put the crown on her head. The crown was golden. The crown was for a princess.

Luna put the golden princess crown on her head.

A **sentence expanding** activity invites learners to use their imagination to add more details to a sentence. Learners must have sufficient metalinguistic awareness to understand the terms attributive adjective, descriptive noun, and prepositional phrase and to be able to create constructions. In this case, a descriptive adjective, a descriptive noun, and another prepositional phrase are added:

> *I bought shoes on my trip.*

> *I bought <u>red</u> <u>tennis</u> shoes on my trip <u>to the city</u>.*

Sentence manipulation can be modeled in class, but students can also learn to employ their awareness of modification while brainstorming or improving a draft paper during the writing process.

Study, Discussion, and Essay Questions

1. Review these terms and add them to your glossary with a definition and some examples if they are not already present: descriptive adjective, attributive adjective, predicative adjective, adverb of manner, gerund, classifying adjective, non-gradable adjectives, participial adjectives, pre-determiner, central determiner, postdeterminer, definite article, indefinite article, possessive determiner, demonstrative determiners, quantifying determiners, wh-words, sentence adverbs, adverbs of frequency.

2. Where do adjective phrases occur when they modify indefinite pronouns like *something* or *somebody*, or the pronoun *one*? Use Lextutor to see if you can find some examples of these constructions.

3. Identify the underlined words in the following expressions as either descriptive nouns or adjectives (either descriptive or classifying). Use the diagnostics and make a note of any difficulties you encounter. The most relevant diagnostics are derivational morphology, potential comparative inflections, use of intensifiers, and the paraphrase for nouns.

> *a <u>global</u> system*
> *<u>communication</u> value*
> *<u>economic</u> goods*
> *their <u>accumulated</u> <u>textual</u> capital*
> *a <u>better</u> <u>material</u> life*
> *<u>language</u> growth and decline*

4. The construction *English speakers* is an example of **lexical ambiguity**. (Lexical ambiguity means that a construction has more than one meaning because the words have multiple meanings and/or belong to more than one syntactic category.) What are the two meanings of English? Hint: one meaning is vastly more common than the other.

5. This chapter suggests that there is a continuum of priming associations in compound nouns, noun–noun collocations, and innovative noun–noun combinations. Create innovative noun–noun combinations by combining words from these lists like this example: *lifeline media*.

> List 1: lifeline, education, competence, pamphlet, negligence, equipment, plant

> List 2: system, strategy, process, media, literature, rhetoric, expert, matter, task

What does each word mean on its own? What does the combination mean? Do definite or indefinite determiners make a difference in their meaning?

6. What is "wrong" with these modifying constructions? What kind of knowledge did you use to fix them? What problems did you have doing this exercise?

> *the Western generalization differing abilities*
> *text powerful overt events*
> *reciprocal negotiation general patterns*
> *culture large negotiation abilities*

7. Review the three types of adverbs discussed in this chapter and give examples of each from Lextutor.

8. In this quote, identify the part of speech of the underlined forms with the *-ing* ending. Recall that they could be gerunds, participial adjectives, or present progressive verb forms.

> *Students themselves are very concerned about accuracy, and . . . <u>responding</u> effectively to students' grammatical and lexical problems is a <u>challenging</u> endeavor fraught with uncertainty about its long term effectiveness.*

9. Are the underlined examples in these quotes attributive participial adjectives, predicative participial adjectives, or passive verb forms with the helping verb *be*?

> *Ideally one would like to have a rigorous, possibly statistically <u>determined</u> way to define what is <u>meant</u> by a "common" or "frequent" expression.*

> *Most fluent speakers of English seem to know what a word is. They know, for example, that words are <u>listed</u> in dictionaries, that they are <u>separated</u> in writing by spaces, and that they may be <u>separated</u> in speech by pauses.*

10. Why do English learners avoid the passive and predicative participial adjectives and overuse other predicative adjectives?

Activities

1. Read the following paragraph from Recinto (1998, pp. 86–87) and answer the questions below.

> Unlike Canada, which passed the Official Languages Act of 1969, and Australia, with its National Policy on Languages (1987) and the Australian Language and Literacy Policy (1991), the United States has never attempted to articulate, let alone implement, a national language policy. When language matters are addressed at the federal level, usually in legislation or in higher court rulings, the goals usually center around the solution of long-standing social problems, most frequently to redress violations of constitutional and statutory civil rights. Therefore, to accurately characterize language policies, one must situate such government actions within broader social policy issues and sociohistorical processes. For example, to understand the goals of the Bilingual Education Act of 1968, one needs to understand why that legislation was passed when it was passed, whose interests were being served, what the general policy framework was with regard to minority languages and speakers of those languages, what sort of support was or wasn't provided to implement the legislation, what the prevailing social attitudes were at the time regarding bilingual education, and so on.

   a. What does this quote say? Put it in your own words in a paragraph in your Language Notebook.
   b. What language policies do you have (or not have) in your region or nation? Write a paragraph and share it with your classmates.
   c. What characteristics of this text make it an example of Academic English?

d. What specific structures might be difficult for an English learner to understand?

e. In the quotation above, identify all the descriptive and classifying adjectives. Make sure that you distinguish them from descriptive nouns, gerunds, or verbal forms. Use morphology, syntax, paraphrase, and function as cues; don't guess. Use both positive and negative evidence. (If you can figure out that a word is not an adjective, it might be a noun. If it is not a noun, it might be an adjective.) Make a note of any problems you have and discuss.

2. Think of a creative and interesting sentence manipulation activity or game to work with noun–noun compounds, descriptive noun + noun combinations or adjective + noun combinations. Make your grammatical explanation match the grade level you select. If your chosen grade level is fourth grade or lower, or composed of learners with low English proficiency, consider whether to make your activity oral or written. For these learners, the activity can also be based on pictures and not a text to be read. For any other learners, the activity should be both oral and written. How would you assess learning after your activity? Share your activity with your classmates.

3. Create a form/meaning pairing, or construction, for the word *mentally*, as in this excerpt from the corpus: *Every word is <u>mentally</u> primed for collocational use.*

Form: syntactic properties
morphological properties
phonological properties
orthographic properties

$[[X]_{ADV}]$
_____
_____
_____

↕   ↕

Meaning: semantic properties
pragmatic properties
discourse properties

_____
_____
_____

Verbal Constructions **10**

VERB [14c: from Latin *verbum* word] A class of words that serve to indicate the occurrence or performance of an action, or the existence of a state or condition: in English, such words (given here in the infinitive with to) as *to climb, to cultivate, to descend, to fish, to laugh, to realize, to walk.* Although many verbs in English have the same base form as nouns (*climb, fish, hound, love, walk*), they are morphologically and syntactically a distinct word class and one of the traditional parts of speech. There are two main types: full verb, auxiliary verb. In terms of form, full verbs divide into regular and irregular verbs. Auxiliaries may be further divided into primary auxiliaries (*be, have, do*) and modal auxiliaries or modal verbs (*may, can, will, shall, must, ought to, need, dare*).

(McArthur, 1992, p. 1083)

McArthur's introduction to verbal constructions touches on the prototypical communicative function for verbal constructions; they are predicates of action or state. Predication is a way that people indicate the relationships among the entities in a focal situation, the mental or physical actions that they perform, or the mental or physical states that they find themselves in. McArthur tells us that there are **finite** verbal constructions like *he climbs, she fishes, they love* as well as **non-finite** verbals which do not have any inflectional markings for time or person.

Finite verbal constructions generally have person and tense inflections that make them quite different from their homonym noun forms (*climb, fish, love*). Finite verbal constructions involve two types of words: main verbs and auxiliaries. Verbs are resource words, but auxiliaries are system words. There are two types of auxiliaries. **Primary auxiliaries** are the words *have*, *be*, and *do*, used to support the system of aspects, voice, tense, and negativity in English. **Modal auxiliaries** interact with this same system, lending nuances of probability, possibility, ability, obligation, futurity, and conditionality. In speech people pronounce auxiliaries with less stress and emphasis, so they blur into the words surrounding them. When people write informally, this "blurring" of speech is represented with contracted forms such as *he's*, *she's*, *it's*, *isn't*, *don't*, *hasn't*, *can't*, *won't*, and so on. Writers often avoid such contracted forms in academic style.

Finite Verbal Constructions

Main verbs: *climbs, fishes, loves, . . .*

Primary auxiliaries: *have, has, do, does, did, be, am*

Modal auxiliaries: *can, could, will, would, . . .*

Non-finite Verbal Constructions

Infinitives with *to*: *to climb, to fish, to love, . . .*

Bare infinitives: *climb, fish, love*

Present participle: *climbing, fishing, loving*

Past participle: *climbed, fished, loved*

Verbal constructions are very numerous in informal registers like conversation, emails, and fiction but less numerous in academic prose. In these examples, the finite verbal constructions are underlined and the non-finite

Informal Text

A woman <u>walks</u> into the kitchen TO FIND her husband STALKING around with a fly swatter.
"What <u>are</u> you DOING?" she <u>asks</u>.
"HUNTING flies," he <u>responds</u>.
"Oh. KILLING any?" she <u>asks</u>.
"Yep, three males, two females," he <u>replies</u>.
Intrigued, she <u>asks</u>, "How <u>can</u> you TELL them apart?"
He <u>responds</u>, "Three <u>were</u> on the TV, and two <u>were</u> on the phone."

verbal constructions are in capital letters. In conversations, stories, and emails, the present tense refers to past time (as in jokes or news reporting), present time (as in sports), or future time. The **progressive** aspect, formed with the primary auxiliary *be* and the non-finite verbal with the inflection -*ing*, is common in informal writing and conversation.

> **Academic Text**
>
> *The rationale of acquisition theory <u>has</u> CHANGED accordingly, if the child <u>has</u> TO LEARN the irregular and peculiar aspects of language by general learning mechanisms, these mechanisms <u>should</u> SUFFICE TO LEARN the more general and predictable patterns of that language as well.*

In contrast, in academic prose, the present tense expresses facts that are not limited to a specific timeframe. The **perfective** aspect is used in academic prose to refer to past ideas, theories or experiments still relevant to the present idea, theory or experiment. In the example in the box, there are two uses of the form *has*. The first one is the primary auxiliary *has* paired with the past participle to express the perfective aspect. The second one is a main verb *has* combined with the non-finite form *to learn* (an infinitive) to express obligation or necessity. The last example, *should suffice to learn*, is a complex verbal construction that combines a modal auxiliary (*should*), a non-finite main verb in the form of a bare infinitive (*suffice*), and another non-finite form, an infinitive (*to learn*). In this example, it is possible to see that in academic prose, complex NPs are more common than verbal constructions.

> **Present:**
> **0 marking on verb:**
> *I, you, we, they provide*
> **3rd person singular marking:**
> *he, she, it provides*
>
> **Past:**
> *provided*

Finite Main Verbs

These examples of simple finite main verbs from the corpus show tense markings in inflections. They are marked for either present or past in form even though there are sometimes no overt signs of inflection. Finite main verbs are prototypical in that the subject of the verb is the agent of the action, so these verbal constructions are called active (i.e. not passive, discussed later). Recall from Chapter 7 that these prototypical verbal constructions can have different colligations; they can be transitive or intransitive, or they can involve a linking verb with a subject complement.

> [C]lassroom L2 writing teachers [**provide**] their learners with both oral feedback as well as written feedback on the more "treatable" types of linguistic error on a regular basis.

> If we [**believe**] that learning an L2 [**is**] a process of socialization where we are learning to construct new sociocultural identities and to reshape our subjectivity, then we [**need**] a theory of language that enables us to understand how grammar is implicated in such processes . . .

> Practice [**gets**] a raw deal in the field of applied linguistics . . . For some, the word [**conjures up**] images of mind-numbing drills in the sweatshops of foreign language learning, while for others it [**means**] fun and games to appease students on Friday afternoons.

(In the example sentence with the verb *get*, the subject is arguably not the logical agent but rather a recipient.)

Finite main verbs are also coupled with non-finite verbal constructions, sometimes with an object NP or prepositional phrase, as in the example *rely <u>on formulaic language</u> to get themselves started*. Sometimes the NP after the main verb is understood as the subject of the following infinitive, as in the example *enables us to understand*. Not all verbs can occur freely in these constructions, but constructions with to-infinitives or bare infinitives are very productive. On the other hand, examples of main verbs with the present participle are rare in academic writing.[1]

Complex Main Verb Colligation

$$[[V] + ([NP]) + [V]_{TO\text{-}INFINITIVE}]_V$$

> The special characteristics of language, language groups and their accumulated textual capital [**help to explain**] the dynamics of language acquisition . . .

---

1. However, one example from the database deserves a mention: *Numerous definitions have been offered and <u>found wanting</u>*, which is a formula with an archaic collocation within it. *Found wanting* means "to be lacking," based on the archaic equivalence of "want" with "lack."

*. . . native speakers [**seem to find**] formulaic . . . language an easy option*

*Learners [**rely on** formulaic language **to get themselves started**] . . .*

*. . . we need a theory of language that [**enables** us **to understand**] how grammar is implicated in such processes . . .*

*. . . for others it [**means** fun and games **to appease**] students on Friday afternoons.*

*Innate linguistic structure [**helps** the child **overcome**] the (possible) underspecification of language structure in the input.*

*Parents [**make** their kids **practice**] their piano skills at home.*

Complex Main Verb Colligation

$$[[V] + ([NP]) + [V]_{\text{BARE INFINITIVE}}]_V$$

Primary Auxiliaries and Main Verbs

Primary auxiliaries mark verb phrases with information about tense, negativity, and aspect. Negative sentences use the primary auxiliary *do* with a bare infinitive. Perfect aspect, with *have* and the past participle of the main verb, indicates that the situation talked about occurred in the past, but it is still relevant to the present. Progressive aspect, with *be* and the present participle, indicates that the situation described is still in progress, and not completed.

Perfect aspect:	*The rationale of acquisition theory [<u>has</u> changed] accordingly.*
Progressive aspect:	*the type of progress every nation . . . [<u>is</u> trying] to achieve*
Negative:	*to disqualify all arguments which [<u>do</u> not fit] the mainstream ideological stance*

The forms of *have*, *do*, and *be* also occur as main verbs, and not just as auxiliaries, as shown in these examples from the database.

Bare infinitive *have*:	*the categories or principles of core syntax do not [<u>have</u> to be learned]*

Main verb *be*:	*Language [is] a dynamic system.*
Infinitive *do*:	*I find it better to try [to <u>do</u>] more (and more varied)*
	empirical research.

Primary Auxiliary do

Emphatic/Negative Colligation

When a main verb occurs with the primary auxiliary *do*, the auxiliary is marked with

$[do] + (not) + [V]_{\text{BARE INFINITIVE}}$

inflections and the main verb is a bare infinitive form. This is a mixed construction that combines lexical items (*do*) in inflected forms (*do, does, did*) and a variable for any appropriate verb in bare infinitive form. If this verbal construction is not negative, it is meant to signal emphasis and contrast with a previous idea, as in these examples from the database. Note also the use of the primary auxiliary *do* with the negative adverb *not* (underlined).

> *First, the teacher must realize that a mistake has been made. The well-known problems involved in proofreading show that this step cannot be taken for granted . . . If teachers [**do recognize**] an error, they still may not have a good understanding of the correct use—questions regarding grammar can be very difficult, even for experts, and someone who writes or speaks English well **<u>does not</u>** <u>necessarily</u> **<u>understand</u>** the principles involved . . . Thus, teachers may well know that an error has occurred but not know exactly why it is an error. If they [**do understand**] it well, they might be unable to give a good explanation; problems that need explaining are often very complex.*

Have and Perfect Aspect

Perfect Colligation

When *have* is the auxiliary, and the non-finite main verb is the past participle, the

$[[have] + [V]]_{\text{PAST PARTICIPLE}}]_{V}$

verb has **perfect aspect**. This is a mixed construction that combines lexical items (*have*) in inflected forms (*have, has, had*) and a variable V for any appropriate verb in the form of a past participle. Perfect aspect is an invitation to view the relationship expressed by the verb with respect to another vantage point of time, usually the present (*They <u>have</u> already <u>eaten</u>*), sometimes the past (*They <u>had</u> already <u>eaten</u> before going to the movie*), or the future (*They <u>will have</u> already <u>eaten</u> before they arrive here*). Between 5 and 10 percent of all verb forms in conversation, news, fiction, and academic prose have perfect aspect. Here are some verbs often in perfect tense in academic prose and news (Biber et al., 1999, p. 463).

agree	*draft*	*witness*
appoint	*experience*	*document*
campaign	*pledge*	*implicate*
circulate	*prompt*	*master*
criticize	*vow*	*report*

In these examples, the connection between the past and the present that is the basis for the perfect aspect is obvious.

> *In contrast, the so-called emergentist and usage-based approaches to language acquisition, that [**have become**] prominent in the past decade . . .*

> *Asking what morphemes a word contains and what they mean is asking what the coiner of the word had in mind when he coined it and possibly what unforeseen associations it [may **have built up**] since.*

> *First and foremost, the ability to examine large text corpora in a systematic manner allows access to a quality of evidence that [**has** not **been**] available before.*

Be *and Progressive Aspect*

When *be* is the primary auxiliary, and the main verb is the present participle, the verb has progressive aspect. This means that the relationship expressed by the verb

Progressive Colligation

$[be + [V]_{\text{PRESENT PARTICIPLE}}]_V$

is to be viewed as in progress, or as continuing over a period of time. (Sometimes this verb form is called **continuous**.) This aspect is less frequent than the perfect aspect in news, fiction, and academic writing, but in conversation progressive aspect is twice as common as perfect (Biber et al., 1999, p. 462). It is also a very regular form. Perhaps that explains why native-speaking children learn this verb form early and English learners have fewer problems with it. Certain verbs, especially verbs of mental state, rarely appear in the progressive because their meaning is not compatible with an "in progress" aspect: *understand, believe, know, comprehend, mean, doubt, want,* and *prefer.* There is diversity in this feature in World Englishes, as discussed further in Chapter 14.

Progressive is a mixed construction which combines the primary auxiliary *be* in its various persons and tenses and a verb in the present participle form. Perfect and progressive can be combined in a more complex verbal construction, but these are somewhat uncommon. In the following examples from the corpus, the progressive meaning is obvious:

> *On the other hand, various advanced syntactic constructions that are commonly associated with academic texts seem to [**be** largely **missing**] from NNS essays . . .*

> *I [**had been reading**] about formulaic language in the context of language proficiency, and had been struck by three observations made in the literature.*

Be and Passive Voice

In passive constructions, the subject is not the agent; rather, the entity that would normally be the direct object is the subject of the passive verb. Passive constructions are mixed constructions with the auxiliary *be* and the past participle of the main verb.

> *. . . **established norms** . . .[are naturally maintained] by a process of self-regulation.*

> *A process of self-regulation [naturally maintains] **established norms**.*

Authors use passive verbs when they are trying to convey a certain detachment and objectivity in their writing. They choose the passive to de-emphasize the agent, especially if they aren't sure who it is. If the agent is present, it appears in a prepositional phrase with *by*, underlined in the first example below. Passives are very common in academic prose, but they are rare in conversation. The perfect passive combination also occurs frequently in academic prose and news, sometimes with main verbs like *get* instead of *be*, as shown in the last example.

Passive Colligation

[be + [V]PAST PARTICIPLE]V

> *The morpheme at best continues to live a parasitic life within the word. It remains half alive for one speaker and dies for the next; or it [**may** be revived] by education.*

*I find it better to try to do more (and more varied) empirical research on how ELF [**is** actually **used**]* . . .

*The present multicultural character of English [**is** clearly **revealed**] in its uses around the globe, especially in creative writing.* (But note the difficulty in distinguishing between passive verbs and participial adjectives.)

*. . . the input [has to **be mapped**] onto innate linguistic categories*

*. . . it [**has** recently **been suggested**] that they are connected*

*Once a learner's consciousness of a target feature [**has been raised**] through formal instruction . . .*

*Learners rely heavily on formulaic language [to **get** themselves **started**].*

The following passive verbs are common in academic prose and news (Biber et al., 1999, p. 477):

done	explained	injured	designed
born	formed	jailed	distributed
told	identified	killed	documented
said	illustrated	named	estimated
expected	introduced	released	extracted
held	limited	revealed	grouped with
achieved	noted	shot	intended
associated	observed	sold	labeled
defined	presented	aligned with	linked to/with
expressed	recognized	based on	located at/in
measured	regarded	deemed	plotted
obtained	replaced	effected	recruited
performed	represented	entitled to	stored
related	studied	flattened	transferred
applied	suggested	inclined	viewed
calculated	accused	obliged	coupled with
chosen	announced	positioned	associated with
compared	arrested	situated	attributed to
derived	beaten	stained	classified as
designed	believed	subjected to	diagnosed as
developed	charged	approved	
discussed	delighted	composed of	
examined	hit	confined to	

Modal Auxiliaries

Modal auxiliaries (e.g. *can, could, will, would, shall, should, must*) are frequent constituents of verbal constructions; they are system words and finite verbals because they carry the tense in the verbal construction, even though it doesn't show in any inflections. They are called auxiliaries because they support the main verb and they are called modals because they contribute to the **mood** that the verb has. Mood refers to concepts like ability, possibility, future, conditionality, permission, obligation, necessity, hypothesis, and so on. *Can, may, must,* and *should* are common in academic prose, possibly because they lend a speculative mood of logical possibility to scientific claims. (Semi-modal constructions are *ought to, had better, used to,* and *be supposed to.* These are more common in conversation than in academic prose. There is diversity in the use of some of these, indicating some instability. For example, people often say *He better go,* but the standard for writing is *He'd better go.*)

Modals combine with bare infinitives. In these examples, the modal auxiliary is in bold print, and the bare infinitive is in capital letters.

We [**shall** CONSIDER] the word as an uninterruptible unit of structure consisting of one or more morphemes and which typically occurs in the structure of phrases.

But innate structure, as rich as it [**may** BE], [**cannot** ACCOUNT] for the acquisition of language-specific properties.

These results suggest that parsing decisions [**may** DEPEND] in part on the person's history of experience.

Only by adopting an integrative, dynamic framework [**will** we UNDERSTAND] how they come about.

This means that the task of "learning a language" [**must** BE reconceived].

In the end, teacher trainers and teachers [**may** NEED to be reminded] that the academic skills they themselves require in teaching and learning are not far removed from those of their NNS students.

Modal auxiliary meanings are subtle and the differences among them are very fuzzy. Because they are unstressed in spoken English, they can be hard to hear, so students may lack oral knowledge of them to apply in their writing.

When they write, they may avoid using modals altogether because they seem complicated.

Discovery Procedures

Valency (V) refers to the number of syntactic elements, or **arguments**, that are required or permitted by verbs. The first argument is outside the verb phrase; it is the subject of the sentence. The other arguments are the referential NPs in the verb phrase (e.g. objects and prepositional phrases). Descriptive nouns, subject/object complements, and adverbials are not arguments of the verb because they don't refer to people or entities in the focal situation. There are a few verbs that permit four arguments, like *bet*, but they are unusual. *Bet* is V^4 because its valency allows four possible arguments: <u>*My brother*</u> *bet* <u>*me*</u> <u>*5 dollars*</u> *on* <u>*that candidate*</u> *to win.* However, most verbs are V^0, V^1, V^2, and V^3.

V^0 verbal constructions are impersonal constructions that have an *it* placeholder or dummy subject.

V^0 <u>*It*</u> *[is reasonable].*

V^1 verbal constructions have one argument, the subject of the sentence. They are intransitive verbs, linking verbs with a subject complement, or passive constructions without a *by*-phrase.

V^1 <u>*My past*</u> *[is my tradition].*

V^2 verb phrases are **transitive** verbs with a subject and a direct object.

V^2 <u>*Correct English language use*</u> *requires* <u>*the possession of a competence*</u> . . .

V^3 verb phrases are **ditransitive** verbs with a subject, a direct object, and an indirect object. In this case, the pronoun *it* refers to English; it is given information, not new.

V^3 <u>*The users*</u> *give [*<u>*it*</u>*]*$_{IO}$ *[*<u>*a distinct identity of their own*</u>*]*$_{DO}$ *in each region.*

Ditransitive verbs like *give* offer another option for English users, a verb phrase construction called the **prepositional dative** because it involves the use of *to* or *for* as a marker for the indirect object. The objects appear in reversed order.

Ditransitive VP: *The users give [English]*$_{IO}$ *[a distinct identity]*$_{DO}$
Prepositional dative VP: *The users give [a distinct identity]*$_{DO}$ *[to English]*$_{IO}$

Examples of ditransitive or prepositional dative sentences are rare in the corpus used in this book, but they are used in general to highlight different information. They are options for speakers and writers as they choose how to express their ideas in discourse. The paraphrases have different senses, in terms of what is given and what is new information. The first sentence is about the given information, English, and says something new about it; the second sentence is about the users transferring their identity to English, the new information.

[The users] give [English] [a distinct identity of their own] in each region.
[The users] give [a distinct identity of their own] [to English] in each region.

The choice of the ditransitive construction or the prepositional dative construction comes down to the relative degree of given or new information. The established or given constituent occurs near the verb, while the new or emphatic information occurs later as the second object (as direct object or the object of a preposition).

Both the ditransitive VP construction and the prepositional dative VP construction are productive in modern English but they are not necessarily common. Their usage is item-based because verbs have different preferences or probabilities for their occurrence in one construction or the other. For instance, although *give* and other common verbs allow both VP construction options, *donate* is primed to appear in the prepositional dative VP construction. In general, verbs of Latinate origin are less acceptable in the ditransitive construction and more acceptable in the prepositional dative.

Ditransitive preference: *ask, allow, refuse, charge (money), wish, cost*

Prepositional dative preference: *donate, explain, acknowledge, admit, announce, communicate, declare, describe, introduce, point out, prove, repeat, report, speak*

Both: *give, bring, deny, do, grant, leave, offer, pass, pay, promise, read, send, serve, show, take, teach, tell, write*

Prepositional dative: *The students donated the books to the school.*
Ditransitive: **The students donated the school the books.*

Some common verbs, like *ask, allow, refuse,* and *wish,* are primed to occur with a ditransitive preference:

> Ditransitive: *The students asked the teacher the question.*
> Prepositional dative: **The students asked the question to the teacher.*

Because these constructions are item-based, they are acquired through usage, exposure, and ample practice.

Verbal Awareness

Academic texts employ fewer verbs than do conversations, fiction, and informal writing. Except for those written about historical events, academic texts are predominantly simple active or passive, present or perfect, or combination verbal constructions as shown in this example from the corpus:

> *The need to achieve an adequate proficiency in English language use [**has** never **been**] greater. Its position as the primary language of international communication in almost every field of professional activity [**means**] that its acquisition at a sufficiently advanced level [**is expected**] from graduates of secondary and tertiary education. Correct English language use in speech and in writing [**requires**] the possession of a competence which [**includes**] the knowledge of grammar rules and vocabulary items, as well as the ability to use them in real-life contexts.*

In the corpus for this book, there are no texts exclusively written with past tense, but occasionally academic texts shift back and forth from past to present depending on the perspective of the author. In the example below, the author establishes a point in the distant past with the past perfect progressive form and the past perfect passive form in the first sentences. The first two observations made by the author are then placed in a recent simple past form, but the verbal constructions that follow the past tense verbals are placed in the present tense (*seem, rely*) because they are viewed as facts that are always true. The third observation is placed entirely in the past, perhaps to match the past tense in the rhetorical question. These switches from past to present and back are subtle rhetorical devices to signal the author's attitude and perspective.

> *I [**had been reading**] about formulaic language in the context of language proficiency, and [**had been struck**] by three observations made in the literature.*

*The first [**was**] that native speakers [**seem to find**] formulaic (that is, prefabricated) language an easy option in their processing and/or communi-cation. The second [**was**] that in the early stages of first and second language acquisition, learners [**rely** heavily on formulaic language **to get** themselves started]. The third observation, however, [**seemed to fly**] in the face of the first two. For L2 learners of intermediate and advanced proficiency, the formulaic language [**was**] the biggest stumbling block to sounding nativelike. How [**could** [something that was so easy when you began with a language, and so easy when you [**were**] fully proficient in it], **be**] so difficult in between?*

Hinkel, in her study of L2 undergraduate writers-in-training, found that the writers were not as accomplished at switching from past to present, as these examples show:

*For example, I **used to think** that I am good at science. However, after I **evaluate** myself and **receive** some inputs from my teachers, I am convinced that science **is** not the study field I am good at . . .*

*My uncle **studied** hospitality in Switzerland. He just **found out** that hospitality **does not fit** him when he **had** the job in the field.*

In general, the perfect aspect and the passive voice constructions are hard for NNSs to acquire and use in appropriate contexts, and they avoided using them in the texts they wrote. They also avoided the use of the modal *would*, when compared to the native-speaking writers-in-training. The L2 writers used the linking verb *be* with predicate adjectives and made statements that were simplistic and not dense or complex. In the corpus used in this book, the use of linking verbs is common, but they are far from ideationally simple. The linking verb appears with complex predicate adjectives and predicate noun phrases, as shown in the example below. This example also exemplifies the predominance of very complex noun phrases (underlined) over verbal con-structions (bold) in academic texts:

*Psycholinguistic and cognitive linguistic theories of language acquisition **hold** that all linguistic units [**are**] abstracted from language use. In these usage-based perspectives, the acquisition of grammar [**is**] the piecemeal learning of many thousands of constructions and the frequency-biased abstraction of regularities within them. Language learning [**is**] the associative learning of representations that reflect the probabilities of occurrence of form-function mappings. Frequency [**is**] thus a key determinant of acquisition because "rules" of language, at all* *levels of analysis (from phonology, through syntax, to discourse), [**are**] structural regularities that [**emerge**] from learners' lifetime analysis of the distributional characteristics of the language input.*

Hinkel found that the more complex the verb phrase construction, the less likely it was to be selected by English learners in their academic writing. In addition, there was an unusually high number of past tense verbs because the learners relied on personal narratives of their past experiences for their rhetorical force and evidence. They also selected public and private verbs that conveyed personal feelings and beliefs and relied on a few common persuasive verbs (*ask, prefer, require,* and *recommend*). Hinkel (2002, p. 117) has this example from an English learner's text:

> *In the first quarter, she complained to me that it was a very difficult major. After several quarters she told me it was not hard as the first time. She said it was the right major for her.*

Types of Verbs

Public: *acknowledge, add, admit, announce, protest, remark, reply, suggest*

Private: *accept, anticipate, determine, discover, doubt, know, learn, remember, prove, study*

Persuasive: *allow, ask, determine, insist, intend, request, require, prefer, recommend*

Logical-semantic relationships: *accompany, approximate, compare, complement, conflict, occur*

Tentative: *attempt, expect, plan, try, want, wonder*

Hinkel strongly recommends that learners try to increase their lexical variety in the choice of verbs as well as the range of verbal constructions that they feel comfortable using. She argues that "whereas in L2 settings it is possible to attain conversational fluency without learning to employ advanced and academic language features, writing an academic essay may require a different set of vocabulary and syntactic constructions that are not found outside academic discourse and texts" (Hinkel, 2002, p. 117).

Study, Discussion, and Essay Questions

1. Review these terms and add them to your glossary with a definition and some examples if they are not already present: non-finite verbals, finite

verbals, primary auxiliaries, modal auxiliaries, perfective aspect, progressive or continuous aspect, passive voice, bare infinitive, *to*-infinitive, past participle, present participle, verbs of mental state, valency, V^0, V^1, V^2, V^3, ditransitive verb phrases, prepositional datives, public verbs, private verbs, persuasive verbs, logical-semantic verbs, and tentative verbs.

2. Verbal constructions are based on the communicative function of predication; what is predication?

3. Why is it hard to pick up information about auxiliaries in speech?

4. Which verb tenses/forms are most common in informal speaking? Which are most common in academic writing?

5. Explain how the primary auxiliary *do* is used for emphasis and negative? Is it also used to form questions?

6. What verbs are not commonly found in progressive aspects in academic writing? Why? Are there some exceptions to this generalization from your usage of English?

7. Convert this sentence from active to passive. What did you have to do? (Besides the usual changes, you need to use the preposition *in* rather than *by* for the "subject" of the passive sentence.) *Proofreading involves well-known problems.*

8. Are passive verbal constructions difficult to distinguish from linking verbs with adjectives derived from past participles? Why?

9. What does each of the modal auxiliaries mean, at least approximately (*may/might, can/could, will/would, shall/should, must*)? What are the semi-modal constructions?

10. Write a sentence with a verbal construction of V^0, V^1, V^2, V^3.

11. Using the verb *take*, write a ditransitive sentence and a prepositional dative sentence. Try to use complex NPs. What differences are there in meaning? Then do the same for the verb *make*. (With *make*, the prepositional dative uses *for*.)

12. Below is one way to correct the sentence: *My uncle studied hospitality in Switzerland. He just found out that hospitality does not fit him when he had the job in the field.*

   Correction: *My uncle studied hospitality in Switzerland. He just found out that hospitality ~~does~~ **did** not fit him when he ~~had the~~ **got** a job in the field.*

   Articulate what changes were made and why you think they were made.

13. What does Hinkel (2002) report about L2 writers' awareness of verbal constructions?

Activities

1. These are some inflectional difficulties that some learners have in their writing. They are subject–verb agreement problems, non-standard or colloquial forms, or missing inflections. Some might be problems in academic writing but not in speaking. In pairs, first say the correct sentence, then explain to your partner which type of problem it is. Explain what the correct form should be. The first one is done for you.

    a. My dad seen a huge truck coming down our street.

    > *Seen* should be *saw. My dad saw a huge truck coming down our street.* The correct past tense for *see* is *saw* and not *seen*. *Seen* is a non-standard past tense form that is not appropriate for academic writing.

    b. Here's the five reasons for buying that stove.
    c. There was too many taxes to pay in that state.
    d. Then I says, "Give me all my money right now."
    e. The deciduous tree lose all its leaves in winter.
    f. My mother going to her office today.
    g. The order was cancel because of lack of funds.
    h. This flower grow best in full sunlight.
    i. They brung their schoolbooks with them.
    j. Those kids done their work already.
    k. The underlying tone of the wall colors were too dark.

2. Passive voice: Some English learners made these mistakes with passive or participial adjective constructions in the paragraphs they wrote. Role play with a partner. Take turns explaining to a learner what his/her error is in a one-on-one writing conference. Errors have to do with missing or incorrect primary or modal auxiliaries, past participles, subjects/objects, prepositions, or other errors. Tell your partner if the errors obscure the meaning the writer is trying to convey (global error) or if they are details that readers notice (local) but do not impede understanding. After explaining the inaccurate usage, tell your partner what the correct sentence is. Ask him/her to make up a similar correct sentence.

    a. Spanish spoken in my country.
    b. My city found in 1800 for missionaries.
    c. This book is suppose to be returned to the bookstore.
    d. They cans be prove the results by the scientists.

e.   The details will added later.

f.   One not smoke here.

g.   He was disturb by the news.

h.   This word is spell wrong.

i.   The paragraph was described the landscape.

j.   The chicken kabob been eaten already.

k.   The president of the company was consider an expert.

l.   The speeder stop for the police.

3.   Use the Lextutor website and the Brown corpus to determine the VP construction preferences for different verbs. Do a search on the verbs *lend, refer, owe,* and *explain* to find out if they seem to prefer the ditransitive construction, the prepositional dative construction, or both. Copy some of the structures you find into your Language Notebook.

Both (like *give*):

Ditransitive (like *ask*):

Prepositional dative (like *donate*):

What difficulties did you have with this exercise?

Sentences   **11**

SENTENCE [12c: through old French from Latin *sententia* a way of thinking, opinion, judgment] . . . The largest structural unit normally treated in grammar. The sentence is notoriously difficult to define; numerous definitions have been offered and found wanting. The classical definition, that a sentence expresses a complete thought, dates from the first Western treatise on grammar, by Dionysius Thrax (c. 100 BC) . . . This traditional notional definition, however, only solves the problem by transferring it: how does one define a complete thought?

(McArthur, 1992, p. 918)

McArthur points out that, just like other concepts in language analysis, the definition of "sentence" is problematic. It became an issue when writing and the study of grammar started taking on more significance for Greeks and Romans around 2,000 years ago. One early solution to the "sentence" problem was to define a sentence as a complete thought, and a complete thought as a unit with a topic and a comment about the topic, or, in other words, a subject (the **topic**) and a predicate (the **comment**). However, it has always been clear that the definition of "complete thought" is different in informal speech or writing. The concept of a complete thought begins at the lowest level of conscious awareness of language, such as the use of inserts like *yes* or *no*.

Complete Thoughts

Analytical processing is the creation of "complete thoughts" using knowledge of abstract pattern-based constructions at the phrasal and sentential level. Holistic processing involves the choice of a formulaic construction that conveys a complete thought. However, a comparison of informal conversational utterances like those in Chapter 1 with informal writing makes it plausible to think that analytical and holistic processing for conversation and writing may differ.

Utterances

The constituents that express "complete thoughts" in informal utterances tend to be words, phrases, inserts, and collocations. Stylistically, there are many questions, pronouns, and verbs. Conversational constituents are dependent on other utterances because each utterance is incomplete on its own but complete when it is understood in the context of other utterances in the conversation. The dependence is based on cooperation between the interlocutors in the conversation, so it involves scaffolding. The units in speech are called **adjacency pairs**, which are utterances that are coherent only in the presence of the utterance that precedes or follows. In the examples from Biber et al. (1999), the academic lecturers intentionally adopt a conversational style to make their explanations more accessible to their listeners.

Now there is no bar to having more than one particle in each state. Quite the contrary.

But what is that? Is it a number? Well . . . yes. It can't be a real number since its square is negative. Of course.

(Biber et al., 1999, pp. 224–225)

Sentences

The ELFA conversation in Chapter 1 (Activities) reflects a style of careful speech, where the interlocutors are conscious of academic norms and therefore they self-regulate to create longer, denser, and more complete sentences. The interlocutors do not complete each other's sentences. Such careful speech is like writing; both are composed of sentences with complete thoughts carefully expressed with subjects and predicates because there is no interlocutor to scaffold the information. Writing, even informal writing, has internal (e.g. within the sentence) and external (e.g. within the text) coherence and completeness requirements, as in this example:

> How you doing? I'm here at work waiting for my appointment to get here, it's Friday. Thank goodness, but I still have tomorrow, but this week has flown by, I guess because I've been staying busy, getting ready for Christmas and stuff. Have you done your Christmas shopping yet? I'm pretty proud of myself. I'm almost finished. Me and L went shopping at Sharpstown last Monday and I got a lot done, I just have a few little things to get. Thanks for the poster, I loved it, I hung it in my room last night, sometimes I feel like that's about right.
>
> (Biber et al., 1999, p. 132)

The example of academic prose from the well-known linguist von Humboldt was written in the early 1830s. It is presented here as a translation from German to English, and it is more literary than modern academic texts. This text is highly informational (not emotional), highly abstract (not concrete), and it explicitly references outside entities, rather than using pronouns or adverbs that refer implicitly. The underlined segment is a **sentence fragment**, or an incomplete sentence, because it is a subordinate sentence. A modern translator might combine the subordinate sentence with the sentence before it because, in strict grammatical terms, it is a subordinate sentence that cannot stand on its own.

> *Its true definition can therefore only be a genetic one, for it is the ever-repetitive work of the spirit to make articulated sound capable of expressing thought.*

This type of sentence fragment is rarely noticed, however, because it is a "complete thought" with its own subject and predicate, and with internal and external coherence. This can cause problems for even the most accomplished of writers.

> Language, taken as real, is something which constantly and in every moment passes away . . . Language is not a work (ergon) but an activity (energeia). Its true definition can therefore only be a genetic one. For it is

the ever-repetitive work of the spirit to make articulated sound capable of expressing thought. Taken directly and strictly, this is the definition of each act of speaking but in a true and intrinsic sense one can look upon language as but the totality of all spoken utterances. For in the scattered chaos of words and rules which we customarily call language, the only thing present in reality is whatever particulars are called forth by individual acts of speaking, and this is never complete. The highest and subtlest aspects of language cannot be recognized in its separate elements; they can only be perceived or intuited in connected speech (which demonstrates all the more that language intrinsically lies in the act of its production in reality). Connected speech is what we must hold before our inner ear as the true and foremost manifestation of language, if we are to be successful in any of our investigations into the living essence of language. Beating it down into words and rules is only a dead artifice of scientific analysis.

(von Humboldt, 1969, pp. 184–185)

Declarative Sentences

The main ingredient for written discourse is the **declarative sentence**, a grammatical unit composed of a subject and a predicate. The declarative sentence states or declares the relationship between different constituents in a focal situation. Generally (but not always) the subject NP of the declarative sentence is the topic, the "given" or already known information, and any "new" information is placed in the predicate VP as a comment. The basic sentence construction comes from the valencies and the meaning of the verb in the verbal construction. In this example with a linking verb and a subject complement, the sentential construction [NP [V NP]]$_S$ sets up an equivalent relationship between the subject and the subject complement.

Linking Sentence Construction

If $[[NP]_{SUBJ} [VP]_{PREDICATE}]_S$
And $[V [NP]_{COMPLEMENT} X]_{VP}$
Then $[NP V NP X]_S$

[English$_{SUBJ}$ *[ceases to be*$_{LINKING\ V}$ *an exponent of only one culture]*$_{PREDICATE}$*]*$_S$

Another prototypical sentence pattern is transitive; it has a subject and a predicate with an active V^2 verb [NP V NP X]$_S$. The variable (X) stands for other constituents of the sentence like prepositional phrases or adverbials.

*[This traditional notional definition]*_{SUBJ} *[only solves the problem by transferring it]*_{PREDICATE}

In the corpus there were numerous intransitive examples because passive sentences do not have a direct object. In this pattern the verb relationship relates the subject to some non-object constituent which is, in this case, a PP.

> **Transitive Sentence Construction**
>
> If $[[NP]_{SUBJ} [VP]_{PREDICATE}]_S$
> And $[V [NP]_{DO} X]_{VP}$
> Then $[NP\ V\ NP\ X]_S$

> **Intransitive Sentence Construction**
>
> If $[[NP]_{SUBJ} [VP]_{PREDICATE}]_S$
> And $[V\ PP\ X]_{VP}$
> Then $[NP\ V\ PP\ X]_S$

> . . . *[we]*_{SUBJ} *[do not communicate by putting together lists of isolated sentences]*_{PREDICATE}

Non-prototypical Sentences

Language users can choose less frequent sentence constructions with non-prototypical word orders. These less frequent constructions involve preposed, inverted, or omitted constituents. **Preposing** is the name for constructions in which a constituent "normally" found in the predicate is found at the beginning of the sentence. **Inversion** is the name for constructions in which an auxiliary and the subject are reversed in word order. Ellipsis is the omission of one or more words that can be understood from the context of the sentence. The following sentence shows both inversion (the modal auxiliary *will*) and preposing (the sentence adverb *only* and the prepositional *by*-phrase).

> *Only by adopting an integrative, dynamic framework will* we understand how they come about.

Inversion and preposing serve a discourse function: to spotlight the new information about how understanding can be accomplished, and put the given information in the background. The inverted sentence is much more interesting and dynamic than its uninverted twin. The prototypical constituent order lacks emphasis, contrast, and rhetorical style:

We will understand how they come about only by adopting an integrative, dynamic framework.

Inversion
Nouns occur as parts of particular units, and <u>so do verbs</u>.
Nouns don't occur in those units, and <u>neither do verbs</u>.

Substitution
Nouns <u>occur</u> as parts of particular units, and verbs <u>do</u> too.

Ellipsis
Nouns don't occur in those units, and verbs don't ___ either.
Nouns can't occur in those units, and verbs can't ___ either.

Compound Sentences

When *and*, *but*, or *or* conjoin two or more sentences, the resulting sentence is **compound**. As in the case of coordinated words and phrases, the coordinating conjunction appears only at the beginning of the last conjunct. Generally, the conjoined constituents have no punctuation between them if there are only two. If there are more than two, there is an optional comma before the conjunction. However, these examples from the corpus have punctuation that separates each conjoined sentence into an independent thought, and the second is a comment on the first.

Rather, they occur as parts of particular units, and these units in turn play particular roles within the sentence.

I had been reading about formulaic language in the context of language proficiency, and had been struck by three observations made in the literature.

It remains half alive for one speaker and dies for the next; or it may be revived by education.

Parallel Structure

The examples below illustrate the use of the conjunctions *and*, *or*, and *but* to conjoin two or more complete sentences. They are examples of **parallel structure**, a stylistic strategy used by writers to show that ideas have the same importance or function. Some people believe that parallelism in writing increases readability or comprehensibility.

> [Parents dutifully take their kids to soccer practice] **and** [professional athletes dutifully show up for team practice, sometimes even with recent injuries]. [Parents make their kids practice their piano skills at home] **and** [the world's most famous performers of classical music often practice for many hours a day, even if it makes their fingers hurt].

> That is, [the effects of practice are greatest at early stages of learning] **but** [they eventually reach asymptote]. [We may not be counting the words as we listen or speak] **but** [each time we process one there is a reduction in processing time that marks this practice increment] **and** [thus the perceptual and motor systems become tuned by the experience of a particular language].

Conjunction by Punctuation

It is not always necessary to use conjunctions to join sentences. Closely related sentences can be joined by punctuation, most commonly a semi-colon, but sometimes a colon. Both the semi-colon and the colon are common in Academic English, but rare in informal writing styles.

> The first places us in the forefront of intellectual and educational progress; the second proves that we are scientifically and technologically in the lead; the third points the way to a better material life for everyone concerned.

> Languages represent a very special class of economic goods: they are not only collective goods but also display network effects . . .

A colon is also used with a list.

> There are two main types: full verb, auxiliary verb.

When two sentences are conjoined with a semi-colon, they often have a **transition** or sentential adverb in the second sentence, as in the example below in bold. This sentence could also be broken up into two sentences with a period after *syndrome* and a capital letter on *That is*.

> Conversely, if we teach discourse (i.e. meaning and functions) without reference to grammar, our learners will produce discourse reminiscent of Kroll's (1990)

college-level ESL composition students who exhibit the +rhetoric/–grammar syndrome; **that is,** *they write logically organized and coherent texts but with such a high number of morphosyntactic errors that native speakers find it difficult, if not impossible, to read and understand their texts.*

Other Communicative Functions

Speakers and writers select other types of sentences and word order alternatives to convey other communicative functions besides stating or declaring. These less prototypical sentences make use of preposing, inversion, deletion, substitution, and insertion of other words or special collocations to accomplish their purpose. In **questions**, preposing and inversion mark an utterance or sentence that solicits a response from an interlocutor such as information or agreement. **Negative sentences** insert an adverb or other words to convey something that is not the case with respect to a focus situation. Imperatives use deletion of a subject, and exclamations involve fragments or the use of collocations like *what a.*

Questions

Types of Questions

Questions rely on preposing and inversion to mark how they are different from declarative sentences. There are four types of direct questions, or direct requests to another person for a response or for certain information.

Intonation
Yes/no (inversion)
Information (inversion and preposing)
Tag (discussed in Chapter 14)

Intonational questions are formed by special rising tone at the end of the question. **Yes/no questions** show inversion of the auxiliary. **Information questions** show both inversion of the subject and the auxiliary and insertion and preposing of wh-pronouns. There are also **tag questions**, such as this hypothetical example: *I can legally open a shop, can't I?*

Direct questions are rare in written Academic English, and when they appear, they are used for rhetorical purposes, since no answer from an interlocutor could be possible. In the second example, ellipsis, or the omission of a constituent to avoid repeating the identical words, is also involved.

How could something that was so easy when you began with a language, and so easy when you were fully proficient in it, be so difficult in between?

If even idolized, spoiled, and highly paid celebrities are willing to put up with practice, why not language learners, teachers, or researchers?

Intonational questions are phrases or declarative sentences pronounced with rising intonation at the end, symbolized by the question mark, as in this example from the conversation cited earlier.

Yes/no questions are formed by inverting the subject and the primary auxiliary (*do, have,* or *be*), the modal auxiliary, or the main verb *be.* If there is a main verb other than *be,* with no primary or modal auxiliary, the auxiliary *do* occurs in the inverted place at the beginning of the question.

Information questions use pronouns like *who, what,* or *whose,* wh-adverbs like *where* or *how,* and wh-determiners + NPs like *what man* or *whose car.* Wh-questions require inversion but, in addition, the construction places the wh-word at the beginning, in highlighted position.

Negative Sentences

The word *not* is a sentence adverb, and as an adverb there are a number of places it can occur in a sentence. In these examples, there are some common system collocations (*whether or not, but not,* and *if not*) as well as a colligation linking *not* to a participial adjective.

Intonational Question

B: *Well—I got it from that travel agent's.*
A: *Oh.*
B: *er the one*
A: <u>*In the precinct?*</u>

Yes/No Question

Can I legally open a shop?

Are English learners willing to practice?

Did you get that at the travel agent's?

Information Question

Where do you go for that?

How could something that was so easy when you began with a language, and so easy when you were fully proficient in it, be so difficult in between?

How does one define a complete thought?

*One must also judge the situational and linguistic context in which the construction occurs to decide [whether or **not**] any given instance of language use is appropriate semantically and pragmatically as well as grammatically.*

*For example, if the question What did you give Jim? (in its unmarked form) is asked of someone, an appropriate unmarked response (pragmatically) is a/the tie or I gave him a/the tie, [but **not**] I gave a/the tie to Jim/him.*

*. . . native speakers find it difficult, [if **not** impossible], to read and understand their texts.*

*. . . there are patterns everywhere, patterns [**not** preordained by God] . . .*

A main usage for the adverb *not* is to negate a sentence by operating on the VP, a main verb *be*, or a primary or modal auxiliary, as in these examples:

Main Verb *be*: *Languages . . . **are not** only collective goods but also display network effects.*

Primary Auxiliary: *. . . the ability to examine large text corpora allows access to a quality of evidence that **has not been** available before.*

Modal Auxiliary: *NNs employ a great number of lexical and syntactic features of text that **may not be** particularly appropriate in constructing academic texts.*

Do Auxiliary: *But the study of grammar **does not end** with learning about structures and functions within the sentence.*

The adverb *not* is placed after a main verb *be* or the auxiliary, and if none of these are present, as in the case of a single main verb (*know, occur, end,* etc.) then the *do* auxiliary is used.

Imperatives

Imperatives, or command forms, are non-prototypical because they usually lack an overt subject, which is otherwise mandatory in English. There are two types of commands. The first is second person with an understood singular or plural *you*. The imperative verb form is simple; it is the

Command

Get in the car.

Be good.

Don't be naughty.

Don't dawdle.

Don't (you) say anything.

Grab that hammer, will you?

Please don't eat the daisies.

bare infinitive. Imperatives with the main verb *be* form their negative with *don't*, as in *Don't be silly*. If the imperative is affirmative, it might have a tag question with *will* or *would* which softens it. Commands also occur with the sentence adverb *please*.

Another type of imperative is softer because it is a suggestion rather than an order. *Let's* is a contracted form of *Let us*, so this command includes the speaker in the suggestion.

According to Biber et al. (1999, pp. 219–222), imperatives of both types are common in conversation but not in fiction, news reporting, or academic prose. In the latter, specialized imperatives serve a rhetorical function to address or include the reader.

> **Suggestion**
>
> *Let's have a party.*
>
> *Let's not spend any money on this.*
>
> *Don't let's spend any money on this.* (in some varieties)

> *In looking for the answers, <u>let us begin</u> with those citizens who have been around for the longest time, the elderly and those in later middle age.*

> *<u>Note</u> that x may occur free and bound in P.*

> *<u>See</u> also Section 5.2.*

> *Let <u><mathematical formula> be</u> the breeding population of blowflies at time t and let <mathematical formula> be the number of eggs produced.*

> *<u>Suppose we</u> believe that the snow is what is muffling the sound of the traffic. (Suppose we is an alternative to Let us or let us suppose that.)*

Exclamations

Exclamations are uncommon in academic prose because their function is to express surprise, warning, dismay, or other strong emotions. One type of exclamation is an insert or a simple phrase with exclamatory intonation or punctuation. Another uses preposing of a sentential adverb (*here/there*) and inversion of the main verb (*comes/goes*). Exclamatory sentences sometimes have singular or plural NPs with various introductory expressions, *what a* or *what* (or *such/such a* in some varieties). The distribution of these expressions is *what/such* with plural or mass nouns and *what/such a* with singular count nouns. Some exclamations prepose NPs out of their sentences and preface them with the introductory expression.

Comparisons

Another common communicative function that has an impact on sentence structure is comparison or detailing the amount or degree of something. The most common comparative constructions in conversation, news, fiction, and academic writing take these structures (Biber et al., 1999, pp. 527–529):

> *Internodes are <u>longer</u> and sheaths <u>relatively and progressively shorter than</u> the internodal length.*

> *But a small sample for comparison is <u>better than</u> nothing at all.*

> *The cost of installing the device would have been <u>higher than</u> the discounted cost of the accident.*

Fiction and informal writing have many different types of comparative expressions, as shown by these examples from fiction cited in Biber et al. (1999, pp. 527–529):

As + adjective + as: *The last tinkle of the last shard died away and silence closed in <u>as deep as</u> ever before.*

So + adjective + that: *His personality was <u>so subdued that</u> it seemed to fit in with anything he did.*

So + adjective + as to: *And if anybody was <u>so foolhardy as to</u> pass by the shrine after dusk he was sure to see the old woman hopping about.*

Too + adjective + infinitive: *I mounted the black scaffold, which was almost <u>too hot to touch</u>.*

Adjective + enough + infinitive: *I was <u>old enough to do</u> it for myself.*

The only examples of comparatives found in the corpus for this book are below. The first example compares two NPs and the second is a rhetorical device to call attention to the inadequacy of even a rich "innate structure" to explain language acquisition. In the third example, the collocation "*such a* NP *that* sentence" highlights the degree or number of errors.

> It is <u>less</u> an analytical question <u>than</u> a question about history.

> But innate structure, <u>as</u> rich <u>as</u> it may be, cannot account for the acquisition of language-specific properties.

> . . . that is, they write logically organized and coherent texts but with [such a high number of morphosyntactic errors that native speakers find it difficult, if not impossible, to read and understand their texts].

Discovery Procedures

Representing all of the details of the abstract form of any sentence is complex, when all of the constituent phrases are spelled out. The simple construction for the sentence *Practice gets a raw deal in the field of applied linguistics* is $[[NP][VP]]_S$. However, when the whole construction is spelled out, it is complicated to the point of obscurity. In order to understand the structure of a sentence, it is sometimes easier to visualize the construction in a different format: the form of an upside-down tree called a **sentence diagram**.

Sentence diagramming or **parsing** has a long history in the study and instruction of English grammar. In the past century, structuralist grammarians perfected sentence diagramming as a part of their theoretical apparatus for generative rules of grammar. Such **phrase structure rules** also became a staple of computational linguistics because such rules are used to program computers to generate well-formed sentences. However, phrase

$[Practice]_{NP}$

$[[a]_{DET} [raw]_{ADJ} [deal]_N]_{NP}$

$[[the]_{DET} [field]_N [[of]_P [[applied]_{ADJ} [linguistics]_N]_{NP}]_{PP}]_{NP}$

$[[NP] [[gets] [NP] [PP]]_{VP}]_S$

$[[Practice]_{NP} [[gets]_V [[a]_{DET} [raw]_{ADJ} [deal]_N]_{NP} [[in]_P [[the]_{DET} [field]_N [[of]_P [[applied]_{ADJ} [linguistics]_N]_{NP}]_{PP}]_{NP}]_{VP}]_S$

structure rules and sentence diagramming have not been used in Construction Grammar as a theory perhaps because of that association. Ultimately, sentence diagramming remains both a discovery procedure and a pedagogical technique, but, like grammar drills and exercises, they are controversial, as McArthur (1992, p. 751) notes in his definition:

PARSING [16c: from the verb parse, from Latin **pars/partis** a part, abstracted from the phrase **pars orationis** part of speech] . . . Analyzing a sentence into its constituents, identifying in greater or less detail the syntactic relations and parts of speech . . . The argument against traditional parsing is threefold: that it promotes old-fashioned descriptions of language based on Latin grammatical categories, that students do not benefit from it, and that it can be a source of frustration and boredom for both students and teachers. The argument in favour of parsing is fourfold: that it makes explicit the structure of speech and writing, exercises the mind in a disciplined way, enables people to talk about language usage, and helps in the learning and discussion of foreign languages. A compromise position holds that the formal discussion of syntax and function can be beneficial, but should take second place to fluent expression and the achievement of confidence rather than dominate the weekly routine.

If McArthur's cautions are kept in mind, sentence diagramming develops metalinguistic awareness because it relates language and thinking, and increases knowledge of parts of speech and skill in grammatical analysis. It is a way to focus on both meaning and message, for example through the analysis of sentences that are structurally ambiguous. It is a way to examine large-scale abstract structures and lexical relationships both analytically and holistically. It may lead to improvement in monitoring and self-regulating skills like proofreading and editing. However, it takes practice.

Figure 11.1 advances the theory that the sentence *Practice gets a raw deal in the field of applied linguistics* can be divided into the subject NP *Practice* and the predicate VP with the main verb *gets* and an object NP *a raw deal*. In addition, the context for the *getting* relationship between *practice* and the *deal* is *the field of applied linguistics*, a complex NP that is the object of the preposition *in* attached under the VP. It is also possible to make some holistic determinations. An examination of the words reveals that there are some common prefabricated units: *a raw deal*, *gets a raw deal*, and *in the field of*. In the context of *a ___ deal*, *raw* doesn't mean *uncooked*; instead, it means *bad* or *unfair*, and *deal* means *treatment*.

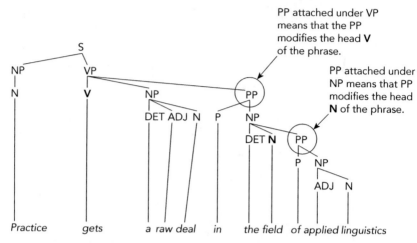

Figure 11.1 A Diagram Presenting a Theory of the Structure of a Sentence

In the sentence below, there is a question about the word *up*. Is it a particle or a preposition? Does it form a constituent with the following NP: *up images of mind-numbing drills*? Or does it form a prefabricated unit with the preceding verb: *conjures up*?

> *The word conjures up images of mind-numbing drills in the sweatshops of foreign language learning . . .*

The latter is the best analysis because of the stronger priming associations and expectations and also because there is a meaning specific to *conjures up*, which is "making something appear by magic." *To conjure up* is a phrasal verb, a compound of a verb *conjure* and a particle *up*. In fact, there are three other compound words in this sentence. There is also a difference in the attachment of the prepositional phrases [*of mind-numbing drills*] [*in the sweatshops*] [*of foreign language learning*] (Figure 11.2).

After looking at the various options for attaching prepositional phrases under verb phrases or under noun phrases, decide where the prepositional phrase in the following sentence is attached. Should the sequences *fun and games* and *Friday afternoons* be considered collocations or compounds? The two trees in Figure 11.3 represent two theories, with triangles used as a convenience to avoid making a claim about structure at this point. Which analysis is the preferred one for the prepositional phrase attachment? What is the reasoning for each analysis?

> *It means fun and games to appease students [on Friday afternoons].*

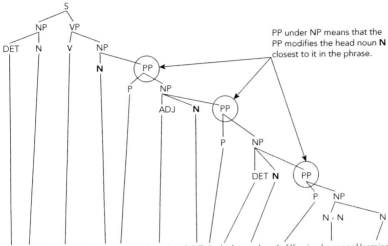

The word [conjures up] images of [mind-numbing] drills in the [sweatshops] of [foreign language] learning

Figure 11.2 A Sentence Diagram with Nested PPs

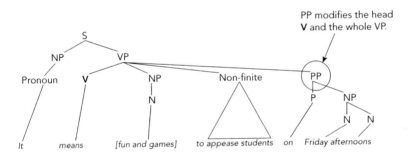

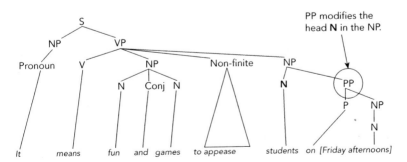

Figure 11.3 Two Sentence Diagrams, Each One Representing a Different Theory of the Structure of the Sentence

The first diagram is consistent with the more straightforward meaning that on Friday afternoon teachers entertain students by playing fun and games in the class. The second diagram has a more specialized meaning that there are some students who come to class only on Friday afternoon and they must be entertained by playing games.

Sentence diagrams lead to the discovery of the commonalities in phrasal and sentential constructions and practicing with them is a good way to develop metalinguistic awareness because it permits a look at underlying patterns once the words are out of the way. There are only a relatively few sentential constructions, and they occur over and over again with different words. If learners look beyond the superficially distracting words, and perceive the common underlying grammatical patterns, they see and understand a linguistic system instead of a random mass of sentences.

The Development of Sentence Awareness

Chapter 3 introduced the idea of a natural order of acquisition and nowhere is a natural order more apparent than in the acquisition of negative sentences and questions. Most second language learners in classrooms are unlikely to have enough usage and exposure to move along from one stage to the next, so direct instruction, practice, and feedback may help learners proceduralize these types of sentences especially for writing purposes. Indeed, extensive feedback and practice may provide sources of priming for the accurate use of these constructions. Grammatical instruction that takes place in response to learner needs and as oral or written feedback to specific errors is the most likely to help since learners may be incapable of noticing and learning forms that are too far beyond their current level of proficiency.

Negation

Berdan (1996) describes the natural order of acquisition of negative sentences. In the first stage, learners simply put *no/not* immediately before the word, phrase, or sentence being negated. In the second stage, learners use *no/not/don't* along with a verb but there is no marking of person, number, or tense in the primary auxiliary *do* or the verb. The third stage negatives show that the main verb *be/have* and the primary auxiliaries are negated correctly, but it is unclear if these forms are analyzed or formulaic. In the fourth stage, the primary auxiliary *do* is acquired and it is marked for person, number, and tense. However, tense marking on the main verb (a bare infinitive) sometimes occurs. Ultimately, in the last stage of acquisition, learners can construct negative sentences with accuracy and fluency, although sporadic performance errors do persist. In addition, there may be issues with double negation, which are discussed in Chapter 15.

1. **No + X:**	*No is happy. Not my friend.*
2. **No/not/don't + verb:**	*He don't have job. They not working.*
3. **Aux + not:**	*I can't play. They aren't there. He don't have job.*
4. **Analyzed do:**	*He doesn't work here. And we don't. I didn't see her. He didn't went.*
5. **Expert accuracy and fluency.**	

Questions

Intonation is the first form of questions for most learners, and its usage persists into expert usage because intonation questions are always natural in conversation. The intonation can accompany single words, phrases, or whole short sentences.

The second stage shows the development of wh-questions. Wh-pronouns like *who, what, which,* or *whom* and wh-adverbs like *why, when,* or *where* (but probably not determiners like *what* NP, *which* NP, or *whose* NP) appear in their preposed position in front of the question. The rest of the question does not reliably show inversion. In the next stage, learners develop their abilities to form yes/no questions. At first, learners have a partial ability to invert the auxiliaries *be* or *have,* and they gradually become able to invert main verbs *be* and *have* and insert the auxiliary *do* and modals with main verbs. At this stage, learners become more and more adept at combining preposing of wh-words with inversion of subjects and auxiliaries.

Stages in the Development of Questions

Stage 1. Intonation with words, phrases, or sentences
Why? This? This is picture? They stay oceans?

Stage 2. Preposing of wh-words
What he is doing? Why he is stopped the car?

Stage 3. Inversion with primary auxiliaries
Does he going home? Is he have neighbor?

Stage 4. Inversion and preposing with main verb *be* and auxiliaries
What is this lady? Where are this place?
What does she hold in her hand? Why did he crying?
Where will she take this?

Stage 5. Negative Questions
You don't like green, are you?
Can't she come in?

Stage 6. Indirect questions
Can you tell me who he is?

(Adapted from Tarone and Swierzbin, 2009, p. 48)

Priming

McDonough and Mackey (2006) studied the effect of recasts and priming on question development and they found that both correlated with question production at a more advanced stage if the learner productively used a question in his or her own way a little while after hearing the recast rather than if the learner simply repeated it. In other words, Learner 2 produced a more advanced question in response to the recast than did Learner 1. McDonough and Mackey (2006) thought that repetitions did not contribute to modified output and language development but that production of a new utterance with the more advanced question did. However, it is also possible that Learner 1 was simply not able to take advantage of the recasts, whereas Learner 2 was able to learn from the scaffolding. In a later study, McDonough and Mackey (2008) confirmed that the learners who advanced to later stage questions were automatizing their knowledge of questions but those who simply repeated questions were at an earlier stage and were practicing the structure. Thus, direct instruction in question formation helps to start the learning process, repetition is good practice to acquire question constructions, but producing questions creatively and analytically in conversations is how learners boost their own internal priming to automatize their ability to produce questions.

Learner 1: Recast Followed by Immediate Repetition

Learner: *Where you live in Vietnam?* (Stage 2 question)
NS: *Where did I stay in Vietnam?* (Recast at stage 4)
Learner: *Where did you stay?* (Repetition at stage 4)
NS: *I started in Hanoi and went down the coast to Hui and Danang and I ended in Saigon*
Learner: *Where the event take place?* (Stage 2 question)

Learner 2: Recast Followed by Primed Production

Learner: *Why he get divorced?* (Stage 2 question)
NS: *Why did he get divorced?* (Recast at stage 4)
Learner: *Yeah* (Acknowledgment)
NS: *Because he knew his wife was having an affair so he didn't want to be with her anymore.*
Learner: *So where did Mr. Smith live?* (Stage 4 question)
NS: *With his friend.*

Indirect Questions

Ultimately, the most advanced question type and the most important from the perspective of academic writing is the indirect question, which, crucially, is not inverted. Indirect questions are subordinate sentences introduced with *if* or *whether* or wh-words followed by an ordinary sentence with ordinary word order.

> *It is reasonable to ask whether <u>grammatical correction is</u> effective and appropriate at all, and if so, what <u>the best ways</u> are to approach it.*

Indirect questions are a type of subordinate sentence and are covered further in the next chapter.

> *I find it better to try to do more (and more varied) empirical research on how* <u>ELF</u> <u>is actually used</u> *and what* <u>it does</u> *to local languages.*

Study, Discussion, and Essay Questions

Write the answers to these questions in your Language Notebook. Create your notebook as a word processing document because you will be using the "find" command to analyze your writing later.

1. Review these terms and add them to your glossary with a definition and some examples: topic, comment, insert, declarative sentence, preposing, inversion, substitution, insertion, parallel structure, sentence diagram, parsing, indirect question.
2. How is the idea of a "complete thought" relevant in different ways to conversations and writing?
3. What is the difference between a semi-colon and a colon?
4. What are the different types of questions?
5. What different types of exclamations are there?
6. How are negative sentences formed?
7. What different types of imperatives are there?
8. Why are sentence diagrams "theories" about the structure of a sentence?
9. What are the stages in the development of negative sentences?
10. How might priming be implicated as learners progress through the stages of question formation?

Activities

1. Read and discuss this essay written in response to an editorial which criticized native speakers who have pronunciation, spelling, and grammar difficulties, and equated non-standard usage with important social problems. Identify the sentence fragments in this essay and suggest editorial changes to integrate them. What other stylistic changes would you make? Rewrite the essay so that it sounds less conversational.

Language Prejudice

I take issue with the guest editorial called "Hello? Is anyone out there speaking proper English?" The author betrays some inaccuracies in her understanding of English spelling and grammar. Not to mention her condescending tone.

First off spelling. Our spelling system is a conservative system, which was frozen in time long ago. And which doesn't match our present day pronunciation well. Many people, not just people who work in discount stores and grocery stores, spell according to the sound of the word. Are bad spellers dimwitted Philistines? Or just people who have failed to master an unpredictable system that relies heavily on visual memory? Or people who don't have spell-checkers handy?

Next, words. Don't be judgmental about young people, including store employees, who don't have extensive vocabularies and may not recognize a word like *gourmet*. Vocabulary learning is developmental. The older the person, the larger the lexicon. Saying *rode* instead of *ridden* reflects people's regional background or socioeconomic origin. Not their intellectual abilities. Saying *weaved* instead of *woven* is following a tradition in English to make irregular verbs regular over time. Like *dreamed* versus *dreamt* or *hanged* versus *hung*.

Then those pesky place names. Place names are notoriously difficult to pronounce. It's a cheap shot to criticize the way someone pronounces a place unknown to them. Examples from my area: Butte des Morts, Fond du Lac, Oconomowoc, Waukesha. Sure how to pronounce them?

Language is social. Its commonalities bind us together. Language is also individual. Because we don't speak the same way. Some people find this inevitable language variation interesting. Not threatening or repugnant.

Language changes over time. Otherwise we would all speak as the characters in Chaucer do. Some people think that language change is degenerative. Others think that change is neutral. Not frightening, not stupid.

Also, to think that spelling errors and non-standard grammar are problems that have emerged in the past 40 years is to deny that there's been a thriving and lucrative spelling and grammar book publishing industry for centuries. This is not a recent "dumbing down" problem. The fact is that mainly upper and middle class people already speak a native dialect similar to Standard English. Lucky for them that our school standard approximates their native speech, making learning easier for them.

On the other hand, the dialects of other populations tend to diverge from Standard English. Such as rural people, second-generation immigrant groups, the urban working or lower socioeconomic classes and minorities. Those who do not grow up speaking standard English in their homes often have a harder time when they get to school. Because they are also grappling with language differences. It especially hinders learners if their teachers consider them stupid or ignorant because of their speech.

Finally, it is absurd to connect spelling errors and non-standard grammar to tasteless popular culture like television, Disney movies, or advances in social networking or technology. And then to "cruelty and stupidity of all sorts: addiction, racism, child abuse, street crime, and demagoguery."

Have you ever misspelled a word? Have you ever committed a grammar mistake? Let he who is without sin cast the first stone. Or him?

2. Using the model sentence diagrams from the chapter, try to diagram these sentences. Pay close attention to the location of the prepositional phrases. Note that in sentence c. there is a prepositional phrase that serves as an adverbial to the whole sentence. Where would you put it in the diagram?

a. *Parents take their kids to soccer practice.*
b. *Professional athletes with injuries show up for team practice.*
c. *Before their concert, the amateur performers practiced the music of classical composers for hours.*

3. Put these direct questions into indirect question form by embedding them into the sentence frames: *I wonder, We are not sure,* or *I asked him.* Compare your answers to your classmates'. The first one is done for you. (Use *whether* or *if* for yes/no questions.)

a. What are the methods that teachers prefer?
    I asked him what the methods that teachers prefer are.
b. How do theorists conceptualize methodologies?
c. Are some instructional methods better than others?
d. Are language learning situations unpredictably numerous?
e. Can any method provide situation-specific suggestions for teachers?
f. Which challenges do teachers confront?
g. When do teachers need to make their own decisions about methods?
h. Where do most ESL methodologies come from?

Complex Sentences   **12**

CLAUSE [13c: from French *clause*, Latin *clausa*, the close of a sentence or formula] In grammatical description, a sentence or sentence-like construction included within another sentence, such as *because I wanted to* in *I did it because I wanted to.*

(McArthur, 1992, p. 220)

Complex sentences contain a main sentence (*I did it* . . .) and at least one dependent "sentence-like" clause (. . . *because I wanted to*) within their structures. The clause is part of the main sentence construction because of a grammatical function called **subordination**. In informal conversation, subordinate sentences take part in adjacency pairs. In writing, subordination permits a clause to play a part in the main sentence construction or to modify constituents in the main sentence. Subordination is a way to create text coherence and cohesion. Complex sentences with such subordinate clauses are common in academic writing because they contribute denseness and elaboration to the prose.

    Subordinate clauses have many of the characteristics of main sentences, such as subjects, predicates with finite verbs, direct objects, and prepositional phrases. The crucial difference between main sentences and subordinate clauses is that subordinate clauses cannot stand alone in formal writing. They are dependent on the syntactic frame created by the main sentence into which the subordinate sentence is inserted. The insertion into the main sentence and the subordinate clause is marked with a **complementizer**. These examples from the corpus illustrate three different types of subordinate clauses. In each case, the subordinate clause is in square brackets and the complementizer in bold:

Noun Clause: *A speaker's sensitivity to previous encounters with language forms and meanings suggests [**that** language use is sensitive to the occurrence of language forms and meanings in the environment]*$_{\text{N CLAUSE}}$

Adjective Clause: *Consequently, there is no date or age [**at which** the learning of a language can be said to be complete]*$_{\text{ADJ CLAUSE}}$

> **Types and Functions of Subordinate Clauses**
>
> **Noun clauses** refer to situations.
> **Adjective clauses** describe nouns.
> **Adverb clauses** add information.

Adverb Clause: *We can only account for collocation [**if** we assume that every word is mentally primed for collocational use]*$_{\text{ADV CLAUSE}}$

The three types of subordinate clauses are different in the function they perform in the main sentence, and the function determines the name of the clause: Noun clauses are referential NPs, adjective clauses describe nouns and are part of NPs, and adverb clauses provide additional information about time, place, conditionality, and so on.

What these subordinate clauses have in common is that they all begin with a complementizer word or phrase. The complementizer for a noun clause is *that* if it is a declarative sentence, or a wh-question word if it is an indirect question. Adjective clauses are introduced with a wh- relative pronoun or pronominal construction with a preposition (e.g. *at which*), and adverb clauses are introduced with an adverbial or connecting word like *if*.

Adjective Clauses

Adjective clauses are subordinate clauses that describe, modify, or clarify nouns or pronouns in the main sentence. The example below illustrates two types of adjective clauses. In the first type, the adjective clause has its own subject (*speakers*) and verb sequence, but it is still linked to the main sentence

> **Adjective Clause**
>
> [complementizer [S]]

nouns by the complementizer *that*. In the second type, only a verb phrase (*occurred*) occurs, linked to the main sentence noun (underlined) with the complementizer.

*In other words, [the exact forms and meanings [that speakers use]*_{ADJP}*]*_{NP} *can be affected by the [language [that occurred in discourse [they recently engaged in]*_{ADJ CLAUSE}*]*_{ADJ CLAUSE}*].*

There is a third adjective clause in the sentence above (*they recently engaged in*), one that doesn't have an overt complementizer. It modifies the noun *discourse*. When an adjective clause has its own subject and verb combination it is permitted a zero complementizer.

There is further variation in the appearance of adjective clauses; there are more complementizers. *Which* is commonly used for nouns that refer to animals or things. *Who* (or the rarer *whom*)[1] is used for people exclusively. *Whose* is used as a possessive determiner most commonly for a human possessor. The wh-complementizers can be used with prepositions, as shown in the underlined examples, and in those contexts the zero complementizer cannot appear. By far the most common complementizers are *that* and zero, but neither can occur with prepositions.

Complementizers

That refers to things or people.

Which refers to animals or things.

Who and **whom** are for people.

Whose is a possessive determiner.

Zero complementizer can occur if there is a subject in the adjective clause.

Can you find a hidden adjective clause inside a noun clause in this sentence?

In the end, teacher trainers and teachers may need to be reminded that the academic skills they themselves require in teaching and learning are not far removed from those of their NNS students.

*Language, taken as real, is something [**which** constantly and in every moment passes away]* . . .

1. *Whom* is rare in most Standard English varieties, but it does occur especially with prepositions as in this hypothetical example: *The languages of the world together constitute a global system held together by multilingual people among whom communication takes place in several languages.*

> To withdraw or abandon the language [**through which** tradition speaks] is to render tradition mute.

> In other words, English is now the language [**of those who** use it].

> . . . the noun phrase "that man" is thereby used as a referring expression [**whose referent** is a specific man [**whose identity** the addressee must either know or be able to determine]].

Commas sometimes occur between the main clause noun and the adjective clause that defines it. Commas are an indication that the purpose of the adjective clause is non-restrictive. In other words, it is meant to add some additional information about the main clause noun. This usage is common in the corpus for this book:

> . . . The growing respect for real examples led in the mid-1980s to a notion of textual well-formedness, [**which** was dubbed naturalness] . . .

> Linguistic theory is concerned primarily with an ideal speaker-listener, in a completely homogeneous speech-community, [**who** knows its language perfectly].

> In contrast, the so-called emergentist and usage-based approaches to language acquisition, [**that** have become prominent in the past decade], are based on the assumption that language structure can be learned from language use by means of powerful generalization abilities.

Sentence modifiers are adjective clauses that modify a whole sentence. In the first example, the adjective clause is in parentheses and it has a nested noun clause inside it. In the second case, the adjective clause is separated from the main clause with a comma.

> The highest and subtlest aspects of language cannot be recognized in its separate elements; they can only be perceived or intuited in connected speech (**which** demonstrates all the more **that** language intrinsically lies in the act of its production in reality).

> These results suggest that parsing decisions may depend in part on the person's history of experience with the structures under scrutiny, **in which case** there might be a general bias in favor of analyses that occur most frequently in the language.

Reduced Adjective Clause Constructions

There are two types of clause-like constructions related to adjective clauses, as shown in this example in square brackets. The first construction has a participial adjective phrase that modifies a noun phrase in the main sentence.

> *The same applies to word sequences [built out of these words]; these too become loaded with the contexts and co-texts in which they occur.* (This sentence also has a full adjective clause at the end.)

Compare:

> *The same applies to word sequences [__that are__ built out of these words]; these too become loaded with the contexts and co-texts in which they occur.*

The example below has a similar reduced adjective clause (shown in square brackets) as well as five exemplar appositives in parentheses.

> *There are five types of phrases, [named after their main word]: noun phrase (a very bright light); verb phrase (may be eating); adjective phrase (extraordinarily happy); adverb phrase or adverbial phrase (quite casually); prepositional phrase (in our city).*

Appositives are related to non-restrictive adjective clauses since they require some kind of separation by punctuation. The following example is complicated by having a construction inside parentheses and one separated by commas, making one very complex NP construction:

> *The position of each language in this system may be characterized by its "communication value" (Q), the product of its prevalence and its centrality.*

Compare this variant in which the relationships among the various nouns is explicit:

> *The position of each language in this system may be characterized by [its "communication value" (__called__ Q), [__which is__ the product of its prevalence and its centrality]].*

In the following example, the appositives are definitional and occur in parentheses after each noun in the main sentence. These appositives contrast with the examplar appositives in parentheses above because here the paraphrases with a full adjective clause are plausible, whereas with examplar appositives, such paraphrases are less plausible:

> *We thus make a fundamental distinction between competence (the speaker-hearer's knowledge of his language) and performance (the actual use of language in concrete situations).*

Appositives occur with pronouns as subjects or objects, as in this example:

> *We, the speakers of English, should proudly flaunt the banners of cultural imperialism, neo-colonialism, and commercialism.*

Adverb Clauses

Adverb clauses modify their main sentence by adding information about time, place, condition, reason, purpose, and result. Adverb clauses serve very important discourse purposes depending on their location before or after their main clause. Adverb clauses that precede their main sentence highlight timing or other contextual information that is important to the development of a paragraph. They advance the topic of the paragraph by introducing new information, which the main sentence then comments on. The examples in the text below show the range of possibilities for the location of adverb clauses with respect to their main clause; they occur either before or after the main clause, often with a comma separating them.

> **Adverb Clause**
>
> [complementizer [S]]

> *[**Whereas** in the past these two knowledge systems were often treated as separate]*$_{ADV\ CLAUSE}$, *it has recently been suggested that they are connected and that one possible interface is learner awareness or consciousness of particular grammatical features developed through formal instruction . . .*

> *[**Once** a learner's consciousness of a target feature has been raised through formal instruction or through continued communicative exposure]*$_{ADV\ CLAUSE}$, *the learner often tends to notice the feature in subsequent input . . . Such noticing or continued awareness of the feature is suggested to be important [**because** it appears to initiate the restructuring of the learner's implicit or unconscious*

*system of linguistic knowledge]*ADV CLAUSE · · · *[When a language point is noticed frequently]*ADV CLAUSE, *learners develop awareness of it and unconsciously compare it with their existing system of linguistic knowledge, unconsciously constructing new hypotheses to accommodate the differences between the noticed information and their L2 competence.*

The adverb clauses that follow their main clause are dependent on their main clause and therefore less crucial to the development of the overall text. The *because* adverb clause in the paragraph above proposes a potential causative connection between noticing and implicit knowledge. These examples also make it clear that the complementizers for adverb clauses are numerous and varied.

Time	Contrast	Intention
after	*although*	*in order that*
as	*even if*	*so that*
before	*unless*	
now that	*while*	**Condition**
since	*whereas*	*as long as*
until		*if*
when(ever)	**Cause**	*provided/-ing that*
while	*as long as*	
	because	
	inasmuch as	
	since	

Noun Clauses

Noun clauses embed sentences as the subject, object, or subject complement of a main sentence or as an appositive. In the first example below, an indirect question is the subject and a declarative noun clause is the subject complement. In the second example below, the declarative noun clause is an appositive that renames or re-expresses what the definition is.

*[What experience should teach us]*N CLAUSE *is [that we must work towards an interactive model of grammar and discourse]*N CLAUSE · · ·

*The classical definition, [that a sentence expresses a complete thought]*N CLAUSE, *dates from the first Western treatise on grammar . . .*

Declarative noun clauses report speech or thought within the context of the author or speaker's opinion, attitude, perception, or experience. Declarative noun clauses often accompany verbs that have communicative, perceptual, or mental meanings such as *suggest* or *remind*:

> **Noun Clause Construction**
>
> [complementizer [S]]

> *In the end, teacher trainers and teachers may need to be reminded [**that** the academic skills they themselves require in teaching and learning are not far removed from those of their NNS students].*

Such noun clauses are also common with impersonal collocations (or lexical bundles, discussed in Chapter 13):

> *This means [**that** the task of "learning a language" must be reconceived].*

> *It goes without saying [**that** . . . all users of English are equal partners in ELF] . . .*

Indirect questions report a question or embed a question within the speaker's attitude, experience, or memory. Indirect questions can be yes/no questions or wh-questions. Indirect yes/no questions take *if* or *whether* as complementizers; indirect wh-questions take a full range of wh-question words. Indirect questions show preposing of the wh-word as the complementizer, but they do not show inversion of the subject and auxiliaries, as discussed in the last chapter. Thus their structure is not like that of direct questions in English because no inversion of the subject and auxiliary takes place, and the auxiliary *do* never occurs (except in the negative example below). Like declarative noun clauses, indirect questions function syntactically as subjects, direct objects, objects of prepositions, and subject complements.

> **Indirect yes/no question:** *One must also judge the situational and linguistic context in which the construction occurs to decide [**whether or not** any given instance of language use is appropriate semantically and pragmatically as well as grammatically].*

> **Indirect wh-questions:** *Teachers can't teach [**what** they don't know].*

> *Asking [**what morphemes** a word contains] and [**what** they mean] is asking*

*[what the coiner of the word had in mind] when[2] he coined it and possibly [**what unforeseen associations** it may have built up since].*

Reduced indirect questions have only a question word and an infinitive with *to.*

Compare the direct questions:

<u>Is</u> *any given instance of language use appropriate?*

*They asked me [**what** to do] but I didn't know.*

What don't they know?

What morphemes does a word contain?

*The researchers wondered [**where** to go] after completing their experiment.*

What do they mean?

What did the coiner of the word have in mind?

*I told them [**how** to proceed] with their investigation.*

What unforeseen associations may it have built up since? (Note that this is awkward as a direct question.)

For . . . to . . . clauses are similar to noun clauses, as in the following paraphrase for *"that learners need to engage in purposeful interaction."* The for–to clause highlights the noun *need* as the object of the verb *emphasize.*

*In summary, contemporary approaches to English language teaching and learning emphasize the need [**for** learners **to** engage] in purposeful interaction using spoken, written, and visual modes.*

Subordinate Clauses and Conjunction

Conjoined subordinate clauses occur frequently in academic prose and they participate in discourse and stylistic constraints on parallel structures. Sometimes complementizers are not present in all of the conjoined constructions. In the following example, in the first sentence there are three

2. The phrase *when he coined it* is not an embedded question but rather an adverb clause with the complementizer *when* because it gives time information but doesn't ask a question about it.

conjoined noun clauses. In the second sentence, there are four. However, the first sentence includes three complementizers and different subjects, whereas in the second one the same complementizer and subject *it* serves the four sentences.

> *The argument against traditional parsing is threefold: that it promotes old-fashioned descriptions of language based on Latin grammatical categories, that students do not benefit from it, and that it can be a source of frustration and boredom for both students and teachers. The argument in favour of parsing is fourfold: that it makes explicit the structure of speech and writing, exercises the mind in a disciplined way, enables people to talk about language usage, and helps in the learning and discussion of foreign languages.*

In this example, even though the complementizers and subjects are the same in each noun clause, they are repeated each time. Why does this author select for redundancy rather than the shorter alternative below? Is one easier to understand than the other?

> *Most fluent speakers of English seem to know what a word is. They know, for example, that words are listed in dictionaries, that they are separated in writing by spaces, and that they may be separated in speech by pauses.*

> *Most fluent speakers of English seem to know what a word is. They know, for example, that words are listed in dictionaries, separated in writing by spaces, and in speech by pauses.*

Discovery Procedures

For these discovery procedures, it is necessary to return to reduced indirect questions of the *when to go* and *for–to* clauses, because they are two important colligations in which infinitives are used. Infinitives are used in other colligations as well. They can be subjects and subject complements in a sentence.

> *To withdraw or abandon the language through which tradition speaks* is *to render tradition mute.*

They can be the complements to adjectives, nouns, and verbs. To discover the infinitive, it is necessary to examine the co-texts in which it appears.

With adjectives:

They might be unable to give a good explanation.

If even idolized, spoiled, and highly paid celebrities are willing to put up with practice, why not language learners, teachers, or researchers?

They produce texts with such a high number of . . . errors that native speakers find it difficult, if not impossible, to read and understand their texts.

With nouns:

Implicit or procedural knowledge . . . is the ability to speak a language unconsciously developed through acts of meaning-focused communication.

Many students never take seriously the need to improve their editing skills. (Note the shift of the heavy NP + Infinitive to after the adverb *seriously*.)

With verbs:

Once we learn to recognize parts of speech, we can begin to explore how particular types of words interact with certain other types within the sentence.

English ceases to be an exponent of only one culture.

Infinitives also occur in verb phrase constructions [V NP Infinitive], where the NP object is understood to be the subject of the infinitive.

[Parsing] enables people to talk about language usage,

We need a theory of language that enables us to understand how grammar is implicated in such processes.

Another common construction has the meaning of *in order to*.

One must also judge the situational and linguistic context in which the construction occurs to decide whether or not any given instance of language use is appropriate semantically and pragmatically as well as grammatically.

With the meaning of *in order to*, infinitives also occur as absolute expressions, that is, expressions that are outside of the main sentence structure.

To meet this goal, the training of teachers of English as a second language needs to provide a greater focus on language.

Clausal Awareness

Academic prose depends on modifiers like adjectives, adverbs, prepositional phrases, and subordinate sentences to create dense information-packed sentences. However, it is useful to see how that is accomplished and one way to do that is by taking the sentences apart into their fundamental propositional structure. Each modifier is given the status of a sentence, often by adding linking verbs. It is often possible to **deconstruct** sentences in different ways, but here are two examples where complex sentences have been taken apart and the rhetorical structure indicates contrast between ideas.

Contrast:

When we speak or write
We do not communicate by putting together lists.
  Sentences are in lists.
  Sentences are isolated.
We communicate by using sentences.
  Sentences are interrelated.
  Sentences are woven together.
We use sentences in order to form a coherent discourse.

. . . when we speak or write, we do not communicate by putting together lists of isolated sentences but instead by using sentences that are interrelated and woven together to form a coherent discourse.

But the study of grammar . . . does not end with learning about structures and functions within the sentence but rather uses the sentence as a starting point for exploring how grammar can be used in discourse to achieve more effective communication.

Reconstruction activities are similar to sentence unscrambling activities in that students take the propositions and re-form a sentence which they can then compare with the naturally well-formed sentence created by the author.

An alternative is to construct new sentences using models drawn from sentence frames in reading texts:

Contrast:

But	*The study of grammar does not end with learning.*
	Learning is about structures and functions.
	Structures and functions are within the sentence.
But rather	*The study of grammar uses the sentence.*
	The sentence is a starting point.
	The starting point is for exploring.
	We explore:
	How can we use grammar in discourse?
	How can we use grammar to achieve more effective
	communication?

When we _____ or _____, we do not _____ by _____, but instead by _____.

The _____ does not _____ but rather _____.

If these activities are too advanced, learners can combine given elements such as descriptive nouns, attributive and classifying adjectives, and prepositional phrases, or verbs with prepositional phrases, adverbs, and predicate adjectives in fill-in-the-blank or cloze activities. Fill-in-the-blank activities involve sentence level completion but cloze activities are paragraph length. The intention of the activity is for learners to become adept at creating complex NPs or VPs and to use natural word orders.

however   real-life   troublesome   always   students'

Real (L teachers, however, have always known that Studeterrors are troublesom

These activities, if simplified, can be done as oral activities as well. In this example, the teacher's focus is on complex sentences with a main clause and one subordinate clause, in this case adverb clauses of cause and effect. The class was referencing a cartoon that had a rat jumping on a piece of cheese, a candle, a rope, a weight, an apple, and a human face with an open mouth. The caption was "a modern way to eat an apple." The action of the rat jumping on the cheese ultimately leads to the apple falling into the human's open mouth.

1. T: *What happens if the rat or the mouse doesn't jump on the cheese?*
2. S1: *The man . . . doesn't eat the apple.*
3. T: *Doesn't eat the apple?*
4. S2: *The man has to use his hands.*
5. T: *Yes, imagine the man doesn't want to use his hands. The man . . .*
6. S1: *Will not eat the apple.*
7. T: *What happens if the candle doesn't burn the rope?*
8. S3: *The weight . . . the weight will not fall down.*
9. T: *OK, the weight won't . . . (writes down)*
10. S3: *Won't fall down.*
11. T: *What happens after the candle burns the rope?*
12. S: *The weight will . . .*
13. T: *The weight will fall down. Eh . . . use a consequence. Connect one action to another action . . . using a word like eh . . .*
14. S4: *If . . .*
15. T: *If . . . that might be a good example. S4?*
16. S4: *If rat does not eat the cheese the candle won't . . . won't burn the rope . . .*
17. T: *OK, the candle won't burn the rope. Use another word like "when" . . .*
18. S3: *When the rat eats the cheese, the candle will burn.*
19. T: *A . . . hmmm. Use another word like eh . . . "after" . . .*
20. S5: *After the weight fall down, the apple will throw up///*
21. T: *Throw up? S6? Will . . .*
22. S6: *will be thrown up.*
23. T: *Will be thrown up. Right. And use another one like . . . "unless" . . .*
24. S: *The 50 pound weight won't fall down unless the rope is burned.*
25. T: *Good. Yes, . . . (writes on board) You can connect any of these two actions with any of these words. What do you notice about this part?*
26. S: *will xxx*
27. T: *Yes . . . it is always going to have something to do with "will". Do you notice over here . . .*
28. S: *Present.*
29. T: *Always present tense. This is our new unit. We will start with complex sentences of this nature using relationships that involve cause and effect.*

(Kumaravadivelu, 2003, p. 180)

Study, Discussion, and Essay Questions

1. Review these terms and add them to your glossary with a definition and some examples if they are not already present: complex sentence, subordination, subordinate clauses, complementizer, noun clause, for–to clause, adjective clause, adverb clause, indirect questions, reduced indirect question, sentence modifying adjective clauses, reduced adjective clause, and appositive.

2. What is the difference between the declarative noun clause and the indirect question? What difference is there between indirect yes/no questions and indirect wh-questions?

3. Write some examples with the for–to construction. Follow this model: For you to speak English well, you may need to practice orally.

4. What is the difference between restrictive adjective clauses and non-restrictive in meaning? How is this meaning difference marked in speech or writing? Write some examples with these constructions.

5. Read through the example from Kumaravadivelu (2003, p. 180) as a role play.

6. Is the underlined portion an indirect question or an adverb clause?

> _Whether English has been the first or an additional language to the writers_, _they have been addressing an international audience, not primarily ENL communities._

7. What is parallel structure? How is it related to subordinate clauses?

8. Identify the type of the underlined subordinate clauses in these excerpts adapted from the examples in the corpus and articulate why you made that choice:

   a. _English is now the language of those who use it._
   b. _The advantage of the holistic system is that it reduces processing effort._
   c. _The changes in mental representation occur both at the time languages are being used and when they are not currently in use._ (Hint: These are both the same type of subordinate clause but one has an unusual complementizer.)
   d. _The categories or principles of core syntax do not have to be learned because they are there right from the beginning._
   e. _The ability to examine large text corpora in a systematic manner allows access to a quality of evidence that has not been available before._

9. Deconstruct this complex sentence. There is no one correct answer but the best answers maintain the meaning as much as possible.

> *If the child has to learn the irregular and peculiar aspects of language by general learning mechanisms, these mechanisms should suffice to learn the more general and predictable patterns of that language as well.*

10. Reconstruct these sentences that emphasize contrast, using your own words. Two options: Try to make the sentence sound funny or try to make the sentence sound academic. Sometimes more than one word can be inserted in each blank.

> *When we _____ or _____, we do not _____ by _____, but instead by _____.*
>
> *The _____ does not _____ but rather _____.*

11. Create some fill-in-the-blank exercises from some of your sentences from the answers in your Language Notebook.

Activities

1. Identify and discuss the use of the infinitives in the following sentences:

   a. *Language is a dynamic system. It comprises the ecological interactions of many players: people who want to communicate and a world to be talked about.*

   b. *It, to put it simply, breaks the continuity between my past and my present. My past is my tradition and the tradition of my community/society . . .*

   c. *First and foremost, the ability to examine large text corpora in a systematic manner allows access to a quality of evidence that has not been available before.*

   d. *The regularities of pattern are sometimes spectacular and, to balance, the variation seems endless.*

2. Parallel structure has to do with good writing style and not grammatical structure. That is, sentences with non-parallel structure are common and go unnoticed in speaking or informal writing because they are not ungrammatical; in fact, people often conjoin elements that they perceive

to have the same function in the sentence, as shown in the box. For instance, if two constituents are descriptive, people may feel that they can be conjoined even if they are different types of phrases. However, good writers avoid mismatched conjoined expressions and revise them so that they are parallel.

> The temperature was <u>below zero</u> and <u>very frigid</u>.
> He likes <u>to eat</u> and <u>finding new restaurants to eat in</u>.
> They don't know <u>the procedure</u> or <u>how to find out what it is</u>.

In a more precise definition, parallel structure refers to a style in which the various parts of the sentence are parallel to each other in part of speech, verbal aspect, tense, voice, pronoun usage, and direct and indirect speech.

> The temperature was [subzero and frigid]_{ADJP}
> He likes [eating and finding new restaurants to eat in]_{GERUNDS}
> He likes [to eat and to find new restaurants to eat in]_{INFINITIVES}
> They don't know [how to do it or (even) how to find out how to do it]_{ADV CLAUSES}

Non-parallel:	*I like to eat in a restaurant rather than staying home and cooking.*
Parallel:	*I like eating in a restaurant rather than staying home and cooking.*
Non-parallel:	*She is famous for her intelligence, wit, and being fair.*
Parallel:	*She is famous for her intelligence, wit, and sense of fair play.*
Non-parallel:	*Sunday afternoon I played football and the evening was spent doing homework.*
Parallel:	*Sunday afternoon I played football and then Sunday evening I did homework.*

In the following sentences, determine what is non-parallel and discuss how the non-parallel structures can be turned into parallel structures.

a. Write non-parallel sentences and then you need to pass them to your neighbor to fix them.

b. One doesn't understand how challenging teaching is until you have tried it.

c. He hopes to work for that company rather than staying at the same job.

d. Having the will to do something and to actually do it are completely different.

e. It is preferable to quit smoking than continuing the bad habit.

f. The aid workers received the shipment of food and it was distributed by them.

g. I asked why anyone would say that and did they understand it.

h. We can understand the need to fix this problem, but you can't repair everything at once.

i. He is trying to decide what he aspires to and the manner of accomplishing his goals.

j. Her talent and persistence match her having great ambition.

k. He wrote the book quickly and with great ease.

3. Find the non-parallel structures hidden in this paragraph about anglophone universities and rewrite the paragraphs to fix them.

To remediate or not to remediate, that is the question facing many universities around the English-speaking world. The debate concerns both the math skills of incoming students and those who write the English language poorly. Some of the students coming into universities are bilingual immigrants who might be expected to have language challenges and needing remediation by ESL programs and writing courses. However, the fact is that many of the students who need remediation are native English-speaking students. To date, this debate has been framed by the questions why our public schools fail to produce adequate English writers and which institutions should offer remediation: the schools or the universities.

Surprisingly, linguists have questions about this, but the controversy remains uninformed by the questions that might be posed by linguists, namely, why so many English-speaking students fail to learn "proper" writing and could we have growing diglossia in English? Why does the notion of changing writing standards and to modify the curriculum not even occur to policy makers? Why does the mere mention of change evoke virulent opposition from faculty members, who object to "dumbing down" the curriculum and the loss of an integral part of their culture? If we are concerned about student writing, what can you do about it?

Discourse

13

When you study grammar, you learn to analyze language by breaking sentences into separate pieces in order to focus on individual parts, to recognize what the parts are, and to understand how these parts function together to convey meaning. But the study of grammar . . . does not end with learning about structures and functions within the sentence but rather uses the sentence as a starting point for exploring how grammar can be used in discourse to achieve more effective communication. That is, when we speak or write, we do not communicate by putting together lists of isolated sentences but instead by using sentences that are interrelated and woven together to form a coherent discourse. Our study of grammar, then, should help us gain insights into how grammar itself can be a means for packaging effective expressions in extended discourse of various kinds.

(DeCarrico, 2000, p. 1)

DeCarrico points out the continuity between grammar at or below the sentence level and grammar at the level of discourse. Communication takes place, and has always taken place, by means of creating a "text" of interrelated utterances and sentences woven together when speakers create coherent discourse together with others or for others. Because language users have learned a system based on usage and exposure to priming and probabilities, and share that system with other users, their common knowledge, or grammar, serves as the means of organizing the multi-level linguistic choices available to communicate what they want to communicate and in the way they want to communicate it.

The earliest such "texts" during millennia were spoken conversations, stories, songs, orations, ceremonies, and the like. In more recent centuries, speech and spoken discourse have been joined by writing and written discourse, and the latter have become as normal as speech and spoken discourse for many people. Thus, discourse is defined as the individual or collaborative creation of spoken or written texts generally made up of more than one sentence.

The intention of the person(s) creating a text determines its primary characteristic, its structure. People tell a story using a narrative structure, they give instructions in a list of commands, they gather information by conducting an interview of questions and answers, they perform rituals by repeating memorized phrases in a set order, and so on. The text-creator's intention also determines the medium for the communication and the genre as written or oral, formal or informal, on or off the record, and so on. This harks back to the idea introduced in Chapter 1 that oral genres like conversations and informal speeches show a range of discourse characteristics that contrast with those of written genres like letters, newspaper or web reports, and academic essays, but because there is choice, there is also overlap.

For example, the pseudo-cleft sentence structure is frequent in conversations because its discourse purpose is to return to earlier comments to say more about them. In the pseudo-cleft structure, there is a wh-noun clause (usually with *what*) followed by a linking verb and a *that*-noun clause. Paradoxically, although pseudo-cleft sentences are relatively rare in academic prose, this example is from the corpus gathered for this book. Perhaps the author of that particular text meant to write somewhat informally, because it also uses the pronouns *we* and *us*.

> [*What experience should teach us*], then, is [*that we must work towards an interactive model of grammar and discourse*]

The choice of the writer in this case is to summarize earlier comments with the wh-noun clause, emphasize the summary with the adverb *then* set off in commas, and add a new comment after the linking verb. The important characteristics of discourse are based on speakers' intentions, the media selected, the genre and text type, and also internal discourse functions related to purpose, presentation, coherence, and cohesion. These preliminaries affect later choices made in the construction of sentences, colligations, vocabulary; in short, they affect the lexical and grammatical structure of the text itself.

In creating their texts, people try to be **coherent**; coherence means that spoken or written texts have logic and order, making them understandable and relevant to the situation at hand. This is first and foremost: the ideas that are expressed and the content of the text must be comprehensible by listeners and readers. Second, speakers and writers make certain lexical, syntactic, and stylistic choices to convey their ideas and express the content as coherently as possible. They choose word orders, preposing, postposing, and inversion to highlight, downplay, or connect information and topics, and they use specific **cohesive devices**, or lexical, syntactic, and stylistic choices, to show how ideas relate to each other. For instance, they use common lexical bundles to show their stance toward what they are communicating, and they frame their ideas in common sentence builders. This chapter will explore these topics.

Stylistic Choices

Choice is pervasive and involves almost all aspects of English grammar except features of system elements like subject–verb agreement in person and number, plurality in determiner and nouns, and pronominal reference to animate or human nouns as subjects and objects, and the like. Other default choices are the most common or most general features, such as the subject before the verb, the direct object after the verb, the adjective before the noun, the object after the preposition. These pattern-based characteristics of declarative utterances and sentences are so expected, so highly primed, that they have ceased to be conscious choices at all for most speakers and writers. That means that the choice of the unmarked structures of English is so highly regulated by automatic priming and expectations that selection operates unconsciously for most language use. There are also some choices that disrupt normal priming, but they are not unexpected either. For instance, preposing and inversion mark the slightly less typical discourse functions of questioning, exclaiming, or commanding.

In general, options available to the speaker and writer involve the ordering of elements with respect to each other in the discourse, and the selection of frequent or "unmarked" structures or infrequent or "marked" structures. As with other metalinguistic awareness, there is variation in any population in terms of their knowledge of the choices available and their intentionality as they compose utterances and sentences, such as in the selection of passive or active for verbs, past or present tense, the use of one determiner over another, or the position of adverb clauses with respect to their main clauses.

The best speakers and writers know which less typical choices, like progressive or perfect aspects or modals, accomplish in the best way the communicative function they are intending: persuasion, explanation, entertainment, humor, reporting, and many others. The knowledge of these choices is problematic for English learners as they attempt to produce language. For instance, Celse-Murcia (1998, p. 688) points out that English learners may not be aware of differences between ditransitive constructions and prepositional dative constructions:

> the learner's ability to produce the form or construction with linguistic accuracy is only part of the overall production task. One must also judge the situational and linguistic context in which the construction occurs to decide whether or not any given instance of language use is appropriate semantically and pragmatically as well as grammatically. For example, if the question *What did you give Jim?* (in its unmarked form) is asked of someone, an appropriate unmarked response (pragmatically) is *a/the tie* or *I gave him a/the tie*, but not *I gave a/the tie to Jim/him.*

Celse-Murcia's example of the possible alternations of direct and indirect object orders (discussed in Chapters 10 and 11) based on given or new information also shows the effects of determiner choice (*a/the tie*) and pronominal or nominal choice (*him/Jim*). It is impossible to do justice to all of the choices that English offers, but here a few are discussed: the position of adverbs in the sentence in terms of what they can modify and what they mean, the use of the existential *there*, and the position of adverb clauses with respect to their main clause.

Adverbs

The first sentence below reflects the author's choice to use the adverb *simply* to modify the main verb *occur*; in the second (constructed) example, the adverb modifies the negation; in the third example *simply* modifies the prepositional phrase. The difference in each meaning is conveyed by a paraphrase after each one. Indeed, the placement of the adverb *simply* causes some variation in its meaning too, in a range from the more figurative "only" to the more literal "in a simple manner."

Individual words do not [simply occur] as unrelated strings in sentences.
Individual words are more than unrelated strings in sentences.
Individual words [simply do not occur] as unrelated strings in sentences.
Individual words never occur as unrelated strings in sentences.
Individual words do not occur [simply as unrelated strings in sentences].
Individual words occur as something more complicated than unrelated strings.

Postposing: Existential There

There are many examples of existential *there* in the database. Some examples are collocations that create a frame and vantage point for an assertion stated as a noun clause or another clausal type. In these examples from the corpus, the author chooses a construction with existential *there* to express a point of view in a very strong or even arrogant way:

> *To begin with, [there is little question] that English is . . . the carrier of Anglo-American cultural imperialism, neo-colonialism, commercialism. [There is little point] in English speakers, American or British, apologizing for these three things.*

However, existential *there* is most prototypically selected by language user to introduce a new topic or a new entity into the discourse, or, if negative, to assert the non-existence of a new topic or entity.

> *Learning a language is not a question of acquiring grammatical structure but of expanding a repertoire of communicative contexts. Consequently, [there is no date or age] at which the learning of a language can be said to be complete. New contexts, and new occasions of negotiation of meaning, occur constantly.*

The new topic/entity is thus shifted away from subject position to subject complement position to highlight it as the new information in the discourse. The following example is prototypical in that the subject complement is an indefinite noun phrase, as shown by the indefinite article *a*. (This example also shows hedging in that the author chooses to soften a claim into a conjecture by using verbs like *suggest* and modals like *may* or *might*.)

> *These results suggest that parsing decisions may depend in part on the person's history of experience with the structures under scrutiny, in which case [there might be a general bias] in favor of analyses that occur most frequently in the language.*

In academic prose, the new topic/entity is often generic, abstract, or plural:

> *It stands to reason that in written language use, where [there is no possibility] of the overt reciprocal negotiation of meaning typical of spoken interaction, [there is more reliance on established norms].*

> *Yet despite this complexity, despite its lack of overt government, instead of anarchy and chaos, [there are patterns everywhere].*

Existential *there* is used to define or elaborate a topic when the subject complement is related to subcategories of earlier or later topics:

[There are five types of phrases], named after their main word . . .

Preposing or Postposing of Adverb Clauses

As noted in the last chapter, adverb clauses can occur either before or after their main clause. It was suggested that adverb clauses occurring before the main sentence highlight information important to the development of a text and the advancing flow of information, but adverb clauses that follow the main clause are less important to the development of the overall text and simply add information or modify the main clause. In the first sentence below, drawn from the corpus, the adverb clause links the construction *transmuting alchemy* back to earlier text, and summarizes in a two word package the discussion of the changes that have accompanied the spread of English around the world, and the main sentence is a further comment on that. The second (hypothetical) example links *transmuting alchemy* quite specifically to its main clause about the language becoming less culture-specific. In the second sentence, the adverb clause doesn't escape its sentential context.

As this transmuting alchemy of English takes effect, the language becomes less and less culture-specific.

The language becomes less and less culture-specific, as this transmuting alchemy of English takes effect.

If the hypothesis is correct, then unlike what is often presented in grammar books, the position of adverb clauses is not random; they are not simply variations of the same information. In the cases below, the option chosen by the author makes sense, but the hypothetical reversed option is a truism, a statement that must be true because it is obvious or self-evident. Note that there is also interaction with the adverb *only*, which makes the third option (with inversion of the modal auxiliary in the main sentence) a possibility.

We can only account for collocation if we assume that every word is mentally primed for collocational use.

If we assume that every word is mentally primed for collocational use, we can (only) account for collocation.

> *Only if we assume that every word is mentally primed for collocational use, can we account for collocation.*

Adverb clauses are important in organizing the discourse of the text they appear in because they link directly back to information in the text and show important relationships of condition, time, contrast, and causality. In the first example below, the conjunction *but* contrasts the mapping that must occur and the innateness of the categories. In the second (hypothetical) example, the conjunction *but* along with the immediate appearance of the adverb clause heightens the contrast being made. Both of these alternatives are possible, but the author has selected one over the other for discourse purposes.

> *A powerful solution to the acquisition problem is the assumption that innate linguistic structure helps the child overcome the (possible) underspecification of language structure in the input. In this view, the input has to be mapped onto innate linguistic categories, but [the categories or principles of core syntax do not have to be learned **because they are there right from the beginning**].*

> *A powerful solution to the acquisition problem is the assumption that innate linguistic structure helps the child overcome the (possible) underspecification of language structure in the input. In this view, the input has to be mapped onto innate linguistic categories, but [**because they are there right from the beginning**, the categories or principles of core syntax do not have to be learned].*

Cohesive Choices

Cohesive devices are signals that allow a listener or a speaker to follow the meaning of a text and create a mental representation of the message. Cohesive devices include pro-words to replace a phrase or clause for discourse purposes such as *then*, *there*, *here*, verbal *do*, clausal *so*, and the use of **ellipsis** (deletion of identical or recoverable repeated information). In the following text, there are a number of **referential cohesive ties**, including referential noun phrases (indefinite or definite), repetition of nouns, paraphrases of nouns, pronouns and demonstratives, and meta-discourse references.

> *We can only account for collocation if we assume that [every word] is mentally primed for collocational use. As [a word] is acquired through encounters with [it] in speech and writing, [it] becomes cumulatively loaded with [contexts and co-texts] in which [it] is encountered, and our knowledge of [it] includes the fact*

*that [it] co-occurs with certain [other words] in certain kinds of [context]. [**The***
***same**] applies to [word sequences] built out of [these words]; [these] too become*
loaded with [the contexts and co-texts] in which [they] occur. I refer to [this
property] as nesting, where [the product of a priming] becomes [itself] primed in
ways that do not apply to [the individual words] making up [the combination].

Chains of Reference

Cohesive devices create a chain of reference, such as the chain created in the
example above by repetition, pronouns, variation in nouns, and paraphrases:
every word, a word, it (× 5), *other words, word sequences, these words, these, they,*
the individual words, and *the combination.* This chain extends through the entire
text cited. In the middle of this chain of reference, the meta-discourse term *the*
same allows the author to extend the same argument from the word level to
the level of word sequences with subsequent elaboration. There is also the use
of the demonstrative in *this property* to link the discussion in the text to a
specialized term (nesting), which is then defined in a subordinate clause. This
text also contains the use of an indefinite plural referential expression *contexts*
and co-texts, later repeated more definitely as *the contexts and co-texts.*

The following text shows (besides the pseudo-cleft construction) the use of
the pronoun *one* to substitute for and repeat a complex NP in order to elaborate
further.

What experience should teach us, then, is that we must work toward [an
*interactive model of grammar and discourse], **one** that demonstrates the necessity*
and importance of both levels of language to the language learning process and
to the attainment of communicative competence.

Conjunctions link words, colligations, clauses, and sentences in unmarked
ways, but they are also important cohesive devices in that they move the
discourse along and show the relationship among constituents, sentences,
and clauses. The same can be said of subordinating complementizers, in
particular, as discussed earlier, adverb complementizers. In these examples,
along with other cohesive devices, the conjunctions mark important discourse
purposes and the conjuncts must appear in a specific order in order to make
sense:

Language *is a dynamic system. **It** comprises the ecological interactions of many*
*players: people who want to communicate **and** a world to be talked about.*

> *That is,* **when** *we speak or write, we do not communicate [***by** *putting together lists of isolated sentences* **but instead by** *using sentences that are interrelated and woven together to form a coherent discourse].*

These examples show another very common discourse structure, one that is based on parallelisms among the colligational and collocational choices. In the first sentence just above, the parallelism is imperfect but highly effective in that the two conjoined phrases are NPs with a head noun and a descriptive constituent, an adjective clause (*who want to communicate*) and an infinitive phrase (*to be talked about*). The second example has parallel *by*-phrases with gerunds (*by putting together . . . by using sentences*), but also places the prepositional phrases in opposition to each other by using the word *instead*.

Lexical Bundles

Lexical bundles are recurrent sequences of words that have discourse functions in sentences in various textual types but they may not be complete constructions. Lexical bundles are multi-word units that often occur at phrasal and clausal boundaries. There is a lot of priming among the words in lexical bundles, so they are sometimes considered a type of collocation. Lexical bundles can be complex prepositions like *the nature of the, as a result of* or clausal introductions with a verb phrase and the beginning of a complement clause such as *I don't know how, I thought that was*. Like other collocations, lexical bundles are often nested within longer lexical bundles, as in *I don't think* as a part of *well I don't think, I don't think so,* or *but I don't think*.

> **Lexical bundles** are identified as the most commonly or most frequently occurring four word sequences in corpora of conversations and written texts.

> Although they are neither idiomatic nor structurally complete, lexical bundles are important building blocks in discourse. Lexical bundles provide a kind of pragmatic "head" for larger phrases and clauses, where they function as discourse frames for the expression of new information. That is, the lexical bundle expresses stance or textual meanings, while the remainder of the phrase / clause expresses new propositional information that has been framed by the lexical bundle. In this way, lexical bundles provide interpretive frames for the developing discourse. For example,

I want you to write a very brief summary of his lecture.

(Biber and Barbieri, 2007, p. 270)

Biber and Barbieri (2007) identify amounts of lexical bundles in different genres; for instance, classroom teaching has more bundles than academic writing or textbooks. Because they are so varied in their syntactic structure, lexical bundles are best differentiated by their function. In academic discourse, they found three functions for lexical bundles: stance, discourse, and reference. The three functions are differentiated both in their purpose and in where they occur most commonly, in spoken or in written discourses, in lectures or in classroom management speaking, and so on.

Stance functions:
epistemic *the fact that the*
desire *I want you to*
obligation *you have to do*
intention/prediction *what we're going to*
ability *to be able to*

Discourse functions:
topic introduction *what I want to do*
topic elaboration/clarification *has to do with*
identification/focus *those of you who*

Reference functions:
description *the size of the*
time/place/text *as shown in Figure*

Stance bundles give the speaker's or writer's attitude toward a proposition that makes up the rest of the utterance or sentence. They frame the proposition with a depiction of the certainty or uncertainty of the proposition. **Discourse bundles** show the relationships between the pieces of the discourse; for example, they might show the listener how to connect the present discourse to prior discourse or following discourse. **Reference bundles** identify or characterize entities or parts of entities involved in the discourse. As might be expected, all of these types of bundles are frequent in classroom teaching and lecturing.

Lexical bundles are combinations of system and resource words that occur again and again in a corpus of data. If corpora are similar to the linguistic data to which people are exposed as they speak, read, listen, and write, then frequency measures are evidence for lexical priming just as they are for collocations. However, lexical bundles are also clearly related to syntactic priming, in that the choice of a lexical bundle primes the abstract constructions that might go with it. Formulaic expressions like collocations and lexical bundles aid in comprehension and production of speech and writing, because they take advantage of lexical and syntactic priming expectations. For instance, Kuipers (1996, p. 3) says that "[f]ormulae make the business of speaking (and that of hearing) easier. I assume that when a speaker uses a formula he or she needs only to retrieve it from the dictionary instead of building it up from its constituent parts."

Sentence Builders

Nattinger and DeCarrico (1992, p. 90) use the expression **sentence builders** for groups of words that provide a framework for whole sentences like *the ____ er X, the ____ er Y*, as in *The higher you climb, the farther you fall*. They use the term **macro-organizers** for expressions that signal the organization of high-level or meta-discourse information in a text. Macro-organizers mark topics, shifts in topics, summarize, and give examples, relationships, evaluations, qualifications, and asides. Some of their examples are: *"I wanted to mention that X, However X, and also X, but then X, and not only that but X."* Nattinger and DeCarrico think that the integration of sentence builders and macro-organizers into discourse is greater in writing than in speaking:

> Speakers use very small chunks of language when they construct conversations, usually no more than two or three lexical phrases joined to form a response or question, whereas writers, with time to edit and sculpt, produce longer and more complexly integrated utterances. The integration that characterizes written language occurs generally through complexity of noun groups, conjoined parallel phrases, sequences of prepositional phrases, and relative clauses . . . It is particularly signaled by macro-organizers that function to signal clearly distinct levels and patterns of coordination and subordination, as described above.
>
> (Nattinger and DeCarrico, 1992, p. 84)

In many ways, the concepts of lexical bundle, sentence builder, and macro-organizers seem like different names for the same things, but they are all involved directly in the personal choices that speakers and writers make, in communication, to project personality, attitude, and identity. In the following example, the writer's ideas are coherent, and the relationship among the ideas is marked by the appositive, parallel structure, cohesive devices, lexical bundles, sentence builders, and macro-organizers. Although many would not agree with the ideas expressed, the stance of the writer is made perfectly clear:

We, the speakers of English, should proudly flaunt the banners of cultural imperialism, neo-colonialism, and commercialism. The first places us in the forefront of intellectual and educational progress; the second proves that we are scientifically and technologically in the lead; the third points the way to a better material life for everyone concerned.

The following example shows opposition and parallelism at the sentence level, using adverb clauses placed before their main sentences and the sentence builder *conversely.*

. . . if we teach grammar without reference to discourse, our students will fail to acquire the discourse competence so vital for developing effective reading and writing skills. Conversely, if we teach discourse (i.e. meaning and functions) without reference to grammar, our learners will produce discourse reminiscent of Kroll's (1990) college-level ESL composition students who exhibit the +rhetoric/–grammar syndrome . . .

Macro-organizers are a means for meta-discourse commentary, or commentary about the discourse itself:

The integration that characterizes written language . . . is particularly signaled by macro-organizers that function to signal clearly distinct levels and patterns of coordination and subordination . . . [as described above].

[In summary], contemporary approaches to English language teaching and learning emphasize the need for learners to engage in purposeful interaction using spoken, written, and visual modes.

The marginalization of my mother tongue creates a temporal tension in my being-in-the-world—a tension which is the result of the power differential between the two languages . . . It, [to put it simply], breaks the continuity between my past and my present.

A speaker's sensitivity to previous encounters with language forms and meanings suggests that language use is sensitive to the occurrence of language forms and meanings in the environment. [In other words], the exact forms and meanings that speakers use can be affected by the language that occurred in discourse they recently engaged in.

The expression *to put it simply* is an infinitive phrase, and infinitive phrases often appear at the beginning of a phrase for discourse purposes. As an alternative, it could appear as:

> *To put it simply, it breaks the continuity between my past and my present.*

The version selected by the author emphasizes and strengthens the connection between the marginalization of his mother tongue and how it affects him. Infinitive phrases are absolute expressions.

Absolute Expressions

MacArthur (1992, p. 6) defines an **absolute expression** as "a term indicating that a word, phrase, or clause stands apart from the usual relations with other elements in a sentence." Many examples involve non-finite verbals, but some do not, and they can occur at the beginning or at the end of sentences. Only a few absolute expressions are common in conversation, like *weather permitting*, or *present company excluded*. Stylistically, especially in writing, absolute expressions without overt subjects must match their main sentence in subject or else they can be misunderstood. If the subject of the absolute expression doesn't match the subject of the main sentence, the absolute expression is called a **dangling modifier**, discussed in the Activities section of the chapter.

> *The regularities of pattern are sometimes spectacular and, <u>to balance</u>, the variation seems endless.*

> *<u>To meet this goal</u>, the training of teachers of English as a second language needs to provide a greater focus on language—beyond conversational discourse.*

> *Language, <u>taken as real</u>, is something which constantly and in every moment passes away . . .*

> *<u>Taken directly and strictly</u>, this is the definition of each act of speaking but in a true and intrinsic sense one can look upon language as but the totality of all spoken utterances.*

Discovery Procedures

Discovering the discourse structure of a text and its cohesive devices requires a simultaneous meaning- and message-oriented approach. The following paragraph is a densely packed example of academic prose, but it has a rather simple organization starting with a very general topic sentence using a subject / linking verb / subject complement construction. The second sentence mentions, in a general but unique way, what language is composed of and its importance in human culture and communication. A colon links but also separates the somewhat parallel NPs that elaborate on the interactions of many "players" and related ecology and the "world." There is a central chain of reference to **language** as a dynamic system that involves pronouns, paraphrases, and repetitions, and secondary chains of reference to the somewhat opposing concepts of **complexity** and **pattern**, concepts that must be integrated for us to understand language as a dynamic system.

*(1) **Language** is **a dynamic system**. (2) **It** comprises the ecological interactions of many players: people who want to communicate and a world to be talked about. (3) **It** operates across many different agents (neurons, brains, and bodies; phonemes, morphemes, lexemes, constructions, interactions, and discourses), different human conglomerations (individuals, social groups, networks, and cultures), and different timescales (evolutionary, diachronic, epigenetic, ontogenetic, interactional, neurosynchronic). (4) Cognition, consciousness, experience, embodiment, brain, self, communication and human interaction, society, culture, and history are all inextricably intertwined in rich, complex, and dynamic ways in **language**. (5) Yet despite **this complexity**, despite **its lack of overt government**, instead of anarchy and chaos, there are **patterns** everywhere, patterns not preordained by God, by genes, by school curriculum, or by other human policy, but patterns that emerge—synchronic **patterns of linguistic organization** at numerous levels (phonology, lexis, syntax, semantics, pragmatics, discourse, genre, etc.), **dynamic patterns** of usage, **diachronic patterns** of language change (linguistic cycles of grammaticization, pidginization, creolization, etc.), **ontogenetic developmental patterns** in child language acquisition, **global geopolitical patterns** of language growth and decline, dominance and loss, and so forth. (6) As **a complex system**, **the systematicities of language** are emergent and adaptive. (7) Only by adopting an **integrative, dynamic framework** will we understand how **they** come about.*

In the third sentence, there are multiple lists of appositive NPs in parentheses, which, if removed, make a simpler sentence structure with conjoined parallel chunks:

> *[Language] operates across many different agents, different human conglomerations, and different timescales.*

The fourth sentence begins with a very complex conjoined series of NPs and closes with the general term "language."

> *[Cognition, consciousness, experience, embodiment, brain, self, communication and human interaction, society, culture, and history] are all inextricably intertwined in rich, complex, and dynamic ways in* **language.**

Sentence 5 contrasts the ideas of "complexity," apparent lack of "government," and the chaos and anarchy which might be expected from such complexity and lack of government, with the central notion of "pattern" in language. These patterns are not genetic, divine, or learned. The patterns are evident in the linguistic system itself; they emerge from usage and exposure. Language change, language development in children, and language growth and decline are all emergent and yet pattern-based. The author leaves the ending of this complex sentence open to the idea that there are more emergent patterns possible with the meta-discourse construction *and so forth*. Sentence 6 returns to the central idea of language as a system and summarizes sentence 5 with the adjectives *emergent* and *adaptive*. Sentence 7 concludes the paragraph with the suggestion that applied linguists should embrace a concept of language that integrates (and doesn't ignore or discard) the complexities of dynamic performance and actual usage, and that, indeed, is the only way the system of language can be properly studied and understood.

Discourse Awareness

> [I]f we teach grammar without reference to discourse, our students will fail to acquire the discourse competence so vital for developing effective reading and writing skills. Conversely, if we teach discourse (i.e. meaning and functions) without reference to grammar, our learners will produce discourse reminiscent of Kroll's (1990) college-level ESL composition students who exhibit the +rhetoric/−grammar syndrome; that is, they write logically organized and coherent texts but with such a high number

of morphosyntactic errors that native speakers find it difficult, if not impossible, to read and understand their texts. What experience should teach us, then, is that we must work towards an interactive model of grammar and discourse, one that demonstrates the necessity and importance of both levels of language to the language learning process and to the attainment of communicative competence.

(Celse-Murcia, 1998, p. 699)

One weakness in many current English methodologies is that there is a disconnect between them and the learning of writing, where grammatical accuracy, naturalness, and textual well-formedness are especially important. At present, many English language teachers do not teach writing beyond the level of the sentence. Many, if they teach writing at all, limit their instruction to the occasional descriptive paragraph, personal narrative, or shallow opinion piece. Other teachers prefer to emulate literature teachers, spending class time reading and writing poetry, fables, or folk tales in order for students to acquire their own voice in writing. While these are entertaining and educational, they do not lead to fluency and accuracy in the informational, abstract, and dense academic reading and writing that characterizes Academic English, where the author's voice is minimized and oblique.

Writing instruction must take a two-pronged targeted approach. On the one hand, it must facilitate analytical choices and maximize accurate linguistic usage and exposure, so it needs to include rules and generalizations as well as practice and exposure. At the same time, grammar instruction must go hand in hand with learning about naturalness in vocabulary choice, collocations, lexical bundles, discourse organizers, and other constructions appropriate for academic texts and genres. Grammar and word choices are stylistic choices that only make sense when considered in the context of register and genre. For example, using the broad term **amplifier** for usages that add intensity to writing, Hinkel (2002, p. 126) points out that her non-native-speaking students used amplifiers much more often in their essays than did her native-speaking students. She says that:

in rhetorical traditions other than Anglo-American, exaggerations and overstatements are considered to be appropriate means of persuasion, when amplification is intended to convey a high degree of the writer's conviction . . . the reason that the frequency rates of amplifiers were so high in NNS texts may lie in the fact that, in general, NNS writers relied on restricted syntactic and lexical repertoires and, hence, employed other means of conveying their ideas and the degree of their conviction.

Hinkel gives this example of the overuse of amplifiers: *There are a lot of people who totally hate their jobs, and they are very miserable*. This sentence is grammatically correct (and probably true as well), but the number of amplifiers in the sentence make it too exaggerated for academic writing. Discourse awareness must be a new goal of grammar and writing instruction.

Study, Discussion, and Essay Questions

1. Review these terms and add them to your glossary with a definition and some examples if they are not already present: text, pseudo-cleft sentence, genre, coherence, cohesion, preposing, postposing, inversion, cohesive devices, existential *there*, hedging, adverb clause, truism, chains of reference, conjunctions, parallelism, lexical bundles, nesting, sentence builder, macro-organizer, meta-discourse commentary, absolute expressions, dangling modifier, and amplifier.
2. What is discourse? What are some examples of spoken and written discourse that are most familiar to you? What kinds of linguistic choices are involved in those texts?
3. What is the relationship between the text creator's intention and the structure, medium, and genre of the text?
4. What are the aspects of language that do not allow choice?
5. Do you think metalinguistic awareness is related to writing ability? Why or why not? What other abilities do good writers have?
6. What is the difference, in terms of their use in texts, between ditransitive constructions and prepositional dative constructions?
7. What are the different locations for adverbs in sentences? What difference in meaning do they produce? Make an example of the same sentence with adverbs in different places.
8. The "existential *there*" construction is used to postpose a noun phrase. What different rhetorical purposes does this construction have? Look at some examples in a concordance to answer this question.
9. What difference does location have in the use of adverb clauses in texts?
10. What are some examples of cohesive devices? What examples can you find in your writing?
11. What are the functions of lexical bundles? Make up some original sentences with the lexical bundles.
12. "The bigger they are, the harder they fall" is an expression about the political disgrace of leaders who get into trouble. Make up some other examples with this sentence frame: *the _____er X, the _____er Y*.

Activities

1. Thinking back on some conversations you have been part of recently, rephrase some of the information as pseudo-cleft sentences.
2. In dangling modifiers, the implied subject of a sentence modifier or absolute expression doesn't match the subject of the main sentence. With your partner, go over these sentences, taking turns identifying if the sentence has a dangling modifier or not. If it does, explain it to your partner and suggest an alternative that doesn't "dangle." You can either add a subject to the modifier, or rephrase the main sentence (e.g. change active to passive, etc.).

   a. As a child, he learned to speak four languages natively.
   b. The train overcrowded, we had to stand up during the trip.
   c. Found guilty of murder, the judge sentenced the man to years in prison.
   d. When finished cooking, you need to take the roast out of the oven.
   e. Warned of the danger, the sharks frightened the swimmers.
   f. Speeding down the street at 80 miles an hour, the car careened out of control.
   g. To understand the problem, both factors need to be considered.
   h. As a boy, his parents encouraged him to play all sports.
   i. Always a wonderful host, Mark welcomed his guests at the door.
   j. While cooking the potatoes, the water should never evaporate completely.
   k. Obsessed with computer games, their parents forced them to set time limits on their playing.
   l. Realizing that conservation was a must, the lights were turned off.
   m. A total mess after the storm, I turned in at the car wash.

3. Look for chains of reference in a few of your longer answers in your Language Notebook. What other cohesive devices can you find? Rewrite your paragraph if necessary so that there are more cohesive devices. Be prepared to share your paragraph.
4. Discourse affects word choice and word choice creates discourse styles. Identify which of these word sets belong to informal conversational discourse and which are appropriate in more formal academic discourse. How did you make your decisions?

Nouns	*man, woman, day*	*proof, evidence, tests*
Verbs	*have, do, get*	*claim, prove, establish*

Adjectives	*former, obvious, clear*	*happy, depressed*
Adverbs	*very, too*	*absolutely, unmistakably*
Prepositions	*throughout, despite*	*in, to, over*
Conjunctions	*neither . . . nor*	*and, or*

Part III

Unstable Grammatical Features

Chapter 14 is about the flexible and fluid English usages that might be susceptible to change or modification over time. The term instability is a cover term that includes both diverse forms and unstable forms. Diverse forms are features present in varieties of English other than Academic English, such as different resource words or collocations found in regional varieties of English. Unstable forms are used unpredictably in speech or writing, which may be due to incomplete learning or fossilization, such as the lack of inversion in embedded questions. Of course, diverse forms and unstable forms may be exactly the same, and the difference lies merely in the identity and background of the language user. Chapter 15 explores the issue of prefabrication and collocation and further discusses Wray's idiomatic paradox from Part I.

Unstable System Elements

14

I ask why is it that, say, "She say I is not good people" and "She telling I no good fello, no!" are murder to the "educated" except in the ghetto of "creative" contexts, whereas something like "in the conversations that have transpired during our acquaintance, she has intimated to me personally that she cannot bring herself to consider myself to be admirably suitable with respect to my individual character" is only deemed "wordy", but clearly shows a "command" of the language? The hegemony of hep standard languages and cool registers which hide where they are coming from . . . is read for points by these non-standard varieties like and unlike the ones I be mixing and jamming here.

(Parakrama, 1995, p. x)

As noted in Chapter 1, academic and professional writing in the World Englishes setting maintains rigid and highly conventionalized standards, although local and international spoken varieties diverge. This diglossic situation creates problems and, although inner circle speakers may be privileged with respect to it, Academic English must be learned by everyone who wants entry to the academic and professional discourse community because intelligibility among writers of various backgrounds is highly valued. The academic community prefers complicated but impersonal styles that demonstrate authors' facility with homogeneous expressions that hide their diversity, so intelligibility is gained only at the expense of individual identity. In other words, members or would-be members are obliged to self-regulate or edit out their particular linguistic identity and any diversity, in order to accommodate to the existing norms of Academic English. The only way this status quo will change is if writers, editors, and publishers change their expectations.

In the quote above, Parakrama (1995, p. x) asks why the concise and pithy ways that people speak are not acceptable to the "educated" academic community except in creative endeavors like fiction or drama. The norms of academic lexis and structure are rigid and conventionalized because others may not understand local expressions like "is read for points" or "mixing and jamming." If the ideas and concepts put forward by authors are misunderstood, they may be discounted or lost to the academic community and to the wider world. In the academic writing community, there is a competition to express ideas and thoughts, and, in the competition to publish for a wider world, these must be comprehensible.

At the same time, Academic English belongs to everyone. Sand (2004) points out that academic writing must be considered as a variety both internal and external to local and regional varieties. Sand argues that textual conventions like those in academic or instructional writing override the norms in local varieties, but that Jamaican academic writing is Jamaican as well as academic, thus it is as endemic to Jamaica as it is to any other region. Sand questions generalizations made about local varieties in World Englishes on the basis of just one text type with colloquial language usage. In fact, in each area of the globe, there are continua of usage, and attitudes toward usage, that should not be disregarded.

Sand (2004, p. 295) points out that for every author who laments the inability to use his or her regionalisms or localisms in academic writing, there are others who feel that such usages have no place in the codified standards of formal writing.

> Another important aspect that could not be covered here is that of psychological salience . . . acceptability surveys are needed to determine the salience and – possibly – stigmatization of features that proved to be statistically relevant like the use or non-use of articles in certain contexts. The previous research discussed above was conducted by "outside observers" . . . as well as "insiders" . . . Since the local linguists who have worked on article use tend to comment disfavorably on the absence of articles in their varieties in comparison to the British model, one could assume that these usages are indeed stigmatized within the speech community and would not lend themselves to codification.
>
> (Sand, 2004, p. 295)

Academic English is a potentially neutral cultural and linguistic space for the expression of ideas, but only when they are expressed in a certain form.

Academic English is largely successful at effacing the personal characteristics of authors and researchers. Most of the time, it is not easy to determine from the language and rhetorical patterns if a text was written by a man or a woman, by a speaker of an African-American English variety or an African English variety, or by a native speaker or a non-native speaker. References to authors usually contain only the last name and a first initial. Peer review takes place without any personal information at all. Thus, paradoxically, for many writers, Academic English itself becomes one of the few accessible means of resistance to the hegemony of Global English, the only venue where ideas of change like Parakrama's can be attended to and considered by others.

The academic publishing world and discourse community prescribe the language forms that must be used and proscribe or disallow others. In general, the proscribed elements are those unstable and diverse usages that could potentially identify an author by ethnicity, gender, linguacultural origin, or some other personal status. Only the stable or consensus features of Academic English are allowed, but at the same time all languages must change over time, even such a highly conventionalized system as Academic English. As one form of change, spoken language norms from different varieties can bleed into written norms over time. That is what Seidlhofer (in Chapter 1) or Parakrama suggest could happen to Academic English if ELF or local regional norms are accepted.

Linguistic constructions that might be susceptible to change or modification over time have been called fragile or vulnerable areas, or even "breakage points" (Sand, 2004, p. 203), but here the term instability is preferred, as perhaps more objective and neutral since instability is normal. **Instability** is a cover term that includes both diverse forms and unstable forms.

Diverse forms are the stable morphological, lexical, and grammatical features that differ in the varieties of English in the inner circle, the outer circle, and, increasingly, in the expanding circle. It must be recognized that it is impossible to do justice to this topic in such a short treatment here. It is perhaps not surprising that many of the same types of differences are found globally, such as variation in article or preposition usage, the presence or absence of various forms of the verbal *be*, or different norms and functions for verbal aspects like progressive.

Unstable linguistic features are less firmly fixed; they are features that are used more unpredictably or undependably in people's speech or writing, especially in the ELF setting. At present, these may be fleeting features of performance, but they may normalize and affect written English norms. Unstable elements also overlap with diverse linguistic features such as the presence or absence of the third person singular present tense or the definite article. There are, of course, many other pressures on written standards: informal usages found on the internet, texting or IM usages, code-switching, borrowing, and the like, so the discussion in this chapter is meant to be tentative. It is impossible to make any definitive predictions about the direction of any systematic change that might occur.

It is not difficult for new resource elements like nouns, verbs, and adjectives that occur first in speech to be taken up in writing, especially in fiction and news reporting. Much of the diversity in World Englishes is in resource vocabulary because of borrowed words or loan translations from local languages, or other regional innovations. Fisher (2000) reports that Ugandan English has the derived forms *overspeeding* (speeding) and *overdrinking* (drinking too much). In regional varieties, there are also some archaic usages retained from older versions of English, such as the use of *fall* for *autumn*.

Some diversity in resource elements stems from differences in meaning. For instance, Kachru and Smith (2008, pp. 90–91) note that the stative and dynamic distinction in verbs is different: "It is, therefore, common, in the Outer and Expanding Circle varieties of English, to ignore the distinction between stative and dynamic verbs. Sentences such as the following are perfectly grammatical in, e.g. South Asian varieties: *He is having two cars*; *I was not knowing him then*; *She is not recognizing you.*" In addition, in line with the flexible parts of speech in World Englishes in general, there is diversity on how words are used in different areas. Gyasi (1991) reports innovative functional shifts like *Your behavior tantamounts to insubordination* and *It doesn't worth the price.*

Morphology

Third Singular

The third person singular present tense is stable among the many varieties of Standard English because of its immense frequency of occurrence and consequent priming, but it shows both diversity and instability in World Englishes. Its presence or

> . . . so this is one practical possibility which also **go** in the same direction . . .
> . . . because it **last** three years . . .
> . . . who is the body that **legalize** or **accept** a joint program . . .
> . . . I suppose it's possible that the thing **function** in both possibilities . . .
> . . . but I think if the community **ask** to us to push this kind of initiatives . . .
>
> (Breiteneder, 2009, p. 259)

absence is an important social marker in inner circle countries, as is its extension to forms that ordinarily don't take it as an inflection. It is also an unstable morpheme among even expert English users of ELF or ELFA, where its lack is quite common, indeed perhaps normal.

Breiteneder (2009, p. 260) notes that use of the third person singular inflection often seems to occur with formulaic or highly practiced expressions like *that means*, as in this example of a conversation between a Norwegian speaker and a Czech speaker (in which I have simplified the transcription). It is possible that the inflection is missing in constructions that are the result of analytical processing, where priming is less.

S8: *that means* if he *make* disser- dissertation work in er french
S1: hm
S8: he *get* the diplom of charles university and french university can give him also the diplom

Breiteneder (2009, p. 260) also notes several instances of repetition; repetition is an important aspect of ELF talk, to confer prominence, to show listenership, and to establish cohesion and intelligibility. In this example of a working group discussion among six speakers from different European countries discussing housing, there are seven repetitions of *if the program decides*, mainly, but not exclusively, by one speaker, S7. In this example, which I have adapted for readability, [. . .] means that there are intervening conversational turns.

S14: *if the program decides* that it's important for the students it's one of the learning outcomes
SS: hm
      [. . .]
S7: *if if the program decides*
S1: an- and i i
S7: *if the program decides* NOT imposed to program. this is very important
      [. . .]
S1: and er i i suppose you
S7: *if the program decides*
      [. . .]
S1: it's a recommendation and it's and some programs . . .
S4: mhm

S7: **If the program decides**

   [. . .]

S1: *maybe made so that it's a support of the and i suppose you all have the experience that you won't get an american student into a*

S7: **If the program decides**

S7: *it is the problem (of the)*

S1: *a course if it's not credited and and and marked*

   [. . .]

S13: *want to put forward the recommendation that we should consider ways of integrating the linguistic competences so to speak in during or before you start you enter the program and **if the program decides** already requires it. the students should be of course be credited for the work load that comes with it*

(Breiteneder, 2009, p. 260)

These examples illustrate the effect of practice on the acquisition of collocations and other prefabricated constructions, and the importance of these for accuracy in speaking. At present even in ELF formal writing, the third person singular present tense is present, but in informal writing it may be absent.

Participial Forms

The past participle and forms derived from it are both unstable and diverse. There are three areas where instability is present. The first is the use of unmarked participial adjectives in attributive position, which has become acceptable in some cases. The second is the use of unmarked regular past participles with perfect or passive constructions or participial predicate adjectives. The third instability, and perhaps the most dramatic change, is the use of past tense verb forms or non-standard participles, sometimes with *shoulda, woulda, coulda* in the U.S. and perhaps extending to other areas of World Englishes.

Unmarked participial adjectives are examples like *ice tea* instead of the more traditional *iced tea*. It seems that the loss is permitted at least in part because of the frequency of descriptive nouns as modifiers. The first example below, a hypothetical one, shows a particularly vulnerable context for the loss of the inflection. When an attributive participial adjective like *old-fashioned* occurs before a word that begins with [d] or [t], the sound of the inflection is not distinguished in the flow of speech, so it is frequently not written. The second example (*advanced level*) shows a context where the consonant cluster at the meeting point between the two words (pronounced n-s-t-l) makes simplification in pronunciation common and therefore it may not be represented in written form.

> *It promotes old-fashion descriptions of language . . .*

> *Acquisition at a sufficiently advance level is expected from graduates of secondary and tertiary education.*

Unmarked past participles and predicate participial adjectives show similar effects of pronunciation. In many cases, but not all, the loss of the inflection is facilitated by the presence of a word that begins with a [t] or a [d] sound, as in this hypothetical example:

> *these norms are adhere to* → *these norms are adhered to*

Past Tense with Coulda

Greblick (2001) argues that examples like *coulda bought* are derived from *could have bought* but they are now ambiguous because there are two possible syntactic analyses. In one, they reflect their original structure as "modal-reduced primary auxiliary-main verb in past participle form." In the other analysis, *coulda bought* has been reanalyzed as a single constituent (*coulda*) and the main verb *bought* as a finite past tense form. Further, Greblick argues that *coulda* and its linguistic cousins *woulda* and *shoulda* have undergone reanalysis as adverbials like *kinda* or *sorta*. It is possible that for many people this process of reanalysis is complete but others are in an intermediate stage where only the primary auxiliary has been reanalyzed as *of*.

Nevertheless, this form occurs only with modals because the present perfect itself remains structurally the same, although there is some diversity in participle or past

Stages of Reanalysis

could have gone	(standard)
could of gone	
coulda gone	
coulda went	(colloquial)

tense morphology on the main verb. At present, these forms are seen increasingly in writing, although they are stigmatized, as in these examples from Doolan and Miller (2012, p. 19).

If I knew that taking high school seriously would help in college I would of taken it seriously. I would of studying for all my exams I had in high school.

Putting a lot of effort would probably helped me in college with some of the same materials. It could of helped me if I had planned my career better in high school rather than in college.

Plural -s

U.S.	*The committee is committed to change.*
U.K.	*The committee are committed to change.*

There are many instabilities in the system of subject–verb agreement that holds between noun phrase plural and singular forms and their combination with verbs. One is the diversity in British and American usage with collective nouns such as *committee* or *family*. Similarly, in outer and expanding circle contexts there is diversity in the use of count and non-count nouns. In particular, what would be non-countable in Standard Englishes becomes countable and plural: *homeworks, furnitures, correspondences, advices, breads, equipments, informations, behaviors, sceneries, beddings, vocabularies, grammars.* In some examples, there is a lack of redundant plural inflection with numbers as determiners, as in this example from Singapore English *I got three sister and two brother,* cited in McArthur (2002, p. 340). The plural is unstable in ELF with *every*; there are numerous examples like this one from Doolan and Miller (2012, p. 21): *I think every Chinese students have different evaluations about high school in China.*

Determiners

Determiners were discussed as modifiers in noun phrases in academic writing in Chapter 9. After noting some of the complexities of determiner usage, and especially the definite and indefinite article usage, in English and in other languages, Kachru and Smith (2008, p. 89) point out:

[I]t is not surprising that the Outer and Expanding Circle varieties of English do not use articles in the same way that the Inner Circle varieties do. Since there is no one-to-one correlation between the forms (i.e. a, the, some) and the meanings they signal, it is difficult for learners to arrive at the principles underlying the use of articles. The picture is further complicated by the fact that depending upon speaker intentions, the choice of articles may vary in what appears to the learners as the same context.

It is quite possible that not only is there no one-to-one correlation between the use of the articles and any meanings or functions they have, but there may simply be no principles underlying the use of the more common articles. In other words, for native speakers in an inner circle country, the different functions and meanings of *a/an*, *the*, and *some* are acquired unconsciously from the usage and exposure that they are surrounded by and participate in during their formative years. They use them based on their priming associations and probabilities of occurrence in different grammatical contexts, colligations, and collocations. They use them to convey very subtle and overlapping nuances of meaning. It is not usually the case that article usage is simply right or wrong, as Kachru and Smith point out in their analysis. Instead, in many contexts, different choices may be equivalent or they may make little difference in the interpretation of an utterance. In short, the normal use of articles may not be pattern-based at all.

If determiner usages are not pattern-based, it is no surprise at all that there is diversity and instability in their usage in World Englishes. For instance, *less* is the comparative of the quantifier *little* and *fewer* is the comparative of the quantifier *few*. In formal or academic usage, *less* is used with mass nouns and *fewer* is used with plural count nouns. However, this usage shows diversity, with *less* overtaking *fewer* in all contexts (*less taxes, less problems*).

However, of the determiners, the most common (*the* and *a/an*) are especially diverse and unstable. For instance, McArthur (2002, p. 321) gives these examples from Indian English: *It is the nature's way. Office is closed today*, and these examples from Phillipine English: *He is studying at the Manuel Quezon University. I am going to visit United States.* (However, the example with *the Manuel Quezon University* may show influence from the United States, where *I am at the university* is preferred over the British *I am at university*.) Fisher (2000, p. 60) notes some examples of "article dropping" in Ugandan English (see box).

> ## Article Dropping
>
> *AIDS virus is so universal.*
> *Bank of Uganda will ensure that . . .*
> *Story has it that . . .*
> *As a result, scarcity of dollars has been reversed.*

In ELF, *the* and *a/an* are also used in inconsistent ways often because of transfer from first language. Languages like Spanish have different norms of article usage and many other languages don't have articles at all. The examples in the box of ELF academic writing come from Doolan and Miller (2012, p. 18).

> **Article Dropping in ELF**
>
> *None of family had attended*
> *to show teacher how much*

Prepositions and Particles

Like the definite and indefinite articles, prepositional and particle uses are often item-based and not pattern-based so they are highly dependent on learning through practice and automatization. For the same reasons, both prepositional and particle usage are diverse and unstable in the Englishes of the world. The diversity extends through prepositional uses in prepositional phrases, prepositional verbs, and verb and particle combinations in phrasal verbs.

Prepositions in Prepositional Phrases

To start with, there are some consistent differences between American usage and British usage. Many of these are idiomatic expressions. McArthur (2002, p. 253) gives these examples:

American	*British*
live on a street	live in a street
do something on the weekend	do something at the weekend
be of two minds about something	be in two minds about something
have a new lease on life	have a new lease of life
be in a course of study	be on a course of study

Singapore English (Tongue, 1974, cited in Kachru and Smith, 2008, p. 99):

> *We can give some thought on the matter.*
> *The matter has been studied with a view of further reducing the risk of fire.*

Ghanaian English (Gyasi, 1991, pp. 29–30):

> *The police are investigating into the case.*
> *We will not be deprived from our rights.*

She has gone to abroad.
He has regretted for his hasty action.

Indian English (Nihalani et al., 1979, cited in Kachru and Smith, 2008, p. 99):

He is very well adapted on his job.
He was accompanied with his best friend.
I admire for his courage.

Ugandan English (Fisher, 2000, p. 59):

. . . activities which result into loss of life . . .
. . . Luganda has gone a long way into doing this . . .
. . . a step ahead into forging national unity . . .
. . . the expectations the people have on me . . .
. . . the teachers are demanding for their salaries . . .

In ELF, there are inconsistent uses of prepositions as well, such as these examples from Doolan and Miller (2012, p. 18):

Never in my 18 years in life	*of life*
received that news through my parents	*from my parents*
follow his footsteps	*in his footsteps*
late to register my classes	*register for*

Prepositional Verbs

In standardized World Englishes, some verb + preposition collocations occur so frequently that the words have "fused" into one **prepositional verb** unit. In these examples from the corpus for this book, the accompanying NP may be considered a direct object of the verb, not the object of the preposition.

Very few studies have <u>focused on</u> systematically collecting huge samples of spontaneous speech.

The well-known problems <u>involved in</u> proofreading show that this step cannot be taken for granted.

With a prepositional verb, the preposition and the direct object are not free to shift away from the verb and move as easily elsewhere in the sentence as "normal" prepositional phrases. Biber et al. (1999, pp. 413–421) and Liu (2012, pp.. 30–32) give these common prepositional verbs:

be used in	*think of*	*belong to*
depend on	*add to*	*account for*
be based on	*be known as*	*consist of*
be associated with	*be seen in*	*differ from*
look at	*be regarded as*	*be based on*
look for	*be seen as*	*be involved in*
deal with	*be considered as*	*be associated with*
be applied to	*be defined as*	*be related to*
be made of	*lead to*	*be included in*
be aimed at	*come from*	*be composed of*
be derived from	*result in*	*be viewed as*
be divided into	*contribute to*	*be regarded as*
obtain NP from	*allow for*	*call for*
use NP as	*be required for*	*give rise to*
refer to	*occur in*	*focus on*
be expressed in	*depend on*	*take account of*

There is instability in prepositional verbs, as shown in these examples from ELF from Nesselhauf (2009, p. 18):

> *The Nairobi Action Plan will <u>comprise of</u> all relevant sectors and topics . . .*

> *. . . it seems that an army <u>comprising of</u> professional soldiers would be more efficient.*

> *For years, they have been <u>discussing about</u> it.*

> *. . . whenever I <u>enter into</u> the class they laugh at me.*

> *. . . guys who usually used their cars to <u>enter into</u> the city.*

> *The school should ensure that it collects excess money and have in a save [sic] place for the learners who can <u>request for it</u> when in need.*

Diversity issues with prepositional verbs may be related to analogy to similar uses or other collocational uses. For instance, Nesselhauf (2009, p. 21) says:

It appears from the analysis that a new prepositional verb is usually created when several of these factors coincide. To give just two examples, in the case of *request for*, the corresponding noun takes the preposition in question and there is a semantically related and moreover frequent word that also takes the preposition (*ask for*). In the case of *enter into*, the collocation already exists, related expressions take the preposition in question, and the adding of a preposition makes the direction implied in the verb more explicit.

Particles and Phrasal Verbs

Particles combine with common verbs to form compound verbs called phrasal verbs (see also Chapter 6). Like the simple prepositions they come from, the literal meanings for particles have to do with spatial location and time: *across, back, down, in(to), off, out, over, to, up, (up)on*, and *with*. Despite that, the meaning the particle contributes to its phrasal verb is elusive. There are some tantalizing generalizations. For example, *up* generally means *ascend* or *do something completely*. The particle *down* often means the opposite: *to descend* or *to disassemble*. These examples are from the corpus, but it should be said that, in general, phrasal verbs are much less common in academic writing than they are in spoken varieties of English.

> *The product of a priming becomes itself primed in ways that do not apply to the individual words <u>making up</u> the combination.*

> *The word practice <u>conjures up</u> images of mind-numbing drills.*

> *If we <u>break</u> any sentence <u>down</u> into the smallest independent units, we end up with single words.*

Phrasal Verbs and Equivalents

Phrasal verbs are informal and slangy, and people use them in requests and commands, in conversation and informal written Englishes. Biber et al. (1999, pp. 408–409) list a few phrasal verbs typical of formal written

carry out—accomplish, complete
make up—invent
take up—begin, occupy
take on—become, assume
set up—establish, plan
point out—indicate, signal

prose: *carry out, take up, take on, set up,* and *point out.* Generally each phrasal verb has an equivalent verb with a similar meaning in formal academic writing.

It is a commonplace observation that phrasal verbs are among the most challenging features of English for English learners to acquire because they are not pattern-based. Instead, the combinations of verbs and particles and their meanings are item-based features learned through usage and exposure. Therefore, it is not unreasonable to expect that, in ELF, particles will be used differently or avoided altogether. Similarly, because of their preponderance in spoken language, there is also a lot of diversity in particle usage in World Englishes.

Schneider (2004) did an exhaustive study of phrasal verbs as diverse linguistic features that have nativized or localized their usage norms in World Englishes. He found that there were systematic differences in phrasal verb usage in different varieties of English. They are used "widely and creatively" in Singapore English; the usage exceeds usage in British English. Phrasal verbs are less commonly used in other varieties of English, such as those in India, the Philippines, East Africa, and Tanzania. In these areas, phrasal verbs are used "more hesitantly—less frequently and in a smaller range of uses" (p. 246). Fisher (2000, p. 59) gives some examples where the particle which might be expected is dropped in Ugandan English: *knock (down) a pedestrian, pick (up) a passenger, cut (down) a tree, lash (out) at opponents, his children had grown (up), to keep (up) an appearance, to live (up) to someone's expectations,* and *to pluck (up) courage.*

Pronouns

Subjects

For speakers of English of all types, there is widespread instability and diversity in the use of subject pronouns, especially in spoken varieties. In inner circle countries, there is widespread usage of object pronouns in subject position with conjoined NPs, as in this example from the spoken British National Corpus:

> . . . *me and him'd sit and eat from half past six.*

Some varieties of English allow reduplicated subjects such as the hypothetical example below, where in more standard written varieties the pronoun would be eliminated.

Speakers of English, they are very different around the world.

Sometimes subject pronouns are omitted when they would normally appear in written English. An omitted subject may come from the differences between spoken English, which allows for incomplete sentences, and written English, which requires subjects and complete sentences. Incomplete sentences occur as part of a discourse in conversation, as add-ons to previous sentences, because the "complete thought" may be created over several conversational turns. People are generally very efficient in speech; they don't mention things that are already understood from the context. In writing, the context is lacking, so more information must be clearly referenced.

Expert ELF speakers may have a problem with subjects in English if their first language allows sentences without overt subjects, if it can be recovered from the context. In other languages, it is easier to understand who the subject is because words are marked with inflections. For instance, in Spanish, pronominal subjects can be omitted because they are unnecessary if the verb carries a specific inflectional ending. The verbal ending of *llueve* (*rains*) is sufficient. Subjects can also be dropped if the adjective is marked as masculine or feminine, as they are in many other languages. It is not surprising to find that, in ELF, missing subjects are common and not stigmatized. However, this usage has not become current in more standardized written English. Doolan and Miller (2012, p. 12) provide this example from a second language learner's text:

> *For example, "I wanna go to Mexico" is one way to speak but you can't write like that because is incorrect.*

Indefinites, Plurality, and Subject/Verb Agreement

The quantifying determiner *every* and the compound indefinites with *every* are not plural. They are singular, take singular forms of verbs, and singular other pronouns, as in this example from the database:

> *We can only account for collocation if we assume that every word is mentally primed for collocational use.*

When writers use an indefinite pronoun, they sometimes are unsure about how to finish off the sentence. With singular forms like *someone* or *every student*, the traditional solution was to use the masculine singular pronouns, but more recently "his or her" has been used.

> *There is a growing body of evidence that **an individual's** parsing decisions are influenced in some way by **his or her** prior contact with comparable strings or structures.*

A better option is to simply make all of the references plural and use the determiner *their*.

> *There is a growing body of evidence that **people's** parsing decisions are influenced in some way by **their** prior contact with comparable strings or structures.*

Sentence Elements

Tag Questions

Tag questions are used in spoken English and informal written English, and occur only rarely in Academic English. (See Chapter 11 for a discussion of questions.) There are two types of tag questions among inner circle speakers of English. The first is formed with a copy of the primary auxiliary (*be, have, do*) and a pronoun that matches the subject. There is also an alternation in affirmative/negative forms but the forms shown below reveal the most common forms; affirmative occurs in the main sentence and negative in the tag. These examples are from the written British National Corpus, but they are mainly used in reporting conversations.

> *"This is an adventure, isn't it?"*

> *"The question doesn't arise, because you're on a boat, aren't you?"*

> *"He seems to be making it in the old alternative comedy scene, doesn't he?"* Ash said.

The second type of tags uses inserts or adverbials like *right* or *okay* attached at the end of a sentence; these also occur in written versions of conversations:

> *"Trying the great silence again, eh, Ferg?"*
> *"Aye, but good for him, though, eh?"*

It is safe to say that the first type of tag question is excessively complex when compared to tag questions in other languages, which tend to be more like the second type. In languages other than English, sometimes the word for *no* or *yes* simply follows a declarative sentence. In ELF, variation in the use of both types of tag questions is to be expected.

Double Negatives

Sentences with two negative words are generally not allowed in academic writing unless the meaning is rhetorically positive, as in these hypothetical examples from McArthur (1992, p. 320), given with their meanings:

> *She is not unintelligent.* → She is intelligent (maybe).

> *You can't not respect their decision.* → It is impossible not to respect their decision.

> *Nobody has NO friends.* → Everyone has at least one friend.

Multiple negation with a negative meaning is common in some varieties of World Englishes, especially in spoken language, as in these examples from Biber et al. (1999, p. 178):

> *You've never seen nothing like it.*
> *I told her not to say nothing to nobody.*

This reflects a usage common in other languages of the world, where multiple negative adverbs coexist commonly in sentences as a form of agreement. It comes as no surprise, then, that multiple negation may occur in ELF conversations or local varieties of World Englishes.

Embedded Questions

In Chapter 12, embedded indirect questions in English were shown to have the same uninverted structure as any other noun clause. Their structure is not like that of direct questions because no inversion of the subject and the primary auxiliary takes place.

> *I don't know <u>what he is doing</u>. (What is he doing?)*
> *There is doubt about <u>where he can go</u>. (Where can he go?)*
> *We don't know <u>why he goes there</u>. (Why does he go there?)*

However, direct questions and embedded questions in other languages may have the same structure, with subject/verb inversion. It is possible for the uninverted embedded question to occur in ELF or in other varieties of World Englishes. The following example is from Doolan and Miller (2012, p. 21):

When I go to college then I realized how easy was high school.

Awareness of Diversity

The lastma final word, then, is to go like crazy for the broadest standard and to be psyched up to steady talk in it, teach your head off in it, write like mad in it, despite of its sometime "oddness" to our ears, refusing of the uncomfortable laughter, inspite the difficulty, paying no mind to some non-standard users and their liberal advocates having an attitude about it. The ideal, then, is for what is standard now to become contaminated with what is non-standard now and arse backwards, so much so that everyone will have to know more about what everyone else speaks/writes, and so that not knowing, say, "black english" will be as much a disqualification as not knowing "general american". There should even be room for a certain amount of self-inconsistency, yar, to bring this to the up front level, nehi?

(Parakrama, 1995, p. xi)

What Parakrama is suggesting is that World English users adopt the standards of academic writing at the same time that they attempt to resist the hegemony of academic standards by letting some of their localisms and regionalisms leak into it, just as, at present, standard forms overlap with regional varieties. Of course, recognized authorities, who have proven that they can use academic norms but choose not to, will find it easier to successfully infiltrate and potentially change the strict conventions of academic writing. However, at the very least, teachers may adopt a more open and accepting attitude toward the diverse and unstable usages that occur in World Englishes, and not selectively punish "errors" and lay blame.

Instead, language awareness activities may call attention to regionalisms (resource or system words, morphemes, and collocations) to stimulate appreciation of local norms as well as the ability to choose the construction that is appropriate for the utterance or sentence. Students may check their grammar logs for usages that seem consistent with ELF and decide whether they wish to aim for Academic English or some other variety. World Englishes is a large tent that shelters and includes both instability and diversity.

Study, Discussion, and Essay Questions

1. Review these terms and add them to your glossary with a definition and some examples if they are not already present: instability, diverse forms, unstable linguistic features, stative verbs, functional shift, third person singular present tense, participles, participial adjectives, plural, countable, non-countable, determiners, prepositions, prepositional phrases, prepositional verbs, phrasal verbs, pronouns, reduplicated subjects, indefinite pronouns, tag questions.

2. Explain the diglossic situation between Academic English and local spoken dialects? Do you agree that writers must efface their personal identity in order to be successful writers in the academic discourse community? Do you agree or disagree with Parakrama's expression of frustration?

3. Why does Sand say that Academic English can be considered endemic in local varieties of English?

4. While there are some people who wish that they could use their local usages in Academic English, there are others who do not. Where do you stand on this controversy?

5. If you live in an area where English is spoken locally, what regionalisms do you find in your locality? What resource words are unique to your area?

6. How is the third person singular of present tense verbs a social marker in many anglophone countries? What is its status in ELF?

7. What are some of the causes of instability in past participle and participial adjective usages?

8. Why is it possible to think that the "normal" use of articles or determiners may not be pattern-based? What could the usage be based on? Does this explain the diversity and instability?

9. Explain the difference between "proper" double negation and "improper" double negation.

10. What is the main problem with the structure of indirect questions?

11. What are some of the common "problems" in the use of subject pronouns?

12. What is the difference between the linguistic behavior of prepositions in prepositional phrases and in prepositional verb constructions? Can you make up some examples that show the difference?

13. Why are some indefinite pronouns problematic in terms of their morphological agreement with verbs? How can these problems be avoided?

14. How are tag questions formed in Standard English? Why is there so much diversity?

Activities

1. Looking back at the second quote from Parakrama (1995, p. xi), list and explain the different resource and system words you see. If you don't know what some of the words or expressions mean, how can you find out?
2. Since embedded questions are common in Academic English, check the following sentences to see if inversion is present or not. If it is not present, rewrite the statement with an inverted construction. Are there any other changes that need to be made to make the statement appropriate for an Academic English text?

   a. Asking what morphemes a word contains and what they mean is asking what the coiner of the word had in mind when he coined it and possibly what unforeseen associations it may have built up since.
   b. Ideally one would like to have a rigorous, possibly statistically determined way to define what is meant by a "common" or "frequent" expression. (Note that in this statement, *what* is both the complementizer and the subject of the following VP, so inversion does not occur.)
   c. Grammar instructors need to understand how do different constituents function together to convey meaning.
   d. It is reasonable to ask whether grammatical correction is effective and appropriate at all, and if so, what the best ways are to approach it.
   e. I find it better to try to do more (and more varied) empirical research on how ELF is actually used and what it does to local languages.
   f. English speakers naturally seem to know what is a word.

3. Look through your grammar log. Which of the usages you have identified are due to diversity in World Englishes? Which are unstable ELF usages? Are there any that you wish to change in order to speak or write more conventionally?
4. Review this excerpt from the ELFA conversation cited in Chapter 1. Although it is very comprehensible and largely correct, what unstable or diverse feature(s) do you see?

   > And I mean it's funny thing because the Estonian it was an article I read. It was a famous Estonian tele- television I don't know reporter or something he went on strike on the hunger strike because er the Estonian government they made some kind of simplifying towards the citizenship law for the Russians so he went to the hunger strike because of the(ir) thinking that it's unfair.

Collocations and the Idiomatic Paradox 15

[C]ommunicative competence is not a matter of knowing rules for the composition of sentences and being able to employ such rules to assemble expressions from scratch as and when occasion requires. It is much more a matter of knowing a stock of partially pre-assembled patterns, formulaic frameworks, and a kit of rules, so to speak, and being able to apply the rules to make whatever adjustments are necessary according to contextual demands. Communicative competence in this view is essentially a matter of adaptation, and rules are not generative but regulative and subservient.

(Widdowson, 1989, p. 135)

This chapter is about the stock of "formulaic frameworks" in English that allow native speakers to express themselves fluently and accurately with the least amount of cognitive load. Paradoxically, as Wray points out in a quote cited in Chapter 2, English learners begin with a small stock of formulaic expressions, but when they reach their intermediate and even advanced stages, the lack of easy access to formulas and collocations becomes an obstacle to communicative competence. In earlier chapters, this was attributed to two ideas. The first idea is that English learners, unlike native speakers, do not acquire strong priming associations among words and lexical item-based constructions in order to compose sentences holistically. The second idea is that they don't acquire strong priming associations that allow for rapid analytical processing to combine lexical items with abstract but conventionalized grammatical patterns and constructions.

The term communicative competence is usually defined as a language user's ability to use words and grammatical constructions to accomplish communicative functions (like persuading, instructing, or informing) accurately and appropriately within a social and cultural context. Crucially, in the quote above Widdowson also suggests that another fundamental component of communicative competence is the language user's knowledge of the priming associations for holistic patterns and frameworks like *set the table* or *go green* along with some analytical "rules" that allow the language user to adapt these prefabricated expressions according to the demands of communication and setting: *She always sets the table the way her mother taught her* or *Their farm is going green and organic*.

In this sense, communicative competence is not simply the ability to compose sentences analytically by combining abstract grammatical structures by the open choice principle, but rather it includes the ability to allow the words in prefabricated patterns to dictate the structures holistically, which are then adapted to the grammatical context. Prefabricated expressions assume more prominence in such a theory of grammar, and abstract grammatical constructions only regulate and serve them by providing syntactic frameworks and generic grammatical meanings. However, Wray's idiomatic paradox is that such a view of the language system seems to make communicative competence out of the reach of most English learners. This chapter returns to this paradox later; in the meantime, the basic types of prefabricated expressions used in holistic processing and how they are involved in analytical processing require examination.

Prefabricated Expressions

At the most basic level, prefabricated expressions are groups of words that have strong priming associations with one another. Priming associations among constructions within the neural architecture of language set up expectations about the language being used in communication. The strength of these associations can be studied by examining prefabricated expressions in corpora. The statistics about the frequency that words occur together don't provide direct evidence about the knowledge in the brain, but they do indicate what type of information is in the linguistic/socio/cultural context that people live in. Thus, evidence from corpora is not direct evidence of brain functioning but a kind of secondary evidence of what causes people to form knowledge of a certain type. The evidence from corpora shows that people learn to use prefabricated expressions, and that such usage contributes to what sounds "natural" in language. The words in prefabricated expressions occur so frequently together that the planned use of one word activates the other words almost automatically, so prefabricated expressions have a certain degree of fixedness and limited adaptability.

Prefabrications are directly involved in the personal choices that speakers and writers make, in communication, to project personality, attitude, and identity. Wray (2002, p. 95) suggests that, in general, formulaic expressions serve to promote the interest of the speaker in a variety of ways, including having easy access to information in the form of mnemonic devices and similar, organizing and expressing information fluently, expressing polite requests and commands to achieve something, and showing membership in a speech community / culture. Speakers also use prefabricated chunks to fill in the spaces or to buy processing time while they think about what they are saying.

Formulaic expressions are both highly personal and highly social at the same time, which make them problematic for second language learners. For instance, prefabrications include fixed **pure idioms** (*not my cup of tea*), memorized **quotes** (*One small step for mankind . . .*), culturally loaded **proverbs** (*A penny saved is a penny earned*), political and commercial **slogans** (*Drill, baby, drill*), and more general **catchphrases** (*It's a win-win*). Because prefabrications are personal and localized, they are not common in academic writing, but they occur frequently in speaking and informal writing.

Proverbs, slogans, quotations, catchphrases, and idioms do not aid in language production or comprehension, unless they occur between two people from similar sociocultural backgrounds. Seidlhofer (2007, p. 145) uses the term "unilateral idiomaticity" for the use of these culturally loaded idiomatic expressions that others don't understand, especially within an ELF or ELFA speaking context. It seems that what some people may want to learn (e.g. new idioms or proverbs) to sound "natural" or "native-like," others may see as an unfair linguistic assault.

There are many other types of prefabricated expressions that are more neutral in their usage and they are therefore common in academic writing. Three types have already been discussed in Chapter 13: lexical bundles, sentence builders, and macro-organizers. Recall that lexical bundles are frequently occurring four word long prefabrications such as complex prepositions (*the nature of the*) or clausal introductions (*I don't know how*). Lexical bundles can be nested within longer lexical bundles (*well [I don't think], [I don't think] so*, or *but [I don't think]*). **Sentence builders** are groups of words that provide a framework for whole sentences like *never/seldom/rarely have I seen such . . .* , and **macro-organizers** signal the organization of information in a text by marking topics and shifts in topics, summarizing and giving examples, making relationships, evaluations, and qualifications explicit, and inserting comments or judgments by the author.

Nevertheless, it is not easy to distinguish between culturally loaded and culturally neutral multi-word units. Prodomou (2008, pp. 109–114) identified very frequent two-word clusters of words that combine pronouns and verbals: *you know, I mean, I think, It was, I don't, do you.* These seem like neutral lexical bundles, and so do these (pp. 46–47):

vague markers:	*sort of thing; or whatever; and stuff*
conversational gambits:	*how do you do; nice to meet you*
sentence stems:	*it is interesting/likely/true that. . .*
repeats:	*again and again; more and more*

Other examples in Prodomou's ample lists of prefabricated multi-word units seem more culturally embedded and potentially prone to unilateral idiomaticity (pp. 46–47):

binomials:	*bed and breakfast; salt and pepper; spick and span*
trinomials:	*tall, dark, and handsome; hook, line, and sinker*
unique expressions:	*arms akimbo; by dint of; kith and kin* (also binomial)
metaphors:	*take the bull by the horns; run out of steam*
similes:	*cool as a cucumber; smart as a whip*

Collocations

Collocations are important prefabricated expressions and they combine elements of both lexical and grammatical prefabrication such as the adjective + noun collocations common in academic prose. Howarth (1998, p. 24) defines collocations as "combinations of words with a syntactic function as constituents of a

Adjective + Noun Collocations

good	*judges, readers, separation, communication, relations, fortune, yields, indication*
important	*changes, advances, step, part, consequences, respect, role, point, factor*
special	*cases, process, regulations, class, types, method*
right	*principles, level, relation, direction, answer, criteria*

(Biber et al., 1999, pp. 514–15)

sentence (such as noun or prepositional phrases or verb and object constructions)." One characteristic that serves to differentiate collocations from other
constructions and colligations is their degree of "fixedness" on a range or
continuum of priming, that is, the extent to which they allow (or not) variation
in the wording. Collocations are the result of holistic processing mainly but not
exclusively at the level of phrasal and sentential constructions.

Howarth distinguishes between collocations and **free combinations** of
words that have a lower statistical probability of occurring together, that is,
colligations that are formed through analytical processing. In the following
example, a VP is formed from the free choice of a verb (*spill*) and an object, so
there is a variable that stands for any liquid NP, as in *spill the gas, spill a drink*,
or *spill his coffee*.

Free Combinations	**Restricted Collocations**	**Figurative Idioms**	**Pure Idioms**
$[spill\ [NP]]_{VP}$	$[spill\ [the\ milk]]_{VP}$	$[spill\ [DET]\ guts]_{VP}$	$[spill\text{-}the\text{-}beans]_{VP}$

Restricted collocations have a higher probability of occurring together but
the words are not fused together as a formula, and the meaning is predictable.
This means that the words are primed to occur together; the choice of one
word primes the choice of the next word through activation in the brain. Any
NP could occur in the collocation but it is restricted to the most frequently
spilled NP, assumed to be, for many English users, *milk*. Both free colligations
and restricted collocations have literal meanings that relate to the lexical
constructions and their syntactic structure (word order, functions).

Figurative idioms are more fixed, with a somewhat unconventional but still
fairly transparent meaning derived from the meanings of the words. (*Spill your
guts* means to unload a lot of personal information, usually truthful, to another
person.) The fixed part of the idiom is underlined in the representation, while
the symbol [DET] means that a variety of different possessive determiners can
occur, because figurative idioms can be changed slightly while still maintaining
the idiom, as in *spill your/ his/ her guts*. The priming effects on figurative idioms
are stronger than for restricted collocations.

Pure idioms are opaque in meaning and cannot easily be changed. (The
idiom *spill the beans* means to reveal something that should remain a secret.)
There seems to be more than simple priming going on between the words in
pure idioms; in the representation above, it is fused as a multi-word lexical
unit, with hyphens. Both pure idioms and figurative idioms may cause unilateral idiomaticity. Collocations and idioms follow the same grammatical
patterns as free combinations and sentences except for completely idiosyncratic

constructions which are strongly primed for unusual syntactic structures, as with *ago*,[1] or *enough*, described below.

System/Resource Collocations

It seems impossible to do justice to the wide array of collocations or prefabricated expressions that can be found in academic language, but the collocations discussed here are common among the academic varieties of World Englishes. In general, they combine system (prepositions, auxiliaries) and resource elements (adverbs, noun phrases) in pattern-based constructions. In some cases, the patterns seem to be fusing together, such as the reanalysis from *could have gone* into *could of gone* and into *coulda gone*, which was discussed in the last chapter. In the more or less standard varieties of English, there is instability in the most common prepositional uses of *of* and *in*. There are already, in spoken English forms, *kind of/kinda* and *sort of/sorta*.

Collocations with of

Lewis (2002, p. 145) points out that the word *of* is one of the most functional in English, second to *the* as the most common. It is generally categorized as an ordinary preposition involved with ownership or relevance. However, its most common usage seems to be a way of concatenating noun phrases to make a denser text, and this is especially important in Academic English, so it would seem that as a lexical item *of* heavily primes not just words but also nested abstract constructions like [NP [P NP [P NP]]] and other similar nested structures, such as these from the corpus:

> the direct consequence *of the* inherent limitations *of the* concept *of* method itself
> the piecemeal learning *of* many thousands *of* constructions

Collocations, lexical bundles, and discourse markers also make ample use of *of* and the other frequent so-called preposition *in*. A search of the corpus yielded these examples and there are many more.

---

1. *Ago* is a preposition but it occurs as a "postposition." It is a highly item-based but robust collocation [[number and unit of time] *ago*]: *three years ago, two minutes ago.*

It stands to reason that <u>in</u> written language use, where there is no possibility <u>of</u> the overt reciprocal negotiation <u>of</u> meaning typical <u>of</u> spoken interaction, there is more reliance on established norms, and these are naturally maintained by a process <u>of</u> self-regulation whereby these norms are adhered to <u>in</u> the interest <u>of</u> maintaining global mutual intelligibility . . .

The highest and subtlest aspects <u>of</u> language cannot be recognized <u>in</u> its separate elements; they can only be perceived or intuited <u>in</u> connected speech (which demonstrates all the more that language intrinsically lies <u>in</u> the act <u>of</u> its production <u>in</u> reality).

However, it seems that, in many of these expressions, *of* is often associated, perhaps even fused, with the word before it. That is, the *"word" of* appears to be undergoing the processes based on frequency and priming that create multi-word lexical units out of what were once, perhaps, individual words. Many of these involve quantifying terms and determiners.

Fusion of Constructions with of

<u>some of the</u> papers
<u>much of</u> their meaning
<u>any of</u> our investigations
<u>a (great) number of</u>

Collocations with as

There are quite a few examples from the corpus of collocations that cluster around the system word *as* (in addition to the conjunction *as well as*, discussed in Chapter 7).

Preposition: [as [NP]]$_{pp}$ means "in the role, function, or status of." Sometimes it is related to verbs like *refer, treat, use,* or *recognize.*

I consider explicit knowledge to be a worthwhile, sometimes indeed indispensable, form of knowledge to be used <u>as a resource</u>.

<u>As a predominately top-down exercise</u>, the conception and construction of methods have been largely guided by a one-size-fits-all, cookie cutter approach.

But the study of grammar . . . does not end with learning about structures and functions within the sentence but rather uses the sentence <u>as a starting point</u> for exploring how grammar can be used in discourse.

I refer to this property <u>as nesting</u>.

As + (participial or regular) adjectives

The disjunction between method <u>as conceptualized</u> by theorists and method <u>as conducted</u> by teachers is the direct consequence of the inherent limitations of the concept of method itself.

Whereas in the past these two knowledge systems were often treated <u>as separate</u>, it has recently been suggested that they are connected.

Such as + a list

In general usage, any small group of words within a sentence or a clause, <u>such as</u> "in general usage," "small groups," and "a clause."

Communicative Competence and Processing

The concept of communicative competence emerged in opposition to Chomsky's ideas that competence, the grammatical knowledge that an ideal speaker-hearer has, exists outside of a social and cultural context, and that performance is largely irrelevant to linguistic theory. Hymes (1972, p. 63) originally used the expression "communicative competence" to argue that theories of language must involve both language use in context and the variable knowledge of language users:

> If an adequate theory of language users and language use is to be developed, it seems that judgments must be recognized to be in fact not of two kinds but of four. And if linguistic theory is to be integrated with theory of communication and culture, this fourfold distinction must be stated in a sufficiently generalized way. I would suggest, then, that for language and for other forms of communication (culture), four questions arise:
>
> 1   Whether (and to what degree) something is formally possible;
> 2   Whether (and to what degree) something is feasible in virtue of the means of implementation available;
> 3   Whether (and to what degree) something is appropriate (adequate, happy, successful) in relation to a context in which it is used and evaluated;
> 4   Whether (and to what degree) something is in fact done, actually performed, and what its doing entails.

A linguistic illustration: a sentence may be grammatical, awkward, tactful and rare.

L1 Communicative Competence

Combining Hymes' view with Widdowson's ideas from the quote at the beginning of the chapter, it is possible to hypothesize that language users have a "kit of rules" or abstract grammatical constructions for analytical composition (1), as well as "partially pre-assembled patterns, formulaic frameworks" to make language use feasible and natural (not awkward) through holistic composition (2). Language users make choices, adjustments, and adaptations to their language based on the sociocultural context (3) and based on tacit knowledge of the probabilities that words and constructions will occur together in certain contexts of use (4). For Hymes as well as Widdowson, abstract grammatical competence serves a regulative function to make sure that utterances and sentences conform to notions of formal possibility, feasibility or naturalness, contextual appropriateness, and probabilities of occurrence.

Thus, the customary relationship between grammar and vocabulary is reversed. For generative grammarians, languages users have a mental grammar that is big, rich, and complex, with a universal core and a periphery of idiosyncratic features, while the mental lexicon is a static list of words and morphemes from which sentences are composed analytically. In constrast, in Construction Grammar, communicative competence depends on knowledge in the form of a complex concordance which contains a trace of "every word it has encountered, a concordance that has been richly glossed for social, physical, discoursal, generic, and interpersonal context. This mental concordance is accessible and can be processed in much the same way that a computer concordance is, so that all kinds of patterns, including collocational patterns, are available for use" (Hoey, 2005, p. 11). Recall from Chapter 2 that Hoey describes the concordance as a linguistic system composed of a "thicket" of priming associations and connections that keep track of context and probabilities and that aim for formal accuracy, feasibility of natural production and comprehension, and appropriateness.

Similarly, Prodomou (2008, pp. 8–11) refers to "situated webs of signification" which connect (through priming and meaning associations) lexical items and constructions that occur immediately (within five words to the left or right) around a focal word in collocations and colligations, as discussed in Chapters 5–12. They are related to each other because together they refer, predicate, and modify based on a focal situation. Webs of signification also relate constructions that contribute to cohesion and coherence in discourse, and the language users' attitudes or pragmatic communicative intentions to words, constructions, or collocations in texts, as discussed in Chapter 13. Prodomou (2008, p. xxvi) argues that "[i]t is through these situated webs of signification that L1-users achieve fluency and the promotion of self rather than in the manipulation of isolated idiomatic units in a vacuum. L2-users of English also achieve fluency but do so in ways which both overlap with and diverge from L1 fluency." Thus, it is possible that the communicative competence for the L2 user is both similar to and different from that for an L1 user. Prodomou (2008, p. xxvi) calls this "the conflicting and often contradictory behavior of idiomaticity in L1- and L2-user discourse."

L2 Communicative Competence

A return to Hymes' original conception of communicative competence allows for a restatement of the idiomaticity paradox. L2 learners begin by making use of memorized prefabricated expressions but soon their classroom instruction focuses learning on abstract grammatical constructions for analytical composition or open choice (1). However, there is often insufficient time and practice for priming associations to form so that their "kit of rules" never becomes automatically fluent and accurate. On the other hand, L2 learners often fail to learn the partially pre-assembled patterns and formulaic frameworks that make their language use feasible and natural (not awkward) through holistic composition (2). Although they are able to make choices, adjustments, and adaptations to their language based on the sociocultural context (3), such abilities are imperfect and limited because their knowledge of the probabilities that words and constructions occur together in certain contexts of use (4) is also limited.

However, many L2 learners achieve a high degree of fluency and accuracy through ample practice, usage, and exposure. To begin with, their abstract grammatical knowledge serves a generative function to produce words, phrases, and sentences using open choice. At each point where there is a choice, the choice is truly open as learners slowly learn to access and produce the word that most commonly belongs in that slot. However, with sufficient usage, exposure, and practice, learners accumulate memory traces and priming associations among the known words and structures that are accessed most often.

In some cases, learners are, perhaps, more highly motivated (like student W in Chapter 3), and they receive sufficient explicit instruction and feedback so that their language, although analytically created, becomes fluent and accurate. Still, their use of idioms may be limited to, as Prodomou put it, "the manipulation of isolated idiomatic units in a vacuum," outside of complicated webs of signification. Sometimes learner language is not structurally or lexically correct, in which case the word "fossilization" is applied to stubborn errors that resist correction because of the strong priming they have already received. Learners' language (like Zoila's from earlier chapters) becomes fossilized in an incorrect state because of priming.

In study, work, or other live abroad contexts, or where L2 learners interact frequently with expert speakers, they acquire the prefabricated expressions, collocations, sentence frames, lexical bundles that allow for holistic processing regulated by abstract grammatical patterns. It is at that point where native-like fluency and accuracy are evident. Still, the sheer number and range of prefabrications will defeat many an L2 user and unilateral idiomaticity is always a possibility, as it sometimes happens among native speakers as well. But this raises another contradiction inherent in this topic: if many item-based collocations and idiomatic expressions come from inner circle varieties of English, is knowledge of them good or bad in the lingua franca context?

English as a Language Stripped Bare?

It is, perhaps, with some longing that an ELF speaker like Alptekin suggests that:

> [T]he spread of bilingualism nowadays results mainly from the widening use of English not as ESL and EFL but as an international language . . . Unlike local/national languages, ELF is an international medium of communication. It has no native speakers and no proper culture of its own to speak of. In this sense, it is everyone's property. In the absence of native speakers and a native culture, it lacks idioms, puns, connotations, slang, humour, and culture-specific pragmatic dimensions.
> (Alptekin, 2010, pp. 101–102)

Seidlhofer (2002, p. 273) is another proponent of this idea. She argues that:

> While cultural "neutrality" of a language is clearly an impossibility, there are nevertheless degrees of cultural "loadedness", with proverbs and idioms at the culture specific end of the spectrum. As distinct from the use speakers make of it, the ELF model as such should be as free as possible of such "prefabricated" cultural baggage taken over from ENL cultures, because the primary cultures of, say, the U.K. or the U.S. have, by definition, no privileged status when English is used as a lingua franca by speakers from a variety of cultures. In that sense, "language stripped

bare" . . . could actually be taken to denote a desirable quality—not in order to limit people to an instrument that can only handle bland and boring talk, but precisely the opposite, to create space to enable them to infuse the code with their own cultural peculiarities.[2]

Over time, two distinct types of English users could emerge. Some English users will engage in analytic processing using grammatical and lexical resources as well as holistic processing using existing prefabricated resources. Their usage and exposure in a sociocultural community will mean that their priming associations will be similar to those of others, maintaining the integrity of a language. On the other hand, at some future time, some English learners will engage mainly in analytical processing through open choice principles by relying on priming among abstract grammatical structures. In the quote above, Seidlhofer suggests that ELF could become a code with its own cultural peculiarities; what this means is that ELF would acquire, besides its own pronunciation, morphological, and syntactic norms, its own collocations and prefabricated expressions. Nevertheless, there may be little common ground of lexical and semantic priming for collocations and prefabricated expressions, unless there is sufficient common interaction in ELF, something that is questionable, at least for the present, given the number of ELF speakers and their fleeting and transitory interactions.

Unless the future of ELF involves the development of its own code, culturally loaded expressions, or collocations, spoken ELF may turn out to be an unnatural language indeed. Prefabricated expressions make composing a sentence easier because the formulaic expression simply needs to be retrieved from the concordance instead of combined analytically. The possibility exists that ELF, because of its temporary and ephemeral communication, will not develop its own common prefabricated chunks and collocations to assist in production of speech. Prefabrications may be conversation-specific; perhaps that is why there is so much repetition in ELF conversations, with the more fluent speaker establishing the norms. For the listener, too, dealing with word

---

2. Jesperson, the great Danish linguist and lover of English, may be objecting from beyond the grave. In 1905, he predicted: "Whatever a remote future may have in store, one need not be a great prophet to predict that in the near future the number of English-speaking people will increase considerably. It must be a source of gratification to mankind that the tongue spoken by two of the greatest powers of the world is so noble, so rich, so pliant, so expressive, and so interesting as the language whose growth and structure I have been here endeavouring to characterize" (Jesperson, [1905] 1939, p. 263).

combinations that have high frequencies of occurring together will activate priming effects, which assist in comprehension and make it faster. The cognitive and processing loads associated with comprehending ELF may create more difficulties than any natural "native" language because holistic processing is associated with increased comprehension, especially under stressed circumstances.

Still, there is a way to resolve this paradox in ELF usage, in that prefabrications are not the same in terms of their amount of cultural baggage. Pure idioms can't be understood by building up a meaning as the sum of the words, and figurative idioms might be on the borderline of comprehensibility. Pure idioms may cause "unilateral idiomaticity." Proverbs, slogans, catchphrases, and quotations are highly personal and are ways that people project their identities and affiliations and recognize similarities and differences in others. These can be avoided in ELF, but ELF users cannot avoid all collocations and lexical bundles, because knowing them means that they can speak, and especially write, more fluently as well as comprehend more easily. So the paradox is resolved if ELF users, be they native or non-native speakers, stick to the frequent, more culturally neutral combinations and avoid personalized idiomatic use. If spoken ELF becomes a conventionalized variety of World Englishes, it may be as rigidly depersonalized and decontextualized as Academic English is in its own way.

Collocational Awareness

> The more one considers the matter, the more reasonable it seems to suppose that lexis is where we need to start from, the syntax needs to be put to the service of words and not the other way around.
>
> (Widdowson, 1989, p. 111)

Taking his inspiration from quotes like the one above, Lewis (2002) proposes an approach to grammar pedagogy that blurs the lines between grammar and vocabulary and places equal importance on collocations and colligations in producing and comprehending language. Teachers present vocabulary in their most common co-texts, that is, as lexical chunks composed of the focal words and their most common word and phrase neighbors, such as the examples in the box (see p. 304), slightly adapted from Lewis (2000, p. 133).

Collocations involve constructions that follow colligational constraints but more importantly they show heavy priming among the lexical items. Some collocations combine fixed combinations of words (*aware-of, interested-in*) and

Various Collocations and the Colligational Constraints

a difficult decision	[[Determiner] [ADJP] [N]]$_{NP}$
radio station	[[Noun] [Noun]]$_{NP}$
submit a report	[[V] [NP]]$_{VP}$
revise the original plan	[[V]$_{TRANSITIVE}$ [NP]]$_{VP}$
examine thoroughly	[[V] [ADVP]]$_{VP}$
extremely inconvenient	[[Intensifier] [Adjective]]$_{ADJP}$
on the other hand	[PP]
a-sort-of . . .	fixed phrase with an object NP
aware-of . . .	ADJP PP

grammatical categories because primed object is not a specific thing but merely anything that is a noun, adjective, or verb.

Collocations are taught as words and with their common co-texts, but Lewis (2002, p. 151) argues that they can be successfully learned from relatively decontextualized exposures to language like word lists, vocabulary notebooks, and pattern practice in drills, followed by free practice in communicative activities. It seems that collocational awareness is a way to combine vocabulary learning and grammar learning and practice holistic as well as analytic composition. It can also be applied to intensive reading and writing classrooms with dictionary and translation work, using context clues for meaning, and the creation and study of linguistic corpora and concordances.

Conclusion

The term "World Englishes" is a new way to talk about an idea whose existence goes back to centuries ago when British sailors, explorers, soldiers, and settlers stepped off of their ships' gangplanks and set foot on other regions of the world. The impact of those early endeavors on the languages of the world cannot be denied but it can be resisted and altered. Similarly, the language awareness curriculum includes the past and the present: traditional time-tested teaching methods of increasing metalinguistic awareness with ideas of rote and meaningful practice to improve language based on new ideas of holistic and analytical processing. And Construction Grammar discards ideas of innateness, competence, grammaticality, and native speaker dominance and picks up past threads of grammatical analysis to support the more recent usage and exposure hypothesis, priming, naturalness, and the multicompetent language user, as shown in this rhetorical question asked in 1968:

> Is it possible that the brains of speakers and hearers coin and understand utterances on the basis of "abstract patterns" of some sort, extracted over the months and years of language-learning and language-use from actual utterances of similar shapes? . . . To entertain it is not to propose, I believe, an additional independent mechanism of the generation of speech, but only to suggest that analogy may work indirectly, via abstraction, as well as directly with actual sets of stored whole utterances; also, we should then have the possibility that the abstract patterns might themselves give rise, via analogy and blending, to new abstract patterns.
> (Hockett, 1968, p. 95)

Hockett's question reminds us that, although some mid-century ideas have been rejected or superseded, others are in the process of renewal. General learning mechanisms like analogy and abstraction, operating on normal usage and exposure, are under reconsideration as crucial in language learning, along with new ideas like priming, holistic processing, and analytical processing. This is why Construction Grammar promises, in the future, to change common ideas of second language acquisition theories and methods.

Study, Discussion, and Essay Questions

1. Review these terms and add them to your glossary with a definition and some examples if they are not already present: pure idioms, quotes, slogans, catchphrases, proverbs, lexical bundles, sentence builders, macro-organizers, vague markers, conversational gambits, sentence stems, repeats, binomials, trinomials, unique expressions, metaphors, similes, collocations, free combinations, restricted collocations, figurative idioms, pure idioms, fossilization. (In defining these terms, note that they overlap in meaning.)
2. What are the various ways that communicative competence is defined?
3. What is Wray's idiomatic paradox?
4. How do holistic processing and analytical processing combine to produce communicative competence?
5. How is prefabrication in language related to naturalness? How are they related to identity or personality? Can you think of any prefabricated expressions that are linked to your identity or personality?

6. How did the concept of communicative competence emerge? What factors are present in a person's communicative competence? Describe the L1 speaker's communicative competence.

7. How does the communicative competence of the L2 learner begin? How does it develop? How is priming implicated both in fluency and accuracy, on the one hand, and in fossilization on the other?

8. Why might ELF turn out to be an unnatural language? Do you think that ELF will develop its own prefabricated expressions? What might hinder that development?

Activities

1. Write an essay contrasting the ideas expressed by Alptekin and Seidlhofer with those expressed by Jesperson a century ago. After you have done justice to their ideas, express your own opinion or preference in this matter. When you are finished with your essay, proofread it to make sure you have chosen AE usages. Be prepared to share your essay with your classmates.

2. What were some of the early prefabrications you learned in English (or another language)? Do/did you experience the idiomatic paradox firsthand? How?

3. Look over the essays and paragraphs you have written in response to these questions. Do you note any changes in your writing over time? How have your ideas about English or English usage changed?

Bibliography

Alptekin, C. (2010) Redefining multicompetence for bilingualism and ELF, *International Journal of Applied Linguistics*, 20, no. 1.

Andrews, L. (1993) *Language Exploration and Awareness*. White Plains, NY: Longman.

Behrens, H. (2009) Usage-based and emergentist approaches to language acquisition, *Linguistics*, 47, no. 2: 383–411.

Berdan, R. (1996) Disentangling language acquisition from language variation, in R. Bayley and D. Preston (eds.) *Second Language Acquisition and Linguistic Variation*. Amsterdam: John Benjamins, 203–244.

Bialystok, E. (1991) *Language Processing in Bilingual Children*. Cambridge, UK: Cambridge University Press.

Biber, D. (1988) *Variation across Speech and Writing*. Cambridge, UK: Cambridge University Press.

Biber, D. and Barbieri, F. (2007) Lexical bundles in university spoken and written registers, *English for Specific Purposes*, 26: 263–286.

Biber, D. and Gray, B. (2010) Challenging stereotypes about academic writing: complexity, elaboration, explicitness, *Journal of English for Academic Purposes*, 9: 2–20.

Biber, D., Johansson, S., Leech, G., Conrad, S., and Finegan, E. (1999) *Longman Grammar of Spoken and Written English*. Harlow: Longman.

Bitchener, J., Young, S., and Cameron, D. (2005) The effect of different types of corrective feedback on ESL student writing, *Journal of Second Language Writing*, 14: 191–205.

Bolinger, D. (1975) *Aspects of Language*. New York: Harcourt, Brace, Jovanovich.

Breiteneder, A. (2009) English as a lingua franca in Europe: an empirical perspective, *World Englishes*, 28, no. 2: 256–269.

Bromberek-Dyzman, K. and Ewert, A. (2010) Figurative competence is better developed in L1 than in L2, or is it? Understanding conversational implicatures in L1 and L2, in M. Pütz and L. Sicola (eds.) *Cognitive Processing in Second Language Acquisition: Inside the Learner's Mind*. Amsterdam: John Benjamins, 317–334.

Butzkamm, W. and Caldwell, J. (2009) *The Bilingual Reform: A Paradigm Shift in Foreign Language Teaching.* Tübingen: Gunter Narr Verlag.

Cazden, C. (1974) Play with language and metalinguistic awareness: one dimension of language experience, *International Journal of Early Childhood*, 6, no. 16: 12–24.

Celse-Murcia, M. (1998) Discourse analysis and grammar instruction, in D. Oaks (ed.) *Linguistics at Work: A Reader of Applications.* Fort Worth, TX: Harcourt Brace College Publishers, 687–705.

Chandler, J. (2003) The efficacy of various kinds of error feedback for improvement in the accuracy and fluency of L2 student writing, *Journal of Second Language Writing*, 12: 267–296.

Chomsky, N. (1965) *Aspects of the Theory of Syntax.* Cambridge, MA: MIT Press.

Conrad, S. (2000) Will corpus linguistics revolutionize grammar teaching in the 21st century? *TESOL Quarterly*, 34, no. 3: 548–560.

Cook, V. (1995) Multi-competence and the learning of many languages, *Language, Culture, and Curriculum*, 8, no. 2: 93–98.

Croft , W. (2001) *Radical Construction Grammar: Syntactic Theory in Typological Perspective.* Oxford, UK: Oxford University Press.

DeCarrico, J. (2000) *The Structure of English: Studies in Form and Function for Language Teaching.* Ann Arbor: University of Michigan Press.

DeKeyser, R. (ed.) (2007) *Practice in a Second Language: Perspectives from Applied Linguistics and Cognitive Psychology.* Cambridge, UK: Cambridge University Press.

Derewianka, B. (2007) Changing approaches to the conceptualization and teaching of grammar, in J. Cummins and C. Davison (eds.) *International Handbook of English Language Teaching.* New York: Springer, 843–858.

de Swaan, A. (1998) The political sociology of the world language system (1): the dynamics of language spread, *Language Problems and Language Planning*, 22, no. 1: 63–75.

Donesch-Jezo, E. (2011) The use of language corpora and concordancing software to improve grammatical competence in teaching English as a foreign language, *Sino–US English Teaching*, 8, no. 12: 754–765.

Doolan, S. and Miller, D. (2012) Generation 1.5 written error patterns: a comparative study, *Journal of Second Language Writing*, 21: 1–22.

Dunbar, R. (1998) Theory of mind and the evolution of language, in J. Hurford, M. Studdert-Kennedy, and C. Knight (eds.) *Approaches to the Evolution of Language.* Cambridge, UK: Cambridge University Press, 92–110.

Ellis, N. (2008) The dynamics of second language emergence: cycles of language use, language change, and language acquisition, *Modern Language Journal*, 92, no. 2: 232–249.

Ellis, R. (1992) *Second Language Acquisition and Language Pedagogy.* Clevedon, UK: Multilingual Matters.

Ellis, R. (1999) *Learning a Second Language through Interaction.* Amsterdam: John Benjamins.

Ferris, D. (1999) The case for grammar correction in L2 writing classes: a response to Truscott (1996), *Journal of Second Language Writing*, 8, no. 1: 1–11.

Ferris, D. (2002) *Treatment of Error in Second Language Writing.* Ann Arbor: University of Michigan Press.

Firth, A. (1996) The discursive accomplishment of normality: on "lingua franca" English and conversational analysis, *Journal of Pragmatics*, 26: 237–259.

Firth, A. and Wagner, J. (1997) On discourse, communication and (some) fundamental concepts in SLA research, *Modern Language Journal*, 81, no. 3: 285–300.

Fisher, E. (2000) Assessing the state of Ugandan English, *English Today*, 16: 57–61.

Gatbonton, E. and Segalowitz, N. (1988) Creative automatization: principles for promoting fluency within a communicative framework, *TESOL Quarterly*, 22, no. 3: 473–492.

Grainger, J. and Carreiras, M. (2009) Advances in morphological priming: an introduction, in R. Frost, J. Grainger, and M. Carreiras (eds.) *Advances in Morphological Priming*. New York: Psychology Press, 933–941.

Greblick, A.J. (2001) The modal preterite phenomenon (MPP) in colloquial American English: a diachronic and synchronic analysis, *Dissertation Abstracts International, A: The Humanities and Social Sciences*, available at http://search.proquest.com/docview 85559024? accountid=10349 (85559024; 200212580) (retrieved 12/2/2012).

Gyasi, I.K. (1991) Aspects of English in Ghana, *English Today*, 7, no. 2: 26–31.

Hinkel, E. (2002) *Second Language Writers' Text: Linguistic and Rhetorical Features*. Mahwah, NJ: Lawrence Erlbaum.

Hinkel, E. and Fotos, S. (2002) *New Perspectives on Grammar Teaching in Second Language Classroom*. Mahwah, NJ: Lawrence Erlbaum.

Hockett, C.F. (1968) *The State of the Art*. The Hague: Mouton.

Hoey, M. (2005) *Lexical Priming: A New Theory of Words and Language*. London and New York: Routledge.

Hopper, P. (1998) Emergent grammar, in M. Tomasello (ed.) *The New Psychology of Language: Cognitive and Functional Approaches to Language Structure*. Mahwah, NJ: Lawrence Erlbaum Associates, 155–175.

House, J. (2003) English as a lingua franca: a threat to multilingualism? *Journal of Sociolinguistics*, 7, no. 4: 556–578.

Howarth, P. (1998) Phraseology and second language proficiency, *Applied Linguistics*, 19: 124–144.

http://www.britishcouncil.org/learning-ielts-what-is-it.htm (retrieved 4/3/2012).

http://www.ets.org/toefl (retrieved 4/3/2012).

http://www.etscanada.ca/students/ (retrieved 4/3/2012).

Hulstijn, J. (2003) Towards a unified account of the representation, processing and acquisition of second language knowledge, *Second Language Research*, 18, no. 3: 193–223.

Hymes, D.H. (1972) On communicative competence, in J.B. Pride and J. Holmes (eds.) *Sociolinguistics: Selected Readings*. Harmondsworth: Penguin, 269–293.

Jackson, H. and Amvela, E. (2000) *Words, Meaning and Vocabulary: An Introduction to Modern English Lexicology*. London: Cassell.

Jesperson, O. ([1905] 1939) *Growth and Structure of the English Language*, 9th edn. Garden City, NY: Doubleday.

Jessner, U. (2006) *Linguistic Awareness in Multilinguals: English as a Third Language*. Edinburgh: Edinburgh University Press.

Jessner, U. (2008) A DST model of multilingualism and the role of metalinguistic awareness, *Modern Language Journal*, 92, no. 2: 270–283.

Johns, T. (1991) From printout to handout: grammar and vocabulary teaching in the context of data-driven learning, *English Language Research Journal*, 4: 27–45.

Kachru, B. (1985) Standards, codification, and sociolinguistic realism: the English language in the outer circle, in R. Quirk and H.G. Widdowson (eds.) *English in the World: Teaching and Learning Language and Literatures*. Cambridge, UK: Cambridge University Press, 11–30.

Kachru, Y. and Smith, L. (2008) *Cultures, Contexts, and World Englishes*. New York: Routledge.

Kazmi, Y. (1997) The hidden political agenda of teaching English as an international language, *Muslim Education Quarterly*, 15, no. 1, available at: http://www.tesolislamia. org/articles.html (retrieved 4/18/2008).

Krashen, S.D. (1987) *Principles and Practice in Second Language Acquisition*. Englewood Cliffs, NJ: Prentice-Hall International.

Krashen, S.D. (1988) *Second Language Acquisition and Second Language Learning*. Englewood Cliffs, NJ: Prentice-Hall International.

Kroll, B. (1990) *Second Language Writing: Research Insights for the Classroom*. Cambridge, UK: Cambridge University Press.

Kuipers, K. (1996) *Smooth Talkers: The Linguistic Performance of Auctioneers and Sportscasters*. Mahwah, NJ: Lawrence Erlbaum.

Kumaravadivelu, B. (2003) *Beyond Methods: Macrostrategies for Language Teaching*. New Haven, CT: Yale University Press.

Lewis, M. (ed.) (2000) *Teaching Collocation: Further Developments in the Lexical Approach*. London: Heinle.

Lewis, M. (2002) *The Lexical Approach: The State of ELT and a Way Forward*. Boston, MA: Thomson/Heinle.

Lichtkoppler, J. (2007) "Male. Male." – "Male?" – "The sex is male." – The role of repetition in English as a lingua franca conversations, *Vienna English Working Papers*, 16, no. 1, available at: http://www.univie.ac.at/anglistik/views.htm (retrieved 10/13/2012).

Liu, D. (2012) The most frequently-used multi-word constructions in academic written English: a multi-corpus study, *English for Specific Purposes*, 31: 25–35.

Liu, D. and Ping, J. (2009) Using a corpus-based lexicogrammatical approach to grammar instruction in EFL and ESL contexts, *Modern Language Journal*, 93, no. 1: 61–78.

Long, M. and Robinson, P. (1998) Focus on form: theory, research and practice, in C. Doughty and J. Williams (eds.) *Focus on Form in Classroom Second Language Acquisition*. Cambridge, UK: Cambridge University Press, 15–41.

McArthur, T. (ed.) (1992) *Oxford Companion to the English Language*. Oxford, UK: Oxford University Press.

McArthur, T. (ed.) (2002) *The Oxford Guide to World English*. Oxford: Oxford University Press.

McDonough, K. (2006) Interaction and syntactic priming: English L2 speakers' production of dative constructions, *Studies in Second Language Acquisition*, 28: 179–207.

McDonough, K. and Mackey, A. (2006) Responses to recasts: repetitions, primed production and linguistic development, *Language Learning*, 54: 693–720.

McDonough, K. and Mackey, A. (2008) Syntactic priming and ESL question development, *Studies in Second Language Acquisition*, 30: 31–47.

McDonough, K. and Trofimovich, P. (2009) *Using Priming Methods in Second Language Research*. New York and London: Routledge.

Mackey, A. and Philp, J. (1998) Conversational interaction and second language development: recasts, responses, and red herrings? *Modern Language Journal*, 82: 338–356.

Malakoff, M. (1992) Translation ability: a natural bilingual and metalinguistic skill, in R.J. Harris (ed.) *Cognitive Processing in Bilinguals*. Amsterdam: North Holland, 515–530.

Matthews, P. (1997) *The Concise Oxford Dictionary of Linguistics*. Oxford, UK: Oxford University Press.

Mauranen, A. and Ranta, E. (2010) *English as a Lingua Franca: Studies and Findings, Newcastle upon Tyne*. Cambridge, UK: Cambridge Scholars Publishing.

Meierkord, C. (1996) *Englisch als Medium der interkulturellen Kommunikation: Untersuchungen zum non-native/non-native speaker. Diskurs*. Frankfurt/Main: Peter Lang.

Nattinger, J. and DeCarrico, J. (1992) *Lexical Phrases and Language Teaching*. Oxford, UK: Oxford University Press.

Nesselhauf, N. (2009) Co-selection phenomena across New Englishes parallels (and differences) to foreign learner varieties, *English World-Wide*, 30, no. 1: 1–26.

Nihalani, P., Tongue, R.K., and Hosali, P. (1979) *Indian and British English: A Handbook of Usage and Pronunciation*. New Delhi: Oxford University Press.

Nunan, D. (1989) *Designing Tasks for the Communicative Classroom*. Cambridge, UK: Cambridge University Press.

Parakrama, A. (1995) *De-hegemonizing Language Standards*. New York: St. Martin's Press.

Pei, M. (1967) *The Many Hues of English*. New York: Knopf.

Phillipson, R. (2007) English, no longer a foreign language in Europe? in J. Cummins and C. Davison (eds.) *International Handbook of English Language Teaching*. London: Springer, 123–136.

Prodomou, L. (2008) *English as a Lingua Franca: A Corpus-Based Approach*. London: Continuum.

Ramirez, G., Chen, X., Geva, E., and Yang, L. (2011) Morphological awareness and word reading in English language learners: evidence from Spanish and Chinese speaking children, *Applied Psycholinguistics*, 32, no. 3: 601–618.

Recinto, T. (1998) National language policy in the United States, in T. Recinto and B. Burnaby (eds.) *Language and Politics in the United States and Canada*. Mahwah, NJ: Lawrence Erlbaum, 85–112.

Richards, J.C. (2002) Accuracy and fluency revisited, in E. Hinkel and S. Fotos (eds.) *New Perspectives on Grammar Teaching in Second Language Classrooms*. Mahwah, NJ: Lawrence Erlbaum, 35–49.

Sand, A. (2004) Shared morpho-syntactic features in contact varieties of English: article use, *World Englishes*, 23, no. 2: 281–298.

Schneider, E. (2004) How to trace structural nativization: particle verbs in world Englishes, *World Englishes*, 23, no. 2: 227–249.

Seidlhofer, B. (2001) Towards making "Euro-English" a linguistic reality, *English Today*, 68: 14–16.

Seidlhofer, B. (2002) The shape of things to come? Some basic questions about English as a lingua franca, in K. Knapp and C. Meierkord (eds.) *Lingua Franca Communication*. Frankfurt/Main: Peter Lang, 269–302.

Seidlhofer, B. (2007) Common property: English as a lingua franca in Europe, in J. Cummins and C. Davison (eds.) *International Handbook of English Language Teaching*. London: Springer, 137–150.

Selinker (1971) Interlanguage, *International Review of Applied Linguistics*, 10: 209–231.

Shapira, R.G. (1978) The non-learning of English: case study of an adult, in E.M. Hatch (ed.) *Second Language Acquisition: A Book of Readings*. Rowley, MA: Newbury House, 246–255.

Sinclair, J. (1991) *Corpus, Concordance, Collocation*. Oxford, UK: Oxford University Press.

Sinclair, J. and Mauranen, A. (2006) *Linear Unit Grammar: Integrating Speech and Writing*. Amsterdam: John Benjamins.

Skutnabb-Kangas, T. (2000) *Linguistic Genocide in Education—or Worldwide Diversity and Human Rights?* Mahwah, NJ: Lawrence Erlbaum.

Tarone, E. and Swierzbin, B. (2009) *Exploring Learner Language*. Oxford, UK: Oxford University Press.

Thornbury, S. (1997) *Language Tasks for Teachers of English*. Cambridge, UK: Cambridge University Press.

Timmis, I. (2002) Native-speaker norms and International English: a classroom view, *ELT Journal*, 56, no. 3: 240–249.

Tomasello, M. (2003) *Constructing a Language: A Usage Based Theory of Language Acquisition.* Cambridge, MA: Harvard University Press.

Tomasello, M. and Herron, C. (1988) Down the garden path: inducing and correcting over-generalization errors in the foreign language classroom, *Applied Psycholinguistics*, 9: 237–246.

Tomasello, M. and Herron, C. (1989) Feedback for language transfer errors: the garden path technique, *Studies in Second Language Acquisition*, 13: 513–517.

Tongue, R. (1974) *The English of Singapore and Malaysia.* Singapore: Eastern Universities Press.

Truscott, J. (1999) The case against grammar correction in L2 writing classes, *Language Learning*, 46: 327–369.

Tsuda, Y. (1994) Hegemony of English vs ecology of language: building equality in international communication, in L.E. Smith and M.L. Forman (eds.) *World Englishes 2000: Selected Essays.* Honolulu: University of Hawai'i, 21–31.

von Humboldt, W. (1969 [1830–1835]) Introduction, in P. Salus (ed.) *Concerning the Variety of Human Language and Its Influence on the Intellectual Development of Mankind*, reprinted in *On Language: Plato to von Humboldt.* New York: Holt, Rinehart, and Winston, 178–198.

Widdowson, H.G (1989) Knowledge of language and ability for use, *Applied Linguistics*, 10, no. 2: 128–137.

Wray, A. (2002) *Formulaic Language and the Lexicon.* Cambridge, UK: Cambridge University Press.

Zhang, D. and Koda, K. (2012) Contribution of morphological awareness and lexical inferencing ability to L2 vocabulary knowledge and reading comprehension among advanced EFL learners: testing direct and indirect effects, *Read Writ*, 25: 1195–1216.

Zhao, S. and Bitchener, J. (2007) Incidental focus on form in teacher–learner and learner–learner interactions, *System*, 35: 431–447.

Index